PAUL ROBESON

THE LIBRARY OF AFRICAN AMERICAN BIOGRAPHY

John David Smith, editor

Paul Robeson: A Life of Activism and Art, Lindsey R. Swindall (2013)

PAUL ROBESON

A LIFE OF
ACTIVISM AND ART

Lindsey R. Swindall

ROWMAN & LITTLEFIELD
Lanham • Boulder • New York • London

Published by Rowman & Littlefield
A wholly owned subsidiary of The Rowman & Littlefield Publishing Group, Inc.
4501 Forbes Boulevard, Suite 200, Lanham, Maryland 20706
www.rowman.com

Unit A, Whitacre Mews, 26-34 Stannary Street, London SE11 4AB

Distributed by NATIONAL BOOK NETWORK

British Library Cataloguing in Publication Information Available

Library of Congress Cataloging-in-Publication Data

The hard back edition of this book was previously cataloged by the Library of Congress as follows:

Swindall, Lindsey R., 1977-
  Paul Robeson : a life of activism and art / Lindsey R. Swindall.
    pages cm. — (The library of African American biography)
  Includes bibliographical references and index.
  1. Robeson, Paul, 1898-1976. 2. Robeson, Paul, 1898-1976—Political and social views. 3. African Americans—Biography. 4. African American political activists—Biography. 5. African American singers—Biography. 6. African American athletes—Biography. 7. African American authors—Biography. 8. Harlem Renaissance. I. Title.
  E185.97.R63S948 2013
  782.0092—dc23
  [B]
                                                                    2012046652

ISBN: 978-1-4422-0793-6 (cloth : alk. paper)
ISBN: 978-1-4422-0794-3 (pbk. : alk. paper)
ISBN: 978-1-4422-0795-0 (electronic)

∞™ The paper used in this publication meets the minimum requirements of American National Standard for Information Sciences—Permanence of Paper for Printed Library Materials, ANSI/NISO Z39.48-1992.

Printed in the United States of America

For Coop

CONTENTS

ACKNOWLEDGMENTS

First, many deeply felt thanks go to John David Smith, because without his guidance and perseverance this project would not have been realized. Thanks also to the editors at Rowman & Littlefield who fostered this manuscript through the process of publication. Special thanks to Jennifer Jensen Wallach, whose biography of Richard Wright got me interested in writing for this important series. I am very appreciative to the archivists who assisted me in securing photo permissions, especially the helpful staff at the Tamiment Library and Robert F. Wagner Labor Archives at New York University. Thanks to my colleagues in the history department at Sam Houston State University who were supportive as I refined this manuscript in Texas especially William K. Ferguson III. I am grateful to those mentors, students, former colleagues, and fellow Robeson acolytes who have been interested champions of my work.

As always, I am thankful to have a tribe of friends and family who are consistently encouraging: Marshall and Lisa Swindall, Lizabeth Foster, Edward Foster, Seth Foster, and Charles Bittner. A special note of thanks also to the northern Foster clan, because without their constant hospitality I would not be able to undertake my research in New York. I hope that Jayden Foster will one day read this book and that it might introduce him, and perhaps some of his generation, to the significant life and work of Paul Robeson. I would like to express sincere appreciation to my partner for his kind attentiveness and undertaking of tasks large and small that helped this manuscript to get written. He has enabled me to truly understand the meaning of a partnership. Finally, it is my greatest hope that Paul Robeson's voice comes through in this narrative and that readers not previously acquainted with him will be touched by his story.

Huntsville, Texas
July 2012

INTRODUCTION

For two days before his funeral, a continuous line of mourners filed past Paul Robeson's open casket in a Harlem funeral home. It was, to the casual observer, a notably diverse gathering. A retired child-care provider in her seventies clutched a program from a production of *Othello*. This dignified lady remembered singing in a choir that accompanied Robeson's interpretation of the Depression-era anthem "Ballad for Americans." A man in his thirties recalled humming along to Robeson's records when he was a child. A middle-aged transit worker shared how he had learned about the great artist in a segregated school in South Carolina. Writer John O. Killens reflected that it was Robeson who taught him about Pan-Africanism. He recollected first meeting Robeson when he was helping a group of cafeteria workers form a union. The lunch ladies had been overwhelmed when the famous baritone agreed to sing for a benefit concert for them. The day of Robeson's funeral in January 1976 was damp and cold. Still, hundreds lined the sidewalks to offer their farewells. They included an African American woman who had saved an autographed Robeson concert program for three decades. A Jewish lady spoke of admiring his integrity and courage. A labor organizer reminisced about providing security for Robeson in Peekskill, New York, in 1949. A writer for *Ebony* magazine observed that although Robeson was a film star and a famous concert vocalist, this was no celebrity funeral. "The event, like the man, defied facile characterization," the reporter concluded. These mourners, who were writers, activists, laborers, music fans, and theater lovers of varied ages and ethnicities, felt connected to Robeson. They venerated him in a unique and heartfelt manner.

In a similar way, exceptionally diverse audiences jammed into venues when he was at the height of his fame in the 1940s. The image on the next page from Rockland Palace revealed working people who probably lived in Harlem, men in suits from downtown, women bearing toothy grins, and students from the nearby universities. They were dark skinned, light skinned, and ranged from young to middle aged. What did they have in common? They adored the tall, handsome performer who stood before them. He returned their smiles with warmth and generosity. The admiration glimmering in the eyes of his listeners was something close to awe. It reflected an association that was much deeper than musical talent, although his singing was beloved, and more profound than film or theater glory, although he was a prominent actor. Some called it magnetism, charisma, or a powerful human vibration. He could walk into Madison Square Garden and a thousand faces would turn his way. His deep voice spoke, and it touched people. His presence moved them, and his intellect challenged them. His body possessed the strength and litheness of an athlete, but he exerted impressive control. Scholar C. L. R. James once reflected that to have been in Robeson's company was something that one "remembered for days." The perceptive James suggested that Robeson's outstanding qualities were his "immense power" that was tempered by "great gentleness." Robeson was a man who was not only blessed with magnificent talent but also was one who, in James's words, "gave up everything and committed himself to what he believed was the only way for the salvation of mankind." This observation elicits several questions: What issues and events helped shape his career? To what ideas was Robeson so dedicated? Upon what principles did he take his stand?

Certainly, Paul Robeson was a complex and fascinating public figure whose life illustrated and was influenced by several of the most significant historical movements of the first half of the twentieth century. Acting might have been one of his professional crafts, but he was also an actor on the global stage in the public discourse. His own life had perhaps more dramatic importance than any of the fictional roles he interpreted from scripts. Because he was born near the close of the nineteenth century, Robeson came of age during the era when racial segregation in the United States was sanctioned by the highest court in the land. Booker T. Washington's

Paul Robeson at Rockland Palace in New York. Daily Worker/Daily World Photographs Collection, Tamiment Library, New York University.

philosophy of thrift, hard work, and accommodation had been embraced for a generation. The black church offered sanctuary and uplifted the community in which young Paul was reared. When he came of age in the 1910s, the National Association for the Advancement of Colored People (NAACP) offered a challenge to Washington's leadership. A younger generation was now opting to protest directly against racial injustice. This was a message that Robeson fully embraced. As a young scholar-athlete, he embodied W. E. B. Du Bois's conception of the "talented tenth." This group represented the elite of the African American population who would form an educated, professional class that would guide the community forward.

Robeson moved to the New York neighborhood of Harlem just as the decade of the 1920s began to roar. This relocation proved to be quite auspicious for his future career. When practicing law did not pan out as he had hoped, Robeson was nudged toward the theater at a time when the arts were blossoming uptown. He was a renaissance man in two important ways: he demonstrated his facility in a variety of fields, including acting and singing, and his artistic career was a consequence of the Harlem Renaissance. During these years, he married Eslanda Cardozo Goode, who had been trained as a scientist. She was dedicated to aiding his career and developed into an adept manager. By the time the stock market crash ushered in a decade of economic woe, Robeson was off to England to nurture a promising livelihood in the arts. The couple spent much of the 1930s abroad. London was their home base for travel around the United Kingdom, other parts of Europe, and the Soviet Union. From there, Robeson watched the fascist movement envelope parts of the continent, which cemented his firm antifascist perspective. Even as the political outlook turned bleak, Robeson's celebrity as a world citizen grew. His concert tours, films, and theater projects were, by and large, very enthusiastically received. Fame, recognition, and financial reward were his.

Paul and his wife hurried back to the United States just as war broke out and the battle for Britain was launched. American audiences came out for Robeson's concerts and were mesmerized by his portrayal of Othello on Broadway. During the global conflict, the people's artist dedicated his talents to aiding an Allied victory. When the war concluded, Robeson advocated for colonial independence and peace with the Soviet Union. As the Second World War gave way to the Cold War, his outspoken political views meant that he was branded as subversive during one of the most vitriolic antiradical purges in U.S. history. Robeson, the cold warrior, confronted the maelstrom by fighting the State Department for his right to travel internationally. Appearing before the feared House Un-American Activities Committee (HUAC), he brazenly chided the committee members as being the real un-Americans. He started his own newspaper and recording company when the media vilified his words and concert promoters declined his music. When the prestigious concert halls closed their doors, Robeson kept singing and speaking in black churches and union halls. Refusing to bend in an era of suspicion and blacklisting meant sacrificing financial gain. He opted for values over comfort; struggle instead of ease. By the late 1950s, the Cold War had thawed enough that Robeson regained his passport. He traveled overseas, where he was highly esteemed, to sing and act once again. However, ill health prevented an extended resurgence in his career, and he was largely retired from public life by the mid-1960s. He monitored the civil rights campaigns of the post–*Brown v. Board of Education* era from the sidelines until he passed away in 1976.

If these were some of the major events and movements that shaped his life, what were the main principles that animated Robeson's political ideology? A question that was often posed during his lifetime was whether or not Robeson was a member of the U.S. Communist Party. The short answer is no; although he was involved in campaigns that included Communists, he was close to some leaders in the party, and he recognized their more progressive approach to race relations. It is important to acknowledge that the media from the 1940s to the 1960s overemphasized his socialist leanings. The historical record was, thus, somewhat slanted on this issue because of the second Red Scare during the intense years of the early Cold War. Much of the national media in the United States, with the exception of most black and progressive newspapers, portrayed Robeson as little more than a stooge of the Soviet Union for many years. His name was maligned or largely erased from the mainstream public discourse until a slow resuscitation began in the 1970s. Post–Cold War studies of Robeson, beginning with biographer Martin B. Duberman's book, once again raised public awareness of this significant historical figure. Thus, to boil down his reputation to a single misguided inquiry about communism overlooks several key issues that Robeson championed.

First, as a Columbia Law graduate, he was an ardent supporter of the Bill of Rights. Although he testified under oath about it, Robeson stopped answering the question about Communist Party membership during the Cold War because he maintained that posing it violated his constitutional right to free political association. The Communist Party was a legal entity like the Republican and Democratic Parties, he consistently pointed out. Antifascism probably more closely described his outlook and was a term he regularly used to characterize his political ideology starting in the late 1930s. His anticolonial position dovetailed closely with his stance against fascism. Secondly, Robeson did assert that socialism represented a superior economic system to capitalism, which rests on the idea of production for private profit. Establishing a more equitable distribution of wealth and protecting the rights of the producing classes were issues that were dear to him and ones about which he gave speeches and wrote articles. However, it was Africa, its rich cultural heritage, its people, their descendants in the diaspora, and the cause of independence, that was central to his worldview. Socialism and his relationship with the Soviet Union were also important aspects of his narrative. But to leave Africa out of his story, or marginalize it, would distort the focus of both his artistic career and his political advocacy.

It was in London in the 1930s that he "discovered Africa" and began to consider himself to be an African. As the center of the British Empire, the city was a crossroads for people of African descent. Interacting with them, and then studying African languages, had a huge impact on Robeson. In his memoir, he noted that he "felt as one" with his African friends. He reflected on African and African American culture in a number of articles around that time. Robeson's film and theater projects engaged themes of African and African American culture to varying degrees. He invariably aimed to partici-pate in plays and movies that offered dignified portrayals of dark-skinned people. However, his film work especially yielded mixed results. It was also during this decade that he first journeyed to the Soviet Union. Robeson did so because he wondered whether strategies that had been used to integrate the tribes of central Asia into the Soviet Union could be beneficial for groups in Africa. Upon arriving, he was impressed by the lack of race prejudice and felt for the first time in his life that he was truly accepted as a full human be-ing by the people of the Soviet Union. This was a profound discovery and, because of it, he felt connected to those people until his death.

Robeson's study of black music, such as spirituals, reinforced his con-viction that African American songs were "in the tradition of the world's great folk music." The music of working people and people who had suf-fered oppression was born from a similar place in the human spirit. His repertoire, thus, began to expand to include folk songs from around the world. The kinship he discovered with African people and other groups motivated his stand against fascism in the 1930s. Robeson decried the Ital-ian invasion of Ethiopia, the fascist support for Franco in Spain, and Hitler's maneuvering across Europe. By the 1940s, he wanted to be back among his community in the United States, and he planned to bring them "a message about Africa." He did so through work with groups such as the Council on African Affairs. Throughout the war, Robeson demanded that the rhetoric of self-determination uttered by the Allies be applied to colonized people. In addition, African Americans must be given their civil rights, he argued, after participating in a war against fascism. As the Cold War set in, it was the cause of African independence that branded Robeson a radical. The State Department cited his advocacy for Africans and African Americans abroad as reason enough to deprive him of the right to travel. What was Robeson's response? He firmly maintained that speaking out for freedom for his people was his right. Robeson was stubbornly prepared to forego large salaries and a degree of material comfort before he was willing to surrender his right to free speech for a worthwhile cause.

Thus, this examination of Robeson's public career aims to demonstrate how the African diaspora, its culture, people, and politics, was at the heart of his artistic career and political activism. The ways in which he was involved in or responded to major events in the early twentieth century are crucial to understanding his art and politics. Returning to C. L. R. James, he summarized in the 1970s that Robeson was "a man whose history is not to be understood unless seen in the context of the most profound historical movements of our century." Forces that impacted the lives of black Americans, such as segregation and racial violence as well as the Harlem Renaissance and the civil rights protest, were crucial to his narrative. But global events, including colonialism, the rise of fascism, the Second World War, the Cold War, and the fight for African self-determination, also figured prominently. Although Robeson never got to spend much time on the continent, he embraced his racial inheritance and aimed to "think and feel as an African." He committed his diverse talents to furthering the cause of liberation for all people in the African diaspora, which included the continent in addition to the Americas and the West Indies. Through his art, Robeson wanted to convey the dignity of his cultural heritage. As a political activist, he used his voice, and his celebrity, to advocate for equal justice. Discussions of the principles of full freedom and civil rights sometimes sound hackneyed. But in Robeson's view, they were like precious, living entities. They had to be respected, and it was worth making sacrifices to protect them. It was this legacy that drew the procession of mourners when he died. To paraphrase Shakespeare's *Othello*, a role Robeson immortalized, these people knew the dangers he had passed, and they loved him for it. It was a legacy built on humble, but dignified, origins in a small New Jersey town in the waning years of the nineteenth century.

1

SCHOLAR ATHLETE

In April 1898, newspapers across the United States were filled with vivid headlines proclaiming an impending war with Spain. The nation seemed to be on a collision course with the Spanish over their presence on an island near the coast of Florida. However, a small African American paper, the *Cleveland Gazette*, was concerned with matters closer to home. On the ninth of April, the paper reported that a delegation including activist Ida B. Wells had recently met with President McKinley. Wells, who was known for her frank rhetoric and no-nonsense manner, had for several years been waging a public protest against lynching. A particularly gruesome and public form of mob violence, lynching had become an all-too-common tool of racial oppression in the late nineteenth century.

At this meeting with the president, Wells estimated that ten thousand citizens had been victims of lynching in the past twenty years. She then formally requested legislation against this form of brutality, as the perpetrators were rarely punished. President McKinley agreed that the statistics were troubling and promised action. Regrettably, Congress did not take up Wells's plea, despite her eloquent appeal within the halls of power. Undeterred, she continued her crusade to end this vicious spectacle. Little did she know that a future ally in her quest was just making his way into the world.

Perhaps the news story of Wells's summit with the president filtered down to the frame house at 110 Witherspoon Street in Princeton, New Jersey. That Saturday, April 9, the household must have been bustling as Reverend William Drew Robeson's household welcomed a newborn into the world. The fourth boy of five surviving children, Paul Leroy was Maria Louisa Robeson's last baby. Paul's infant features did not yet reveal the towering figure he would become. Like an actor with impeccable timing, his entrance on the day the African American community learned of Wells's encounter with McKinley was nothing short of poetic foreshadowing.

Over four decades later, as the number of lynchings spiked after World War II, a similar antilynching delegation met with President Truman. Paul Robeson capably led this group. Frustrated that antilynching legislation had still failed to materialize, Robeson did not mince words before the president. In fact, he indicated that African Americans would have to do something themselves to curb the epidemic of violence if the government neglected to address the situation. Following this meeting, an audience of several thousand gathered in a light rain at the base of the Lincoln Memorial to hear Robeson's sonorous baritone fall gracefully upon their ears. He offered a song or two and reminded the audience that despite the Emancipation Proclamation having been signed nearly one hundred years ago, African Americans had not yet experienced full freedom. The spirit of Ida B. Wells must have smiled that September day. If she had been alive she would have seen that even though Washington's politicians never passed a bill to outlaw lynching, an activist no less fiery than she had taken up the torch to advocate for their people.

Paul's arrival into the Robeson house coincided with the United States' appearance as a key player on the global stage. As European nations were busy carving empires across the continent of Africa, the United States was staking its claim in the Caribbean and the Pacific. After defeating Spain in 1898, the United States took possession of that country's colonies, including Puerto Rico and Guam. The United States flexed its imperial muscle by dominating Cuba with the Platt Amendment, annexing Hawaii, and embarking on a bloody campaign to control the Philippines. This hunger for new markets was driven in part by the expanding industrial capacity of the United States at the dawn of the twentieth century.

Giant corporations such as Andrew Carnegie's U.S. Steel and John D. Rockefeller's Standard Oil consolidated their businesses and reaped fabulous profits in the largely unregulated marketplace of the Gilded Age.

Railroad lines enticed settlement away from the swelling cities of the Eastern seaboard to the great plains of the West and all the way to the Pacific coast. European immigrants crowded into Atlantic ports seeking the promise of work in steel mills, meat-packing plants, shipping docks, and factories. Some hoped to cultivate a patch of land somewhere in that seemingly endless expanse of territory. The United States was evolving rapidly, and its capacity for growth was fueled to some extent by the vast pool of available laborers. Unskilled workers came cheaply and were expendable. Job protection did not exist, and laborers were easily replaced. Discrimination against ethnic groups such as the Irish was common, but the most acute forms of prejudice and inequity were aimed at African Americans.

Following the end of the Civil War, the Thirteenth Amendment to the Constitution finally abolished slavery in 1865. During the postwar Reconstruction period, black American civil rights were protected and all men gained the right to vote with the Fourteenth and Fifteenth Amendments. Yet by the 1880s, former slaveholding Southerners loyal to the Democratic Party were regaining political power in the South. Once in control, they virtually recreated the slave system by disfranchising African Americans, coercing them into sharecropping contracts, and enacting a rigid, discriminatory code of racial segregation in all facets of public life. These injustices were enforced through intimidation and violence such as lynching. In 1895 when Frederick Douglass, the fervent abolitionist, breathed his last, the economic and social circumstances for African Americans had not been so dark since enslavement. Another distressing symbol appeared two years before Robeson's birth when the Supreme Court sanctioned segregation law in the *Plessy v. Ferguson* decision in 1896. A new race leader emerged in the 1890s. Unlike Douglass, Booker T. Washington found it necessary to temporarily accommodate to the strictures of segregation. He argued for industrial education as a chance at economic advancement, and he hoped that civil rights would later be restored.

The environment in which Paul Robeson spent his early childhood was influenced by these national events. Segregation was common in the North, especially as African Americans began migrating to urban centers seeking jobs. Princeton, New Jersey, was a small town and had been strongly influenced by the generations of Southern gentry who attended its prestigious university. Social relations in Princeton could be described as reflecting the customs of a southern plantation. On such an estate, a white planter owned a grand house, perhaps encircled by majestic oaks with Spanish moss dangling from their branches. A throng of enslaved black people worked the surrounding fields. In Princeton, the distinguished university symbolized the plantation house. The workers were not slaves but were kept in subservient positions. Most of the black community in Princeton was employed as cooks, maids, coachmen, or laborers for the white faculty, students, and administrators of the university.

Though white townspeople could aspire for one of their children to become a student in those esteemed halls of learning, black Princeton residents could afford no such daydream. This was especially true once Woodrow Wilson, a Virginia segregationist, took the reins as president of Princeton. He adamantly refused admittance to blacks even though a few African Americans had previously attended the seminary. This ritual of discrimination did not discourage Reverend Robeson. He forthrightly sought admission for his bright son and namesake, William, around 1900. His request was steadfastly denied. Still, Reverend Robeson's bold act of defiance served as an example of his leadership and undaunted spirit. Even though he was ensnared in a social structure wracked with injustice, his self-respect was never swayed. The elder Robeson's dignity and steadfastness to his principles made a deep and abiding impression on young Paul.

William D. Robeson was born enslaved on a plantation in Martin County, North Carolina, in 1845 to Benjamin and Sabra. Their surname was an iteration of the town's name, Robersonville, which had been named for the prominent slaveholding family of that region. Some biographers, including Paul's son, have asserted that the Robeson lineage was traced back to the dark-skinned Ibo people of West Africa. Yet others contend that there was no definitive documentation for the Robeson family past Paul's grandparents. It is certain that Paul was conscious of the role that African people played in laying the economic foundation of the United States through the sweat of their labor in fields of cotton, rice, and tobacco. He was also aware of the role that his own family had played in that important history. Thus, Paul resolved to fight for equal rights for all people of African descent on the basis of their blood and unpaid toil. Even if the family connection to West Africa was not substantiated, young Paul's sense of identity was firmly rooted in the African-like communal village of the black population in

Princeton. This strong sense of community among people of African lineage must have influenced the Pan-African ideology he developed later in life.

During his teenage years, around 1858, William Robeson made the bold decision to escape from the plantation. This was a fairly common strategy of rebellion. Scores of enslaved people, perhaps as many as a thousand per year, left the fields in search of liberation. Yet breaking from the slave system was always a heart-wrenching decision. If a slave departed permanently, he might never again see his family or friends. He might face harsh punishments, or he might leave only to be seized and enslaved by someone else. Fortunately, William had a companion: his older brother, Ezekiel.

The two Robeson brothers probably made use of the Underground Railroad to make their getaway. The indomitable Harriet Tubman, known as the "Moses" of her people, sometimes directed runaway slaves traveling via this informal network of safe houses. William successfully left Martin County and settled in the free soil state of Pennsylvania. In his memoir, Paul noted that William's devotion to his mother, Sabra, compelled him to return to North Carolina twice to visit her, which was an extremely risky proposition. Once the Civil War commenced, the gutsy freedman joined the Union cause. William was most likely employed as a laborer, perhaps digging trenches or cooking for soldiers, to support the war effort.

After the war, William Robeson enrolled at Lincoln University, an African American institution, near Philadelphia. He clearly had a resolute belief in the importance of education. Robeson proved to be an ambitious and driven student, completing three degrees, including a bachelor in Sacred Theology, by 1876. Paul's father, who studied Latin, Greek, and Hebrew at Lincoln, no doubt influenced Paul's excellence as a student and his proclivity for languages. William found time for other pursuits while in college, including meeting and courting the lovely Maria Louisa Bustill.

The union of a daughter of the Bustill family to William Robeson, like two ends of a rope, conjoined divergent branches of the African people in America. Robeson had only recently been unshackled from slavery. His education was newly acquired, his family was poor, and his future prospects were unclear. The respected Bustill family, on the other hand, could definitely trace their ancestry back to the early 1600s. The African part of the family had intermarried with Native Americans and Quakers. The Bustills possessed a lighter skin tone, which was considered more advantageous than darker skin, like Robeson's. They furthermore had a distinguished history in the Philadelphia area.

Paul's great-great-grandfather, Cyrus Bustill, was born enslaved in 1732. The enterprising Bustill was apprenticed and became an exceptional baker. His proficiency in the kitchen enabled him to purchase his freedom and build a thriving business. It was said that he had even baked for General Washington's troops during the Revolution. In 1787, Bustill, along with Richard Allen, Absalom Jones, and other free blacks, founded the Free African Society. This was the first African American mutual aid society and an important precursor to the African Methodist Episcopal (AME) church. The Bustill kin network included many professional people, and they viewed the Robeson clan as somewhat humble in comparison. Maria Louisa, a school teacher and several years William's junior, nevertheless set out for New Jersey with her new husband around 1878. Once settled in Princeton, the Robeson family grew as Maria Louisa delivered William Junior, Benjamin, Reeve, Marian, and, finally, Paul. By the time their youngest was born, Maria Louisa was forty-five, William was fifty-three, and the family was well established in the parish house on Witherspoon Street.

Reverend Robeson was well known among the black and white communities of Princeton. In a town of around four thousand people, African Americans represented about one-fifth of the population. Reverend Robeson became the head of Witherspoon Presbyterian Church in 1879. During his tenure it became a center of the black community. African Americans found solace in their homes, churches, and businesses along Witherspoon, Quarry, and McLean streets. In these dwellings, the black community held benefits and potluck suppers. They organized an Odd Fellows Lodge and a local baseball team. The Hampton Singers and the Fisk Jubilee Singers performed concerts of spirituals in Princeton. In 1881, Reverend Robeson delivered a moving eulogy for the assassinated President Garfield. This speech reminded African Americans of Lincoln's untimely death and helped galvanize local support for the Republican Party. The famous Booker T. Washington himself even stopped for a speaking engagement in 1895, much to the delight of the black community.

The close-knit black population of Princeton also had an activist inclination. In 1903, they publicly celebrated the fortieth anniversary of the Emancipation Proclamation. In Trenton three years later, they protested a production of Thomas Dixon's play *The Clansman*, which was a degrading portrait of black Americans that glorified the vigilantism of the Ku Klux Klan. Education for black children in Princeton was segregated, with a black school established on the same street as Reverend Robeson's church. In the 1880s, the New Jersey legislature passed a law to desegregate schools. Yet local jurisdictions immediately sought ways to avoid compliance. The Princeton school board offered the black community a better school with more teachers if parents would agree to keep their students out of the white schools. This issue split the black community. Reverend Robeson supported a stronger black school, arguing that young children should not be sent where they were not welcome. His position was ultimately adopted, and education in Princeton remained racially separated until the 1940s. As a result, Paul attended a segregated grade school and did not have frequent contact with whites when he was very young. Paul recalled in his memoir that the Princeton of his childhood was "spiritually located in Dixie" because it reinforced these patterns of white supremacy.

Unwelcome in most white institutions, the center of Paul's early life was in the bosom of his father's church. Black churches served as a place of emotional and physical release from the daily indignities of segregation and discrimination. At church, everyone could raise their voices without fear of recrimination. The music awakened their senses and lifted their spirits. Rousing sermons stirred the imagination with vivid images of a heavenly reward for the godly and everlasting damnation for evildoers. Paul especially relished the spiritual songs of his people. The sweet rhythm of this folk music emerged during enslavement to nurture a people who otherwise might have drowned in their sorrows. Paul was also immersed in the lyricism of his father's oratory, which came out of the black oral tradition. These fine preachers he referred to as "masters of poetic speech." In her biography, Paul's wife, Eslanda, summarized that "the church, the music, and the people became an essential part of him."

The comfort and security provided by the black community in Princeton were especially significant following the shocking death of Paul's mother. In 1904, Maria Louisa was cleaning near the stove when a stray ember suddenly ignited her skirts. The flames quickly engulfed her. Her body gruesomely burned, Maria Louisa bravely managed to remain conscious until her husband returned home so she could offer him a final good-bye. Amid the chaos, no one in the family was certain whether Paul had witnessed the tragic accident. He later maintained that he had no memory of his mother's death and might have repressed the trauma out of self-protection. In Paul Robeson Junior's biography, he wrote that the loss of Paul's mother left an emotional scar from which his father never completely recovered. Paul, a sensitive child, was wounded by complicated feelings of guilt, fear, and trouble with intimacy for the rest of his life.

Because his siblings were older, Paul was frequently the only child at home. When faced with his mother's absence, he found his father, "Pop," to be a dependable, unswerving companion. Pop's devotion prompted Paul to declare in his memoir that "the glory of my boyhood years was my father." The Robeson family was supportive, while the Bustills distanced themselves following Maria Louisa's passing. Additional care flowed from the black population of Princeton. Although Paul must have been lonesome as a motherless child, his memoir recounted that everyone in the town helped raise him. There was always an extra place for Paul at the dinner table of a neighbor or space enough for him to sleep in the bed of a friend if needed. He remembered that these hardworking people had few material belongings but were rich in their compassion. They lavished affection on the preacher's young son. This bond of kinship with Princeton's black community profoundly touched Paul. Later in life, after fame and wealth had blessed him, he fervently maintained his affiliation with working people. The communal sense of shared values and material possessions demonstrated a kind of socialism to Paul in childhood that deeply resonated with him for many years.

Unfortunately, Paul and Pop were uprooted from the Princeton community in 1907. William had lost his position at the Witherspoon Church. Reverend Robeson had denounced racial violence and had contested the status quo when he requested that his oldest son be admitted to the university. Thus, his ouster probably stemmed from the white power structure of the town feeling threatened by his outspoken nature. After laboring at a series of odd jobs, including hauling ashes, William got another church appointment in 1907. The family then moved about thirty miles north to Westfield, New Jersey.

Separation from the nurturing environment of Princeton was tough for Paul, but he soon began settling into the new town. Westfield was smaller, and the black children attended an integrated school, which was a new experience for him. Consequently, Paul began interacting more with the working-class white community. A couple of years later, Reverend Robeson took a position at St. Thomas AME Zion church in nearby Somerville. He served as pastor there until his death. Had they remained in Princeton, Paul most likely would have continued his education in all-black schools; however, in 1911 he entered Somerville High as one of only about a dozen black students.

Paul proved to be a capable student from an early age. As a child, people in Princeton had often noticed a special quality about him that might one day make him a leader in the black community. Pop encouraged his youngest son's studies. He especially emphasized the importance of languages, literature, and public speaking. Despite the prevalence of Booker T. Washington's theory that African Americans should concentrate on obtaining industrial training, Reverend Robeson rebuffed this notion. That he had supported himself while earning three advanced degrees at Lincoln University attested to this fact. The elder Robeson also fostered his children's pursuit of higher education: William Junior (Bill) became a physician, Benjamin followed his father's footsteps into the ministry, and Marian, like her mother, became a teacher. To all of his offspring, Paul included, William Robeson stressed the idea that success equaled the fulfillment of one's personal aptitude. His message was not to compare yourself to others, but to continually aim for your personal best. When he saw Paul's report card, Pop might ask, "Why get a 95 when 100 is possible?" In his memoir, Paul pointed out that his father did this not because he was obsessed with perfection but to underline that personal integrity was vital to achieving one's maximum human potential.

Accordingly, a positive self-image and mutual respect were the building blocks of relationships in the Robeson household. Pop's example illustrated values of compassion, dignity, and a commitment to principles that Paul absorbed. The youngster understood by observing his father's interaction with the community that all people shared a common humanity that should be acknowledged. Paul imparted in his memoir a revealing anecdote concerning the only time he disobeyed his father. Paul was about ten and had not done something his father requested. The boy darted away when Pop queried him. When the older man ran after Paul, Pop fell and broke his tooth. Young Paul was horrified. He quickly helped his father to his feet as feelings of shame, ingratitude, and selfishness washed over him. Afterward, Paul's impulse toward self-discipline constrained him, and he never had to be admonished by his father again.

Always polite and respectful, Paul became popular in the Somerville neighborhood. In high school, he made white friends whose parents seemed pleased that their children were spending time with a well-behaved scholastic achiever. His buddies, however, were probably more excited about Paul's love of sport and were eager to toss a football around in an empty lot. At Somerville High, several teachers took an interest in Paul and helped to mold his multifaceted talents. He joined the glee club because Miss Vosseller, the music teacher, had observed his fine voice. Anna Miller, an English teacher, introduced Paul to Shakespeare and had the foresight to cast him as Othello. At around six feet tall and 190 pounds, Paul towered over the football field his senior year. He also played guard on the basketball court and catcher for the baseball team.

The specter of racism did, at times, rear its head during Paul's adolescence. In 1914, field officials ignored Paul as football players willfully piled on top of him, leaving him sidelined with several broken bones. Somerville's principal took an immediate dislike to the gifted student athlete and made use of every opportunity to reproach Paul. His son's biography asserted that Dr. Ackerman went as far as to purposely withhold news of a preliminary scholarship test from Paul so he could not compete. Parties and dances often followed the ball games and glee club recitals in which Paul participated. Yet he hesitated to attend these functions at the nearly all-white school. Social life was pretty rigidly segregated and, although Paul had white friends, he was mindful that it could be dangerous to overtly challenge social customs.

During these years, Paul learned to move adeptly between distinctly separate environments: the predominately white school, the white working-class neighborhood, the black church, and the black community in Princeton that he considered home. He did not understand until later in life that his social adroitness was rather unique. His wife described this gift as a "social ease" that would enable anyone to feel comfortable in his presence. Most of his classmates remembered this gregarious, smiling, and courteous side of Paul. On the other hand, he suppressed a deep rage at times. For example, when those vicious football players purposely left him hobbling to the bench with a broken collarbone, he realized that, at his size, physical retribution could be deadly. Instead, he withdrew into a private inner sanctum to avoid such confrontation. Still, Paul would not refuse to stand up to an opponent, if necessary. In the words of his son, there was a staunch resolve behind Paul's outwardly "placid manner." These traits were vividly apparent later in his life when Paul, the activist, confronted government repression during the early Cold War years.

Paul managed to find out about the college scholarship competition that Dr. Ackerman had attempted to conceal. The reward was a full scholarship to Rutgers, the state college of New Jersey. Now a senior, Paul had planned to enroll at his father's alma mater, Lincoln University. However, a four-year scholarship was appealing and would alleviate his aging father's financial responsibilities. Plus, New Brunswick was close enough for Paul to visit Pop regularly. Since he had missed the preliminary test, Paul had to undertake one exam that covered content from all four years of high school. His competitors, in contrast, were writing an exam over material solely from the past year.

Paul buckled down to prepare for the rigorous examination. It was an important sign when his hard work and intellect triumphed. Dr. Ackerman's animosity appeared especially baseless when Paul won the scholarship. In retrospect, Paul believed it was "a decisive point in my life." In the 1910s Rutgers was a fairly small, exclusive institution that had only opened its doors to a handful of African Americans. Paul Robeson would now be counted among them. At this significant turning point in his life, he held firm to the assurance of his self-worth. Paul later wrote, "Deep in my heart from that day on was a conviction which none of the Ackerman's of America would ever be able to shake. Equality might be denied, but I *knew* I was not inferior."

In the spring of 1915, before graduating from Somerville High, Paul entered a statewide oratorical competition. He placed third in the contest. This was commendable, though he had his sights on the top position. More important than his award was Paul's chosen subject. At seventeen years of age, he selected to recite Wendell Phillips's oratory on Toussaint L'Ouverture before a virtually all-white audience. Phillips was a passionate abolitionist from Massachusetts who was known for his candid repudiation of the slave system. The speech that Paul delivered celebrated a prominent leader of the slave insurrection, which led to the establishment of Haiti as a free republic in 1804. To invoke Toussaint L'Ouverture was to acknowledge a powerful emblem of rebellion.

The crowd must have been mildly surprised, and maybe a little uncomfortable, that the well-spoken black student chose to, as Paul later declared, give voice to Phillips's "searing attack . . . of white supremacy." Paul recollected that, at the time, he did not fully comprehend the meaning of the speech. Instead, he concentrated on perfecting his diction. Nonetheless, the occasion generated a potent image of the six-foot-tall adolescent standing erectly in front of a crowd, perhaps a bit anxious but meticulous about his phrasing, as he honored the great general who had attacked the slave system.

This event was a prescient symbol of Paul's future as an advocate for civil rights. Booker T. Washington died the year Paul delivered this speech. A new, more radical group of agitators had recently formed an organization that directly protested for civil rights. The National Association for the Advancement of Colored People (NAACP) represented the emerging vanguard of black activism. They decried disfranchisement, rallied against lynching, and affirmed the right of promising African Americans to pursue higher education. Though too young to have helped found the NAACP, Paul now confirmed his place as a member of the generation that was waging a frontal assault on discrimination. Moreover, the seeds of Paul's character and the kernels of his talents had all germinated during these years in Princeton, Westfield, and Somerville. He concluded in his memoir, "All which came later . . . had their roots in the[se] early years."

By the autumn of 1915, when Paul Robeson entered Rutgers College, Europe had been embroiled in the Great War for over a year. Woodrow Wilson, now president of the United States, promised to keep the nation out of Europe's conflict. This isolationist policy was tested when the Germans sank the cruise liner *Lusitania* that year. Even though over one hundred Americans died in the attack, the United States did not plunge into the conflagration for another two years. Secure from the grisly battles an ocean away, Paul spent the summer of 1915 employed as a kitchen boy at a resort in Rhode Island. Paul's brother, Ben, was there to show him the ropes and play touch football on the beach in their off time. Now six foot two and around two hundred pounds, Paul must have been a striking physical presence when he arrived on the Rutgers campus.

Rutgers was founded in 1766, one of only eight higher-learning institutions at that time in the colonies. The campus tucked next to the Raritan River was originally established to train clergy but expanded when it became a land-grant institution in the 1860s. The student body of about five hundred was still all male when Paul entered. It was also almost exclusively white. Paul was only the third African American to attend the college, and he had no black peers in his entering class. His impressive frame coupled with his dark skin certainly made an unmistakable profile when he strode along George Street. Finding a seat in class or riding on a trolley car near campus must have been an anxious experience for the new freshman.

Paul Robeson Junior's biography pointed out that Paul was not permitted to live in the dormitory his first year since there were no black students to share his room. Instead, the young scholar was welcomed into the home of a black family in New Brunswick. Fortunately, another black student, Robert Davenport, joined Paul his second year on campus. They roomed together in Winants Hall and became fast friends. Davenport was familiar with the surrounding communities where the two African Americans frequently socialized. Despite the difficulties he faced, Paul was often able to submerge his disquiet beneath a composed, good-natured personality. Most of his classmates remembered him as respectful, very musical, and quick with a smile. The social ease he had developed in high school served him well during these years. Visiting Pop regularly back in Somerville also eased Paul's college transition.

By any estimation, his achievements at Rutgers were stunning. The athletic, forensic, and scholastic gifts that surfaced at Somerville High truly soared in college. By the time he graduated, Paul was a nationally recognized college football player and arguably the best player of his time. He amassed no less than fourteen varsity sports letters in track, basketball, baseball, and, of course, football. By his junior year, Paul's academic record was already strong enough to be invited to join the prestigious Phi Beta Kappa honor society. The Cap and Skull Society, a group that recognized the four seniors who embodied the ideals of the college, also honored Paul. He somehow found time to hone his debating technique and lead the debate team to numerous victories. Paul never failed to win an oratorical contest while at Rutgers. The entire college had the chance to appreciate his rhetorical skill when he delivered the commencement address his senior year.

Though he accumulated a remarkable record of accomplishments, the momentum of Paul's college years was also burdened by setbacks. This extremely gifted individual at times collided headlong into what W. E. B. Du Bois labeled "the color line." For example, the Phi Beta Kappa group acknowledged Paul's outstanding grade point average but did not welcome him for social occasions. Similarly, the glee club enjoyed hearing his baritone in their home recitals, but it was too complicated for him to travel with the group because of segregation, and his presence was not embraced at social events following their performances. However, Paul's experience with the football team probably best illustrated the racial hostility he faced in college. This was overcome largely because his indisputable talent could not be ignored.

Before Paul tried out for the team, no African American had ever played football at Rutgers. After his four years, probably no one at the college would ever play football like Paul Robeson again. Securing a place on the team was Paul's first major obstacle. George Foster Sanford, an esteemed coach who was a member of the National Football Hall of Fame, led the squad. Coach Sanford knew of Paul from his high school days and wanted Paul for the team he was assembling. However, the varsity players would not hear of having a black teammate and even threatened to strike. Coach Sanford, aware of Paul's potential, offered him a chance at making the team if he could prove himself on the field. Having been excluded from the preseason practices, Paul must have been slightly apprehensive while gearing up for the first scrimmage.

Paul's aptitude at playing defensive end was readily apparent. Unfortunately, so was the racism of the players who relentlessly pummeled him on the field. At the end of the day, Paul nursed a dislocated shoulder and an array of bruises. More than the silent treatment from the white players, the blatant physical punishment unnerved him. Paul wondered if he could continue to face such cruelty. If lynch mobs could murder black citizens without punishment, how could he expect any protection on a football field? Yet a pep talk from his brother, Ben, reminded Paul of a lesson from their father. Paul later explained that he knew he was not at Rutgers "just on his own." In reality, he "was the representative of a lot of Negro boys who wanted to play football and . . . [he] had to show that [he] could take whatever was handed out."

And show them he did. At one scrimmage Paul was momentarily on the ground after making a tackle. Seeing Paul's vulnerable right hand lying on the grass, a player deliberately crushed his cleat into Paul's fingers, prying out a fingernail or two in the process. Rage seethed through the young athlete's body. Paul had reached his limit of forbearance in the face of direct insult. Burying the pain of his hand, he lined up for the next play. That player, Frank Kelly, was carrying the ball. Kelly was now the focused target of Paul's undiluted muscular force. With his arms extended, the dominance of his absolute, unchecked strength lifted Kelly into the air. Paul recalled, "I got Kelly in my two hands and I was going to smash him so hard to the ground that I'd break him right in two, and I could have done it." Fearful for Kelly's safety, Coach Sanford hollered that Robeson had made the varsity team. Paul then released the player, who must have been flabbergasted.

This episode illustrated that anger was a latent force inside of Paul. Never before had he allowed his rage to flow to the surface with such exhilaration. He managed to contain his rage carefully but also realized its capacity. Paul plainly demonstrated to his teammates that he was capable of defending himself. And when he did so, they could be at risk. This incident was also an apt metaphor for his social activism later in life. Righteous anger churned within Paul over the disfranchisement, segregation, and lynching of his people. The unconstitutional banning of his passport caused him to fume. And few issues boiled inside of Paul with more urgency than securing independence for African colonies. This anger must have bolstered his unparalleled ability to speak out bluntly and courageously to those in power. Frank Kelly's insult had been the target of Paul's anger that day on the college football field. In the years to come, his rage would be focused upon the broader forces of fascism and colonialism.

The football team grew to accept "Robey." This respect was, no doubt, inspired by his unmistakable talent for the game. During Paul's four years, the team had a record of 22-6-3. He excelled at several positions—tackle, guard, and end—but could usually be spotted at left tackle. The crowd in the stands on those autumn days began to notice and talk about this versatile player. Soon, they were excitedly cheering for Robey as he ran in a fumble for a touchdown against Rensselaer and scored on two thirty-yard pass plays against Fort Wadsworth. In a 1917 game played at Ebbets Field in New

York, Paul caught a pass for a touchdown to help secure a 14–0 victory over the heavily favored, undefeated Newport Naval Reserve team.

Paul continued to face racial discrimination despite his athletic prowess. On the road, he roomed with an assistant coach to make sure his safety was not compromised. Paul's locker was often separated from the other members of the team. Worse still, in 1916, Washington and Lee College objected to competing against a black player. Paul was benched, and the southern school tied Rutgers in that game. Many African American fans were outraged. James Dickson Carr, the first black graduate of Rutgers in 1892, penned a scathing letter of protest directly to President William Demarest in response to his administration's yielding to racial bias. The following year, the West Virginia coach made a similar request, but Coach Sanford stood his ground and kept his star player on the field. Paul's game matured, and his proficiency was nationally recognized. In 1917 there was no official All-American team because of World War I, but Paul was listed as a standout player by almost every major U.S. newspaper. The next year, Walter Camp, the father of American football, recognized Paul with a formal place in the All-American lineup. In Camp's words, Robeson was "the greatest defensive back ever to trod the gridiron." Perhaps even more fulfilling for Paul were the games when Pop was sitting in the bleachers rooting for his son.

Sadly, Reverend Robeson's health had been declining during Paul's college years. In the spring of 1918, he beckoned his youngest son to help organize his affairs. Upon Pop's death that May, Paul had to confront his final year of college alone. Now a young man, he was forced to contemplate his future without the input of his steadfast anchor. Reverend Robeson's last request had been for Paul to enter an oratorical contest at Rutgers. Paul mustered the resolve to win the competition with a speech titled "Loyalty and the American Negro."

It was his father who had demonstrated to Paul the significance of principles such as loyalty. Pop's values remained ingrained in Paul and, in a way, fostered a continued relationship between them. Throughout his life, Paul measured himself against the mores of his father. During one of the most trying periods of his career, Paul wrote in a 1952 column, "My Pop's influence is still present in the struggles that face me today. I know he would say, 'Stand firm, son; stand by your beliefs, your principles.' You bet I will, Pop—as long as there is a breath in my body." An obituary for Reverend

William Drew Robeson recorded that he was a man of "strong character" who was "always interested" in the welfare of his people and "quickly resented any attempt to belittle them or to interfere with their rights." Indeed, the same could be said of his youngest son.

Paul's scholarship and social awareness were displayed in two important ways his senior year. His senior thesis showed a promising legal mind, and his commencement address powerfully heralded the entrance of a budding social activist. "The Fourteenth Amendment: The Sleeping Giant of the Constitution" was the title of Paul's thesis. In it, he displayed his familiarity with U.S. legal history and argued for the primacy of this law regarding federal protection of the rights of citizens. Paul pointed out that this amendment for the first time defined the basis of citizenship as "all persons born or naturalized" in the United States. This, he contended, effectively overturned the Supreme Court's 1857 decision in the *Dred Scott v. Sandford* case, which had unequivocally stated that no person of African descent could be entitled to U.S. citizenship.

Given his cogent assessment of the *Scott* case, it was perhaps surprising that Paul did not refer to the *Plessy v. Ferguson* case in his analysis. This 1896 case set the course for widespread de jure, or legal, segregation even as de facto, or traditional, segregation was already evident around the country. In his famous, but lone, dissent Justice John Marshall Harlan perceptively insisted that segregation law did violate the "true intent and meaning" of both the Thirteenth and Fourteenth Amendments as guardians of freedom and citizenship rights. Harlan's interpretation was progressive for its time and perhaps a little too radical for a thesis by a black student with the hope of soon being accepted into law school. It was probably pragmatic that Paul avoided a discussion of *Plessy*, considering his professor made the comment "extravagant" next to his opening statement: "Of all the forces . . . in protecting our civil rights from invasion . . . the Fourteenth Amendment is the greatest."

On the other hand, Robeson's commencement address, "The New Idealism," contained a clear call for social change. He was aware of current affairs and used the wartime context to lay the foundation of the text. The peace treaty between the Allies and the Germans was signed in France the same month, June 1919, that Paul delivered this speech. When the United States had officially entered the war in 1917, President Wilson declared that the country was doing so to make the world safe for democracy to flourish. Knowing the audience would be familiar with that vision, Paul skillfully opened by appealing to the predominantly white crowd's sense of patriotic duty to preserve the ideals of freedom. He then suggested that the close of the war offered an "unparalleled opportunity for reconstructing our entire national life." The use of the term *reconstruct* cleverly invoked the post–Civil War era when the nation first included African Americans as citizens.

At several points, Paul referred to the sacrifice made by the men lost in the war. He alluded to Lincoln's renowned Gettysburg address by noting that the deaths of these men would not have been in vain if the people remained devoted to the cause for which they fought. Paul then subtly transitioned into the contemporary circumstances of African Americans. This last section was truly remarkable. In the space of mere paragraphs he articulately summarized the ethos of black leadership of the previous generation and looked to the future. First, he acknowledged the idea of uplifting the race from within that was proffered in Booker T. Washington's era. Paul recognized that African Americans must "stand or fall by their own merit" and that success would rely on values of "self-reliance, self-respect, industry, perseverance and economy." A laudable message, but it was hardly innovative.

However, the next detail was revelatory and truly challenged the listeners: "But in order for us to successfully do all these things it is necessary that you of the favored race catch a new vision and exemplify in your actions this new American spirit." Yes, he confirmed, African Americans had a role to play in improving their condition. But the black community had not accidentally landed in a position without political power or economic or civil rights. The situation was deliberately imposed through racial subjugation. Social change could not then be a one-way street. Equally vital was the recognition from white America that they had a responsibility to treat their fellow man with compassion, behave fair-mindedly, and extend a "fraternal spirit" to their fellow citizens. Certainly, Paul declared, a new social order must be created in which all who are deserving "receive the respect, honor and dignity due them."

He concluded by reiterating the call that all continue to fight, in the name of those who died in the war, until "in all sections of this fair land there will be equal opportunities for all . . . and until black and white shall clasp friendly hands conscious of the fact that we are brethren and that God is the father of us all." It was a brave and penetrating speech for anyone to have delivered. That he was only twenty-one-years old made his performance all the more impressive. Paul's words were especially courageous given the perilous circumstances of the era. For example, mob violence against African Americans reached epidemic proportions in riots in 1917 and 1919. The government was cracking down on socialists and political radicals during the Palmer Raids of 1918 to 1919. Activists demanding suffrage for women had been met in recent years with beatings and jail time. The current president had segregated federal offices in Washington upon coming to power. Thus, Paul had no way of foretelling exactly how his speech would be received.

The audience had been spellbound. Newspaper accounts of the graduation ceremony wondered if there had ever been such a prolonged ovation for a commencement speech in the history of the college. The fundamental elements of Paul's youth—his father's values, his study of language and history, the honing of his oratorical style, perhaps even a bit of anger—had cohered on this occasion. The speech announced that Paul Robeson was fulfilling the special quality of leadership the Princeton community had seen in him as a small child. It also confirmed Robeson as a member of W. E. B. Du Bois's model of the "talented tenth." This was the portion of a new generation of agitators who were the brightest and most talented in the African American community. According to Du Bois, this group, one-tenth of the population, would form the backbone of the civil rights struggle in the early twentieth century. The promising young Robeson headed to New York in the summer of 1919 to begin law school. He did so with his father present only in spirit but equipped with a strong inner compass to steer his yet uncharted path.

2

RENAISSANCE MAN

In December 1929, Paul Robeson returned to Princeton, New Jersey, the town where he was born, to give a benefit concert at Alexander Hall on the grounds of the university. An enthusiastic audience greeted his interpretations of African American spirituals and folk songs, and they demanded numerous encores from the generous performer. According to a special dispatch to the *New York Times*, such an ovation had "seldom been seen" in the singer's hometown. The proceeds from the event went to aid the local church that William Robeson had ministered during Paul's boyhood. Robeson, the solo vocalist, was now eagerly applauded on the campus that had been strictly segregated in his youth and had denied admission to his older brother. This was his first concert back in Princeton, but Robeson was, by the end of the twenties, well known as an artist. His recitals had been warmly received across the United States and abroad in Europe. Robeson's acting talent had been ignited, and he had achieved fame in leading roles in plays such as *The Emperor Jones* while immortalizing minor roles such as Joe in *Show Boat* with his memorable baritone. It was not unusual for his name to be in print in publications such as the *New Yorker*, which had recently referred to Robeson as "the promise of his race." In 1907, he had moved away from Princeton with his minister-father who had, at times, undertaken odd jobs to support the family. Robeson was now a notable artist who mingled with the glitterati in New York and had tea in Britain's House of Commons. How had this meteoric rise taken shape? What had come to pass in his life that had afforded Robeson the unusual opportunity to return as a bona fide celebrity to the small town whose black community had nurtured his formative years? In the relatively brief span of a decade, Robeson transitioned from studying law to undertaking a multifaceted artistic career with a steady upward trajectory. The narrative started with his arrival in New York ten years earlier.

Paul Robeson ventured to the metropolis in the summer of 1919 to take a place at New York University's law school, although he ended up transferring to Columbia University. The uptown campus of Columbia suited Robeson better since it was adjacent to the thriving African American community of Harlem. Robeson took up residence in the city at a significant time when events initiated during the First World War were transitioning to a cultural rebirth that profoundly influenced the course of his career. After the Versailles Treaty officially ended the Great War, demobilized soldiers were returning to the United States. The all-black 369th Infantry regiment, known affectionately as the Harlem Hellfighters, came home after fighting with the French army. They had spent more time on the front than any other American unit, and several of the Hellfighters were awarded the esteemed French Croix de Guerre for their heroic efforts. These men, and thousands of others, had followed W. E. B. Du Bois's advice to "close ranks" and join the war effort. Writing in the influential *Crisis*, the official magazine of the NAACP, which was based in New York and sold one hundred thousand copies monthly, Du Bois had hoped that demonstrating loyalty by supporting the war would motivate the federal government to protect the citizenship rights of African Americans. If the United States was fighting to make the "world safe for democracy," as President Wilson claimed, surely democratic rights for its black citizens would not be overlooked after the conflagration.

However, the Harlem Hellfighters, and all black returning soldiers, faced increased lynching, continued disfranchisement, limited economic opportunities, and strict segregation back in the United States. Even worse, racial violence swept like a scourge through dozens of cities in what came to be known as the Red Summer of 1919. Racist, anti-immigrant, and antiradical fervor had been stirred up during the war and helped inspire a nationwide resurgence of the Ku Klux Klan. The urban pogroms had also been motivated by an enormous demographic shift, known as the Great Migration, which had occurred as hundreds of thousands of African Americans journeyed out of the South during and immediately following the war.

With immigration from Europe slowed down to a trickle, black Americans turned their backs on the low pay and discrimination of the largely agrarian South and turned northward for wartime industrial jobs. These jobs were in decline as war production wound down, and whites grew increasingly resentful of the mounting African American presence in the urban centers of the North. In addition to racial violence, de facto segregation proliferated in the North, and African Americans could secure housing in only a few dilapidated neighborhoods. Many labor unions refused to recruit black workers, who were sometimes reduced to acting as scabs, the despised laborers who were called upon during strikes. All in all, the desperate social and economic circumstances motivated Du Bois to pen an incensed editorial that year that repudiated lynching, disfranchisement, and the limited employment and educational opportunities afforded black citizens. He famously countered Wilson's lack of regard for racial justice by observing of the African American community, "We return from fighting. We return fighting."

An antiradical posture was also apparent in the wake of World War I. Following the passage of the Espionage Act in 1917, pressure was applied broadly to just about anyone involved in left-wing political activities. Perhaps most famously, Socialist Party leader Eugene V. Debs was arrested and convicted for making an antiwar speech in 1918. Although he maintained that it was his constitutional right to decry the imperialist war in Europe, a jury disagreed and sent him to prison. His sentence was ultimately commuted in 1921, but not before Debs ran again for president from jail and garnered nearly a million votes. The postwar repression of civil liberties was most vehemently demonstrated in the Palmer Raids around 1920, in which thousands were arrested and held without charge. "Big Bill" Haywood, a leader of the radical Industrial Workers of the World (IWW) labor union, was sentenced to prison for supporting striking for fair pay during the war. Emma Goldman, who later became friends with Robeson and his wife, was promptly deported for her anarchist political activism. This "Red Scare" had long-term consequences as left-wing discourse and activity was virtually immobilized. Groups such as the IWW and the Socialist Party practically crumbled under the repressive circumstances. The infant U.S. Communist Party went underground to try to avoid scrutiny. While the United States had been purportedly paving the way for democracy abroad, freedom of speech and political action were effectively squelched at home.

This foreshadowed the anti-Communist hysteria that gripped the American imagination after the Second World War. Although the young Robeson was not yet directly involved in political activism during the Red Scare of 1919, its successor in the late 1940s greatly impacted his life and work.

The war, then, was a political turning point as the U.S. government signaled its strength by taking on unprecedented powers during the era. After the war, the largely probusiness Republican leadership of the 1920s encouraged economic expansion based on manufacturing consumer goods. Automobile production soared. Radios appeared in many homes and apartments, while new appliances such as vacuum cleaners and washing machines eased the domestic burdens of women. Purchasing goods on credit became more common as the American idea of standard of living became wedded to the ability to participate in the expanding consumer culture. Many people seemed to want to forget about the war, and they flocked to amusement parks for entertainment or paid a nickel to see a motion picture in the theater. On the other hand, the passage of prohibition and the rise of fundamentalism pointed to a deeply felt religiosity among Americans, especially in the South and West. These men and women viewed modern urban life as a debasement of traditional moral values such as thrift and temperance.

Another group also rejected the burgeoning materialism of the postwar era. The Greenwich Village neighborhood of New York became a haven for bohemian artists and writers in what has been labeled "the lost generation." While debating the philosophy of Karl Marx or the new psychology of Sigmund Freud in smoky coffeehouses, these people reacted against the reigning paradigm of European culture that had led to the unimaginable horrors of the recent war. They sought an alternative cultural milieu in which to explore the human condition. Some of these writers, such as Ridgley Torrence and Eugene O'Neill, drew upon the African American experience as source material in their quest for artistic renewal. Torrence and O'Neill were considered bold for creating dignified black characters in plays such as *Simon the Cyrenian* and *The Emperor Jones*, which starred Robeson when they were revived later in the 1920s. Although these white writers had little personal knowledge about African American culture, this interest in black culture in the art world helped to usher in a period of intense cultural output in the African American community of Harlem. If white Americans were interested in the African American experience, then here was an opportunity for black artists to render the humanity of their community honestly and, in so doing, help influence the national discourse on race. As historian David L. Lewis has astutely pointed out, the focus on African American culture in the 1920s served very different purposes for these two groups of artists. The bohemian artists of the Village wanted to reshape society before they would embrace it again; whereas for African Americans, art was a means by which they could try to change society in order to be accepted into it. While economic opportunities and political representation were severely limited, African Americans could argue for equality through the theater, concert hall, and publishing house. Just as Robeson was arriving in Harlem, then, a movement was brewing that would ultimately help guide the path of his career.

The demographics of the neighborhood in Manhattan that lies north of Central Park and is known as Harlem started to change in the early twentieth century. Due to a variety of circumstances and the energies of an enterprising black realtor, African American families streamed into the buildings flanking Fifth and Sixth Avenues and the streets around 135th. Though they were charged higher rents than other tenants, many African Americans were happy to leave the crowded midtown neighborhoods of San Juan Hill and the Tenderloin. As more Southerners competed for space during the Great Migration, Harlem's black community fashioned a culture with distinctive Southern American undertones. Eslanda Robeson once noticed that it was almost impossible not to bump into someone from one's hometown when promenading down the avenue in Harlem on a pleasant afternoon. European immigrants still made up the majority of the neighborhood's population even as a vibrant African American community emerged east of Eighth Avenue to the Harlem River and between 130th and 145th streets. A healthy West Indian population added to the Pan-African character of the neighborhood, and by the 1920s it was known as "the Negro capital of the world." In 1916, a West Indian named Marcus Garvey spoke for the first time at the public speaker's corner on Lenox Avenue and 135th Street. Garvey and his Universal Negro Improvement Association (UNIA) wooed the African American masses with a potent message of racial pride. His scheme to purchase a fleet of ships to convey people from the diaspora back to Africa was a spectacular flop. However, Garvey's ability to rally ordinary people around the Pan-African slogans of "Africa for the Africans" and "Up, you might race" was rarely outmatched.

By the time Robeson became a resident of Harlem, West Indian poet Claude McKay, who later became a friend, had acknowledged the racial violence of the era. He declared that there was a new militancy in the postwar generation when he wrote, "Like men we'll face the murderous cowardly pack, / Pressed to the wall, dying, but fighting back!" Political and civil rights groups such as the NAACP, UNIA, and the National Urban League circulated the periodicals *Crisis*, *Opportunity*, *Negro World*, and *Messenger* that were read widely in the community. Magazines such as these were crucial during the cultural renaissance in Harlem since they afforded poets, playwrights, and other writers space in which to publish their work. As a college graduate, Robeson was part of an important minority, which Du Bois had labeled the "talented tenth." Though the number of educated, professional African Americans was, in reality, much lower than 10 percent of the 10 million African Americans in the nation, these were the men and women who were to be called upon to be leaders in the community. These would also be the black Americans at the vanguard of a conscious movement that aimed to uplift the race by using the arts. It would be known as the New Negro Renaissance or the Harlem Renaissance. The emergence of a "New Negro," as implied in McKay's poem, occurred in reaction to the Red Summer and indicated that there was a new, dedicated spirit of protest for obtaining equal civil rights in the black community. This movement of arts and letters was steered by the prevailing civil rights organizations and by the artists themselves, though these two groups did not always agree on what constituted art that would benefit the race as a whole. Through financial backing by white philanthropists and guidance by stalwarts of the talented tenth, many, like Robeson, who had perhaps not considered art as a career option, were encouraged to use their talents to advance a dignified conception of the race. By 1924, Robeson announced in an interview that he believed he could do more for the advancement of African Americans by becoming a "first rate actor" than through propaganda and argument.

When Robeson settled into a flat on 135th Street in Harlem, his position in the neighborhood was unique, since at age twenty-one he was already a celebrity. Children and grown-ups alike congregated on the street to greet the renowned football star from Rutgers. It was impressive that he had been written about in white newspapers and, to top it off, he was also a Phi Beta Kappa scholar. Despite this early public recognition of his achievements, Robeson, like most Harlemites, had to hustle at numerous odd jobs to make ends meet. With both parents gone, he had to work to put himself through law school. The summer before moving to New York, Robeson took a job as a waiter on the Fall River Line steamboat that ran from Boston to New York. Once he rented a place uptown, Robeson moved between two distinct worlds as he had during his boyhood in New Jersey. He glided between Morningside Heights, the largely white, upper-class environment of the Ivy League Columbia University, and Harlem, a bustling, economically impoverished but culturally rich black neighborhood. His ease around people coupled with his unique ability to feel comfortable and at home in most surroundings served him well.

Robeson maintained an intense schedule during his law school years in the early 1920s. He turned to sports both for enjoyment and financial remuneration. In addition to attending classes at Columbia, he returned to Rutgers sometimes on weekends to coach football with his friend George Foster Sanford. His warmth and generosity extended also to Sanford's son, who Robeson tutored in Latin. Robeson briefly joined a basketball team that competed against semiprofessional teams in the New York region for a share of the ticket sales. Down at Lincoln University, his father's alma mater, Robeson coached football with Fritz Pollard, former All-American at Brown University, whom he had faced across the gridiron while playing for Rutgers. It was through Pollard that Robeson began playing professional football, which practically paid his way through law school. Though beloved at the college level, football was a newcomer to the world of professional athletics, which was dominated by America's sport, baseball. Unlike baseball, the emerging pro football conference allowed African Americans to play, and Robeson's friend, Fritz Pollard, became the league's first black coach. In 1920, the American Professional Football Association was formed, and about eight teams across the nation competed against each other. Robeson joined the Akron Pros in the 1920 season as a left defensive end, though he could also act as a pass receiver on offense, and he brought home about two hundred dollars per game. However, it was a rough sport, and Robeson had to maintain a grueling schedule to earn that much-needed money. Players in the days before heavy padding were knocked around quite a bit, so nursing postgame cracked or broken bones was not unusual. To make the Saturday practice and the Sunday game during the season, Robeson sometimes spent all of Friday night on the train and then all of Sunday night on the train again to get back in time for Monday classes. The last season Robeson played, in 1922, the association changed its name to the National Football League.

Back in Harlem, Robeson's social circle included talented young men and women who were college students or recent graduates and were preparing for professional careers in medicine, education, or law. The atmosphere of the cultural renaissance was stimulating and delightful for engaged young people like Robeson. They gathered at dinners, dances, plays, nightclubs, and parties in private homes. Politics galvanized many in the community. There were events sponsored by civil rights groups to attend, readings at the Harlem branch of the New York Public Library, speakers to hear at the corner of 135th Street and Lenox Avenue, political and literary magazines to discuss. He mingled with poets and artists at gatherings in the homes of civil rights leaders. The aristocratic Du Bois sometimes graced these groups with his presence. Poet Claude McKay befriended Robeson, and James Weldon Johnson, a leader in both the NAACP and the New Negro Movement, was influential in Robeson's early intellectual development. Sometimes Robeson sang at private events, and soon enough the tall, handsome young man with the athletic build and smooth baritone voice was recruited into the theater. In 1920, Dora Cole Norman and an all-black troupe called the Amateur Players convinced Robeson to take the leading role in a revival of *Simon the Cyrenian* being mounted at the local YMCA. The one-act play recounted the story of the man from North Africa who had been compelled to carry the cross of Jesus to the site of the crucifixion. It was a stroke of luck that two influential members of the experimental group the Provincetown Players, Kenneth Macgowan and Robert Edmond Jones, were in the audience to see Robeson's performance.

Not surprisingly, soon a young woman in Robeson's social circle had set her sights on him. Although he had been courting Geraldine Neale, who ultimately turned down his marriage proposal, it was Eslanda Cardozo Goode who became Mrs. Robeson in 1921. Essie, as she was known to friends, was three years older than Paul, and though they had different personalities, they shared several commonalities. Both were bright, scholastic achievers, both were the youngest child in their families, and both had lost a parent at a young age. In a number of ways, Essie embodied the new woman that was emerging in the urban United States in the twenties. More women at this time were challenging previous assumptions about gender roles by enjoying a single social life before getting married, working outside the home, and using their own money to participate in the expanding mass consumer culture. Like many cosmopolitan young women, Essie was mature, educated, and independent minded. She was also economically stable since she was working as a chemist in a pathology lab at Presbyterian Hospital at the time she met Paul. But preparing slides was not the extent of her ambition, as she aimed to become a doctor. Eslanda also enjoyed the exciting social life available in New York as well as a certain amount of material refinement. Being light skinned enough to occasionally pass for white could be an advantage in a racially divided city. She was sometimes perceived as having an aristocratic manner, being abrasive, or overly ambitious. Yet Eslanda was definitely proud of her family heritage.

Her great-grandfather, Isaac Nunez Cardozo, was Spanish-Jewish and immigrated to North America in the late eighteenth century. Cardozo married a free woman with black ancestry in Charleston, South Carolina, and had several children. One of their sons, Francis Lewis Cardozo, who was born in the 1830s, led quite a distinguished life. He graduated from the University of Glasgow, became a pastor, and secured a grant through the American Missionary Association, which helped establish the Avery Normal Institute, a school for African Americans in Charleston. During Reconstruction, when large numbers of black citizens were exercising their recently obtained right to vote, Cardozo became involved in politics. He served as Secretary of State and State Treasurer when the South Carolina State Assembly had black representation for the first time in its history. Reconstruction governments, however, were frequently accused of being corrupt because African Americans were now involved in the legislative process. Cardozo was incarcerated for fraud after the election of 1877 and the collapse of Reconstruction, but he was later released due to public outcry. The family then moved to Washington, D.C., where Cardozo's daughter, also named Eslanda, grew up. Though she had light skin and could have remained firmly rooted in elite society, she surprised everyone when she chose to wed the dark-skinned John Goode. Goode died when his daughter

Essie was only four years old. Essie's mother, the enterprising Mrs. Goode, moved her family to Chicago and started a successful business selling beauty products to support her three children. Essie, the only girl of the siblings, graduated from high school at sixteen and was awarded a full scholarship to the University of Illinois. Her scientific mind steered her to study chemistry, and she transferred to Columbia University in New York in her senior year.

Paul and Eslanda married before a Justice of the Peace in Port Chester, New York, in August 1921. Their first shared home was an apartment on 138th Street in Harlem. She continued working in the lab, though it bothered Paul that he was not yet able to support them financially. Friends of the couple might have perceived them as an odd match since they were different in many ways. For example, on a practical level, she was a morning person, while he stayed up late and slept late; he was largely indifferent to clothing and material goods, while she placed more emphasis on appearances; he was notorious for not keeping in touch with friends, while she wrote copious letters and kept a detailed journal. At a deeper level, she was pragmatic and liked to make plans, while he relied on inner revelation to guide him; she went out and tried to make things happen, while he waited for the right opportunity to come his way with a quiet confidence; he rarely said a mean word to anyone, while she could be frank or even rude if she deemed it necessary. However, they each provided the other with something vital. It had not been long since Paul had lost his father. Eslanda could offer stability, her scientific mind could organize the household, handle the finances and, later, help manage Paul's artistic career. And it would be Paul's career that largely determined the course of their lives. She sensed that this remarkable man who possessed a rare magnetism and unmistakable dignity of spirit was going someplace special. His potential was apparent, and Essie got to see firsthand where it would lead. One of the first places it led her was around town to locate the men's stores that carried good-quality clothes in Paul's size.

In 1922, Robeson returned to the stage in a role in the play *Taboo*, written by Mary Hoyt Wiborg, a white socialite. He had agreed to participate only after some nudging from Dora Cole Norman as well as Eslanda, who was beginning to sense brighter prospects for him in the arts rather than law. A well-received stint with a quartet, The Harmony Kings, who sang in the popular musical revue *Shuffle Along*, also seemed to indicate that Robeson might have a future on stage. The play *Taboo*, which received mostly unenthusiastic reviews, was set on a southern plantation and flashbacked to Africa. Robeson's performance, however, as a wandering minstrel character was viewed favorably in much of the press. A few months after the very brief run in New York, the show was picked up for an engagement in England. Robeson would get to perform with Mrs. Patrick Campbell, an acclaimed British actress, who revised the play for the overseas production.

That summer, Robeson sailed to the United Kingdom for the tour of the play now renamed *Voodoo*. Visiting Blackpool, Edinburgh, Glasgow, Liverpool, Plymouth, and London, Robeson absorbed his first glimpses of the people and cityscapes of England and Scotland. The play received mixed reviews, but Mrs. Campbell was encouraging of his talent and Robeson almost immediately felt at home in England. He considered pursuing a career abroad as he soaked in the sights of the British capital and attended theater productions as well as tennis matches. While in London, Robeson stayed with a fellow musician from Harlem, John Payne, who had another boarder at the time, Lawrence Brown. Brown, a pianist and skilled arranger, was currently accompanying the well-known tenor Roland Hayes. Robeson and Brown teamed up to entertain at a private party one night and in doing so foreshadowed a fruitful musical partnership that would last several decades. However, their collaboration would not begin in earnest until the mid-1920s. Meanwhile, back in New York, Eslanda was quite ill. In her characteristically independent manner, she had not alerted Paul that she had to have an operation while he was away. Instead, she wrote a series of upbeat postdated letters for a friend to mail while she was in the hospital. Her husband was left confused as to why her letters never responded to any of the questions he posed in his letters, and Paul became worried. After a month-long stay in the hospital, Essie divulged the truth to a stunned Paul. *Voodoo* was sputtering, so Paul shortly booked passage to return home and to the bedside of his wife, where he stayed until she was able to go home from the hospital. By autumn, she had improved enough to start keeping dates on their social calendar.

The Robesons still needed a steady income, and Paul picked up work where he could in early 1923 as he finished law school. He sang in another musical revue, put in some hours at a post office branch, played a bit of football, and turned down an offer from a boxing promoter. In February, Robeson finished his degree and had to decide whether to pursue a clerkship and study for the New York state bar exam or to focus on building a career in the theater. After some consideration, and with no theatrical prospects on the immediate horizon, law won. Robeson was hired by a Rutgers alumus, Louis W. Stotesbury, who led a respected firm that specialized in estate law. The firm was litigating a will from the powerful Gould family when Robeson joined the all-white office. He worked diligently, even preparing a brief for the Gould case, but tension over the presence of an African American in the firm gradually mounted. One day, a stenographer caustically refused to take dictation from Robeson, hurled a racial epithet in his direction, and fumed out. Robeson took the issue to Stotesbury, who counseled Paul that his race would impede the trajectory of his career in the legal profession. Most white clients would consider a black lawyer to be a detriment before a white judge. Stotesbury suggested that Robeson might open and manage a branch of the firm in Harlem where he could work with black clients. However, Robeson would not undertake a career where his options would be so constrained at the outset because of his race. The theater, though uncertain, still held possibilities. So it was the stage, in the end, that ultimately piloted Robeson's course.

Robeson's intuition to abandon law served him well and before too long a promising theatrical opportunity surfaced. Following a letter of introduction from Augustin Duncan, who had directed *Taboo*, Robeson was approached by Kenneth Macgowan of the Provincetown Players about reading for a part in Eugene O'Neill's new play *All God's Chillun Got Wings*. Macgowan had seen Robeson in *Simon the Cyrenian*, and the Provincetown Players were, in Eslanda's words, "one of the most intelligent, sincere, and non-commercial of the artistic groups in America." Robeson's graceful presence impressed the group at the audition, and he got the part of Jim Harris. The Provincetown Players, based in Greenwich Village, had been formed by a group of artists who shared their work while vacationing on the Massachusetts coast, hence the name, in 1915. Early participants included writers Susan Glaspell and her husband, George Cram Cook, set designer Robert Edmond Jones, and writer John Reed, who invited Eugene O'Neill to join the group. These artists aimed to produce new and experimental American plays that dealt with serious themes in contemporary society and offered an antidote to the melodramas popular on Broadway. Their productions explored issues such as class, race, politics, family, and the plight of immigrants while also giving unusually weighty roles to women. The Players helped inaugurate the careers of playwrights Glaspell and O'Neill, who both won multiple awards for drama, including the Pulitzer Prize. By the time of Robeson's audition, the Players had taken up residence in a brownstone on MacDougal Street in the Village in which they had constructed a stage and benches for the audience. The group had also undergone a shift in leadership that had put the trio of Kenneth Macgowan (director of the playhouse), O'Neill, and designer Robert Edmond Jones at the helm.

All God's Chillun Got Wings, whose title came from an African American spiritual, was a study of an interracial relationship between Jim Harris, Robeson's character, and Ella Downey, played by Mary Blair. Ella, having internalized the racist sentiments of society, slowly descends into madness after marrying Jim, who remains steadfastly true to her until the end. In this play, Robeson saw a narrative of two people struggling "against forces they could not control" that accentuated the "spiritual force" of the husband and the "humanness" of mankind. Due to contractual obligations, the production of the play had to be postponed to the spring of 1924 after the play was published by *American Mercury* magazine. In the meantime, Robeson stayed busy around New York, singing for events at places such as the YMCA and at social engagements for groups such as the NAACP. He was given a role in a revival of the play *Roseanne* by Nan Bagby Stevens at the Lafayette Theater in Harlem. This production by the Lafayette Players, a troupe of black actors founded by Charles Gilpin, starred Robeson as a crooked Southern preacher who was redeemed by the upstanding title character, played by Rose McClendon. The revival played briefly in New York and Philadelphia. The critics, while not complimentary of the play itself, noticed Robeson's performance and wondered what he might do with more substantial roles.

The opening of *All God's Chillun Got Wings* had to be put off again because Mary Blair had fallen ill. To further complicate matters, once the play appeared in *American Mercury*, there was a public backlash against its theme of miscegenation. One of the chief complaints by reactionaries, who knew that a black actor would be playing Jim across from a white actress, was the scene in which Blair's character kisses her husband on the hand. Splashy newspaper headlines predicted riots at the opening. The vitriolic reaction to the play from some quarters was perhaps not surprising given the strong racist and nativist sentiments prevalent in the early twentieth century. In the 1920s, there was a surge in Klan membership into the millions across the country. Eugene O'Neill tried to downplay the outcry, noting in a *New York Times* interview that he did not actually advocate intermarriage in the play. As a dramatist, it was rather the individual characters, "the [racial] gap between them and their struggle to bridge it" that he wanted to explore. As coverage of the play swelled, the news clipping service used by the Provincetown Players gave up using envelopes to contain the piles of clippings and opted for shoeboxes. In the interim, since Mary Blair was in the hospital, Macgowan and the Provincetown leaders decided that mounting a different play could deflect attention from the controversy. Another O'Neill play, *The Emperor Jones*, was selected and, thus, Robeson ended up portraying two leading characters with the Provincetown Players in May 1924.

The Provincetown Players had first produced *The Emperor Jones* during their fifth season in New York in 1920 to 1921 with the brilliant Charles Gilpin in the lead. This had been one of their most successful plays and was moved from MacDougal Street to the larger Princess Theatre uptown. Gilpin had been acclaimed in the role, and it could help launch Robeson's burgeoning career. However, he had to swiftly learn his lines for *The Emperor Jones*, which opened just weeks before *All God's Chillun Got Wings* was scheduled open. Essie ran lines with Paul morning, noon, and evening to the point that her mother, who was staying with them, announced that she had committed much of the script to memory. The play focused on the life of Brutus Jones, a cunning Pullman porter, who traded in a rural southern life for the fast-paced city and its opportunities for wheeling and dealing. Jones ends up on a chain gang but escapes by killing a guard. He ultimately finds his way to a small island in the Caribbean, where he wrests control and becomes emperor. As his power erodes, Jones flees into the jungle, where he slips into madness, or descends back to the primitive. Despite its focus on primitivism and individual psychology, *The Emperor Jones* was one of the first major American plays to undertake the portrayal of a black lead character in a thoughtful and serious manner. The fact that the play was not vaudeville or minstrelsy made it an especially rare and enticing prospect for a black actor. In her biography, Eslanda described how director James Light allowed Robeson to "feel his way" through the scripts and would "sit down on a soap-box beside him on the empty stage" when Robeson struggled with a speech so they could examine it "thought by thought and word by word."

After breaking down each passage, Robeson would then build it back up for himself with greater understanding.

Robeson's diligent work in such a condensed period of time paid off, and *The Emperor Jones* filled the house for the weeks before *All God's Chillun Got Wings* opened. Robeson commented in an interview that Brutus Jones's "exultant tragedy" made for a "great part" and one of "the great plays." Many critics dubbed Robeson as a "worthy successor" to Gilpin's interpretation of the role and took note that a significant new African American talent had emerged on the stage. Some even began to wonder if the young actor would soon tackle Shakespeare's *Othello*. Later in the month, Robeson appeared as Jim Harris in the long-awaited production of *All God's Chillun Got Wings*. It was a tense opening due to the controversy that had erupted, and Robeson observed in an interview that "many an anxious moment" had passed prior to the curtain. Police surrounded the theater in case there was trouble. However, the play went off virtually without a hitch, much to the relief of everyone at the theater, and the crowd was "exuberant" at the end. Even though Robeson received mostly glowing notices, the critical response to the play itself was lukewarm. It was described as both "tiresome" and "painful," and the *New York Times* pointed out that if its "enemies had been less diligent" the play probably would have garnered scant public attention. Some in the black press criticized the play as making an implicit argument against interracial marriage, though the dean of the editorial page, W. E. B. Du Bois, reflected that it was constructive that O'Neill had written a credible and human black character.

The publicity from both plays led to increased press interest in Robeson. In interviews with him in this period, he was beginning to form an ideology about the role of art in American society. During the New Negro or Harlem Renaissance, there was a continuing dialogue between black artists and leaders in civil rights organizations as to how African American life and culture should be depicted artistically. The aim of many artists and civil rights leaders was to help uplift the race. Most agreed that emphasizing the dignity and humanity of black Americans was beneficial to the ultimate aim of ridding the United States of segregation, discrimination, racial violence, and disfranchisement. The poetry of Langston Hughes, for example, gracefully underscored the nobility in the everyday lives of black working folk who labored during the day and relaxed by sitting on their stoops in the evening listening to a little jazz music waft down the avenue. However, when Claude McKay's novel *Home to Harlem* came out, some of the black intelligentsia felt he had painted black life as gritty and debauched. Where was the line between unsentimental realism and plain filth? One's class status often figured prominently in where one stood on such issues. White portrayals of the black community also fueled debate, such as Carl Van Vechten's novel *Nigger Heaven*. What was Robeson saying about art in the 1920s?

In terms of his role as an artist, Robeson remarked in a 1924 interview that the best way for him to help the race was to thoroughly develop his talents. Working as an actor, he felt he would have more opportunities than as a lawyer, but he hoped that in the future black actors would not be limited only to black roles. Robeson went on to suggest that if he did "become a first-rate actor" it would be more valuable to the race than "any amount of propaganda and argument." In another interview, he developed his thoughts on the value of African American culture further. He commented, "One of the great measures of a people is its culture, its artistic stature. Above all things, we boast that the only true artistic contributions of America are Negro in origin. We boast of the culture of ancient Africa." Significantly, Robeson pointed to Africa in identifying the derivation of African American culture. He would develop this position further in the 1930s after more study and interaction with people from the African diaspora. Others, like Du Bois in his book *The Gift of Black Folk*, also advocated the centrality of African American contributions to American art forms. Spirituals, for instance, had been created by African Americans who were not simply mimicking European art but expressing the singular experiences that were rooted in their African origins. Robeson offered singer Roland Hayes, who sometimes sang spirituals, as an example: "So today Roland Hayes is infinitely more a racial asset than many who 'talk' at great length. Thousands of people hear him, see him, are moved by him, and are brought to a clearer understanding of human values." Robeson anticipated that if he could achieve something like that, he would "be happy." Interestingly, many years later, Robeson's friend and biographer Lloyd Brown made a strikingly comparable observation about the "transforming power" of Robeson's artistry. According to Brown, Robeson's magnetism and the "velvety lushness" of his voice worked like magic, and during a concert "people seemed to like themselves more, and to like each other more and to revel in the experi-

ence." Though his talents were just blossoming in the cultural renaissance
of the twenties, Robeson ultimately became quite accomplished at communicating dignity and a shared humanity through his work.

Robeson's success in the two plays for the Provincetown Players indicated that his star was rising. *All God's Chillun Got Wings* ran off and on to full houses through the summer, which buoyed Robeson both professionally and financially. Working on MacDougal Street had exposed Robeson to the bohemian art world of Greenwich Village with which he continued to interact. He posed for photographer Nickolas Muray and for Italian American sculptor Antonio Salemme. Sometimes Robeson socialized with Salemme and his wife as well as the artists who dropped by Salemme's studio in the Village. Up in Harlem, the Robesons were quickly moving to the center of influential social circles that included artists, philanthropists, political activists, and socialites. They were invited to parties at the apartment on Edgecombe Avenue of NAACP leader Walter White and his wife, Gladys, and were friends with James Weldon Johnson and his wife. A night out on the town might include a visit to Harlem spots such as Smalls' Paradise or Connie's Inn or maybe dancing to Fletcher Henderson's big band. Some nightclubs, like the famous Cotton Club, did not allow black patrons, but the Sugar Cane was a club just for African Americans and did not play "crisp Broadway jazz" but kept a "low-down, insinuating, pulsing beat" such that no one could keep still. An evening of social events for the Robesons might include rubbing shoulders with people such as writers Jean Toomer, Countee Cullen, Jessie Fauset, or singer Roland Hayes. Soon the Robesons were also mingling with Carl Van Vechten and his wife, Fania Marinoff, and going to events at publisher Alfred Knopf's home. Van Vechten had been the music critic for the *New York Times* and was a prominent figure in the New York cultural scene, with many important contacts. Van Vechten was keenly interested in African American life and art and helped launch Robeson and Lawrence Brown's first concert of spirituals. One particularly memorable marathon night out with Eugene O'Neill and some others from the Provincetown group was recorded in Eslanda's diary. First, there were cocktails at the Robeson's 127th Street flat followed by dinner at Craig's, a popular Harlem restaurant, and a dance performance at the Lincoln Theater. Then later the group listened to a midnight set at the Lafayette Theater, went dancing at Smalls' Paradise, and stopped for ice cream before enjoying more late-night banter back at the Robeson's. The group broke up after breakfast the next morning.

Robeson's next acting project was in an emerging medium: film. In late 1924, arrangements were made for Robeson to star in black director Oscar Micheaux's silent film *Body and Soul*. Micheaux, a resourceful entrepreneur, was the first African American filmmaker credited with a feature-length film. Of the forty-five films he made, about half were silent, but only four of those, including *Body and Soul*, have survived. In this early era of film, many race movies for black audiences, like those made by Micheaux, were both educational and entertaining. Pearl Bowser, Micheaux's biographer, has noted that Micheaux used the medium of film to both address negative black stereotypes and to critique the black community. For example, he often put himself in his films briefly in a cameo to advertise that the film was made by a black director. He also used images with which the audience would have been familiar. In addition, many shots of the righteous, hardworking protagonist of *Body and Soul*, Sister Martha, included photos of black heroes, like Booker T. Washington, that were pasted on the wall of her room. Whether or not the audience could read the film's subtitles, they understood and could relate to the values of Sister Martha.

The plot, reminiscent of the play *Roseanne*, centered around the dream of a virtuous parishioner, Sister Martha, in which her preacher was a devious con man who stole her life savings and assaulted her daughter, Isabella. Upon waking, Sister Martha was relieved that Isabella was safe and sound, preparing to marry the upright and educated young Sylvester, who had a solid future ahead of him. The film allowed Robeson to expand as an actor by playing both the cunning, evil preacher and the honorable young suitor. He had to modify his acting technique to conform to the quirks of filming as opposed to stage acting. For example, rarely did Micheaux indulge second takes. Robeson also had to adjust to communicating primarily through body language rather than spoken language in the silent medium. At least the central motif was quite familiar to Robeson: the black church. Micheaux's script was critical of corrupt church leaders who were fraudulent and raped their acolytes of their earnings just as the two-faced preacher raped Isabella. (Micheaux perceived his father-in-law as a duplicitous preacher and made that a recurring theme in his work.) *Body and Soul* also gently mocked the church women, like Sister Martha's friends, who flattered their preacher excessively and gave the church most of their money whether or not they could afford it. At the end of Sister Martha's dream, she understood that she could invest her money in the community in other ways, such as by supporting Sylvester, rather than by always giving so much to the church. The film enabled Robeson to grow as an actor while working with a director who aimed at representing the black community honestly. On the financial side, Micheaux's deal gave Robeson a small portion of the gross profits.

In the mid-1920s, Robeson's musical career also gained momentum. In addition to singing at private parties, Robeson gave a formal recital in November 1924 at the Copley Plaza in Boston upon the invitation from socialite Mrs. Guy Currier. Harry Burleigh, the prominent African American arranger and composer, helped Robeson prepare for the concert. He was accompanied on piano by Louis Hooper and, according to the program, offered mostly selections of African American spirituals, including arrangements by Burleigh, Lawrence Brown, and J. Rosamond Johnson. The concert was well received and demonstrated Robeson's potential in the concert arena. In early 1925, Lawrence Brown returned to the United States, and he and Robeson renewed their acquaintance. They performed several spirituals, with Brown on piano and harmonizing his tenor with Robeson's baritone, at a gathering at Carl Van Vechten's, much to the delight of those assembled. The idea of a formal concert with Robeson and Brown was immediately proposed, and Van Vechten's connections in the art world helped secure arrangements for an April show at the Greenwich Village Theater.

Lawrence Brown, five years Robeson's senior, was born in Jacksonville, Florida, in 1893. Like Robeson, his father, Clark Brown, had lived during enslavement, and his mother died when he was young. He first journeyed to Boston to study music and then went abroad to London, where he studied musical composition at Trinity College and voice with Amanda Aldridge, daughter of the famous actor Ira Aldridge and a former pupil of Jenny Lind. As he matured into a professional accompanist, Brown played with numerous artists, including Roger Quilter and Marian Anderson. Brown spent four years working with Roland Hayes and had even played before royalty at Buckingham Palace. He believed deeply in the importance of black folk music and devoted much of his energy as an arranger to working with spirituals. By the time he met Robeson, he had already published an arrangement of "Steal Away," and he went on to produce more than thirty arrangements of spirituals in his career. Robeson was also drawn to the spirituals, and this was the music that formed the basis of their fruitful partnership that lasted into the 1950s and was beloved by audiences. In an interview, Brown once described Robeson's singing as having "no affectation" but possessing a unique "tenderness" not usually found in deep, male voices.

The spirituals were a form of folk music that was born out of the experience of African American enslavement. W. E. B. Du Bois, and other artists and intellectuals, argued that the spirituals were significant as one of the few examples of truly original American music. Du Bois eloquently characterized the spirituals as not only "the rhythmic cry of the slave" but "the most beautiful expression of human experience born this side of the seas." In addition to their labor, which helped construct the cities and harvest the farmland of this country, African American creativity made a singular contribution to the culture of the land to which they were brought. These songs acted as a kind of oral history by recording the daily experiences of the enslaved as well as their rich emotional lives since they had few outlets to express themselves. The music also spoke to universal themes found in folk music from around the world, like suffering as well as joy, and a complex spiritual belief system that searched for comfort, redemption, and hope for the future. James Weldon Johnson maintained that the spirituals were based on African forms, such as call and response, making them a communal music. These songs were first written down by white northerners, like Thomas Wentworth Higginson, who interacted with African Americans around the time of the Civil War. In the late nineteenth century, the spirituals were widely acclaimed when the famous Fisk Jubilee Singers toured in the United States and Europe singing these songs that had been passed down through their forebears. Concerts given entirely by African Americans that focused on African American music were fairly new and not always welcomed in the United States. Mark Twain heard the spirituals in the 1890s in Switzerland and wished it was a foreign musical form so that people back in America would bestow it with more money and praise.

In the early twentieth century, artists and audiences revisited the spirituals. Du Bois wrote about them tenderly in both *The Souls of Black Folk* and *The Gift of Black Folk*. Arrangers were reworking their music into new formats for solo and duo performance. In 1925, many of these arrangements were collected in James Weldon and J. Rosamond Johnson's *The Book of*

American Negro Spirituals, which also featured Lawrence Brown's work. A second volume soon followed. In a 1929 article poet Countee Cullen elucidated the origins of the spirituals and asserted that they had now "assumed an international importance." The spirituals hummed in the ears of approving audiences in the United States and abroad when performers such as Roland Hayes, Marian Anderson, Jules Bledsoe, and Paul Robeson gave them voice. In an interview published in the *New York Times* in 1925, Robeson noted that his ambition as a singer was to concentrate on the music of his community and "to show the people the beauty of" black folk songs, work songs, and spirituals. A 1927 interview demonstrated that Robeson had put considerable time into his study of the spirituals. He pointed out the skillful way in which the spirituals used Old Testament themes. Enslaved African Americans "saw their own history reflected" in the stories of the Hebrews. The process of creating the spirituals, then, showed how the "naturally artistic" African American people had "grasped the ideas" of the Bible and then translated them into another form "for their own inspiration." Having been exposed to this music since his childhood, Robeson aimed to sing them the way he "felt their meaning."

Robeson and Brown's historic first concert in April 1925 helped advance the contemporary interest in spirituals, as their program consisted entirely of African American folk music. Critics enthusiastically received the recital, and the audience in the hall was packed to standing room only. Lawrence Brown did not exaggerate when he later recalled that the concert made Robeson an "immediate favorite." The *Amsterdam News* informed readers that those who have heard the spirituals rendered in a "sanctimonious" or "lugubrious" manner will be pleasantly surprised by Robeson and Brown's varied interpretations of songs such as "Joshua Fit de Battle of Jericho" and "Ev'ry Time I Feel the Spirit." Many critics noted Robeson's earnest and sincere approach to the music, which one reporter described as his "overwhelming inward conviction." One particularly inspired reviewer felt Robeson's performance communicated a "universal humanism that touches the heart." A follow-up concert was swiftly organized, and was also warmly embraced.

That summer, Robeson and Brown channeled the popularity of their concerts by making their first joint recordings of spirituals on Victor Records. When the records were released in late 1925, over fifty thousand copies sold in four months, which brought in royalties as well as offers to appear on radio. The appeal of the spirituals was not universal, however. African American writer Zora Neale Hurston critiqued the trend of singing spirituals solo in a formalized, Western-style recital as being disconnected from the communal origins of the music. Other African Americans shied away from this folk music because it was associated with the shame of enslavement. Nevertheless, Robeson's early success on the concert stage seemed to indicate that it would be feasible for him to build a career by balancing both singing and acting jobs. The contract for Robeson to play the lead in a British production of *The Emperor Jones* enabled the Robesons to move into a better apartment on West 145th Street. Eslanda was no longer compelled to work in the lab but could help manage Paul's career.

The Robesons sailed for England late in the summer of 1925 in preparation for the September opening of *The Emperor Jones*, which would be directed by James Light, one of their friends from the Provincetown Players. Eslanda had enlisted assistance scouting the London area for accommodations, and the couple settled into a flat in Chelsea. Though cordially received, the play did not resonate with British theatergoers, who were more accustomed to class-based comedies of manner, and it closed after a five-week run. One review noted that audience reaction to *The Emperor Jones* seemed to be divided over Robeson, who they adored, and the play itself. The Robesons stayed on in London and then traveled to Europe for the next few months as they enjoyed the social scene and found the comparative lack of racial prejudice to be uplifting. They became friends with Emma Goldman, the anarchist who had been deported from the United States, and met Ira Aldridge's daughter, Amanda. In Paris, luminaries, including ex-patriot Ernest Hemingway and writer James Joyce, turned up when Robeson gave a concert of spirituals. Paul and Essie met the widow of French painter Henri Matisse, had tea with Gertrude Stein, and saw African American dancer Josephine Baker perform. Baker's routine was quickly becoming a Paris phenomenon, although Eslanda found some of her "uncalled for wiggling" to be off-putting. The Robesons then spent several weeks vacationing in the village of Villefranche on the Riviera, where they rested and socialized with many of the writers and artists who were in the area, such as Claude McKay, radical journalist Max Eastman, and English writer Rebecca West. The warm Mediterranean weather coaxed the Robesons to relax and aided Paul's proclivity for catching colds. One evening when the Robesons were having drinks in the hotel lobby with Rebecca West, all the lights abruptly went out. Paul started singing while the power was being restored, and the hotel owner compared the sound of his baritone penetrating through the darkness to the voice of an angel.

Paul and Eslanda traveled back to New York in December. In January and February 1926, Robeson and Brown were scheduled to perform in several U.S. cities. After a concert in New York, the team went by rail to Detroit, Philadelphia, Pittsburgh, and Indianapolis. Then later they visited Chicago, Milwaukee, and Green Bay. The overall reception of this first tour was mixed. The house was packed in Indianapolis, and one reviewer from there waxed that Robeson had illuminated the sixteen selections he offered in all of their "true beauty" and "true force." A critic in Pittsburgh was complimentary of the recital but refrained from judging Robeson's voice, since he clearly had a cold. In Chicago, the crowd was "unpleasantly small" according to a reviewer, who praised Robeson's "depth of feeling" and hoped word of mouth would encourage a larger crowd next time he came through town. The color line was also a persistent issue. One hotel reluctantly allowed the African American guests to stay only if they were as unobtrusive as possible. Back in the New York area in late February, the audience hardly filled half of the seats at the Academy of Music in Brooklyn, prompting one reviewer to speculate that Robeson was not as well known on the other side of the East River as he was in Manhattan. All in all, the demands of touring had been draining for Robeson physically and had not been very rewarding financially. Robeson soon engaged a voice coach who helped improve his vocal stamina, but the unpredictability of his income as a young artist would be a persistent concern.

In the autumn of 1926, Robeson took the lead role in the play *Black Boy* written by Jim Tully and Frank Dazey and produced by Horace Liveright at the Comedy Theatre in New York. It was a melodrama about a boxer that was perhaps loosely based on the life of Jack Johnson. Brooks Atkinson, who was fairly new to the drama desk at the *New York Times* but would hold that office for decades to come, charged the playwrights with having "substituted cheap and meretricious theatrical flourishes for real analysis of character." He suggested that Robeson's "fine-grained" interpretation probably approached the authors' conception of the character more closely than "the play of their own composition." While the reviews of Robeson's performance were mainly complimentary, the play itself received mixed notices and ran for only a few weeks. In the play, Fredi Washington, an attractive, light-skinned African American actress, played Black Boy's white girlfriend. The rumor mill buzzed that Washington and Robeson had an affair during the run of the play. Indeed they had, and their close relationship would continue, off and on, for many years.

This was not Robeson's first liaison outside of his marriage. He also had an ongoing intimacy with Freda Diamond as well as brief affairs with other women. Paul and Eslanda had now been married for five years, and their relationship was, at times, strained. Eslanda felt insecure about their relationship, while Paul was restless and sometimes discontented in the marriage. In his biography, the Robesons' son pointed out that Paul did not want to be his wife's possession. Even though much of his career's success was dependent on Eslanda's managerial skill, Paul did not want to feel that she owned him. By this time, both Robesons sensed that their marriage was facing a turning point. However, they did not divorce, and they continued to attend social events together as a couple. Their partnership was necessary for the advancement of Paul's career: he needed her to organize travel details, handle the money, and negotiate contracts while she would never have had the opportunities to travel, interact with influential people, or be so well connected in the art world if they parted. As Paul Jr. later explained, the couple "suppressed their dark mood and cultivated their glittering image for the world to see."

In 1927, Robeson returned to the concert stage on a tour with Lawrence Brown. Roy Wilkins, a future leader in the NAACP, organized an engagement in Kansas City. Even though the theater was not segregated, which defied typical arrangements, a large audience turned out to hear Robeson. Following the concert, a letter to the editor was published in the local African American newspaper, the Kansas City *Call*, that criticized Robeson's repertoire of spirituals as drawing attention to the humiliating past of enslavement. Despite such occasional criticism from the black community, Robeson remained true to his vision of interpreting African American folk songs for, as he noted in a 1924 interview, he felt that African Americans were "too afraid of showing all phases of our life." Robeson and Brown gave successful concerts through the summer in cities in Ohio, New Jersey, and New York. Reviewers praised Robeson's poignant presentation of the music of his people. One critic in Rochester, New York, observed that "it was as if a whole people spoke last night through the medium of one man on whom exceptional gifts have been bestowed." Concert work was also bringing in necessary income. By the end of the year, it was publicized that Robeson was making over $1,200 per engagement.

In the autumn of 1927, Robeson signed with a concert manager for an overseas tour with Brown that was scheduled to commence in Paris. When Paul climbed aboard the ship that took him to Europe, he left behind Eslanda only a few weeks before she was due to give birth to their first and only child. However, she had encouraged him to go on the tour knowing it would be good for his career. When Eslanda had informed Paul of her pregnancy back in the spring, he had been somewhat surprised since she had not mentioned that she was trying to conceive. The European tour, then, helped assuage the need to begin providing financially for a family. The first show on the tour was a triumph. Fifteen hundred seats were full at the Salle Gaveau concert hall, and at least five hundred Parisians who wanted tickets had to be turned away. Given the enthusiastic response, a follow-up concert was arranged right away.

In early November, Eslanda gave birth to a healthy baby boy, but she became gravely ill following the delivery developing, among other ailments, a severe case of phlebitis. She concealed this from Paul, however, who was thousands of miles away and assumed she was recovering. Eslanda's mother later cabled Paul of his wife's acute condition, against her daughter's wishes. Paul headed back to New York straight away, leaving his European tour suddenly without a soloist. The care of Paul Jr. was given over to his maternal grandmother, Mrs. Goode, who looked after him for much of his childhood. Eslanda's recuperation was protracted, and her health did not completely return until the following spring. In the meantime, having abandoned the tour abroad, Paul knew he needed to find work. He jumped at the chance to join a production of DuBose Heyward's *Porgy* in the role of Crown, which being vacated in the spring of 1928. Robeson had previously turned down this role, but now the weekly salary was too good to refuse. Several musical numbers that had been cut were restored when Robeson entered the cast, but the nature of the production drained his vocal reserves.

Fortunately, Robeson only had to stay with *Porgy* for a few weeks until a better opportunity came along. The hit musical *Show Boat* was going to open in London in April, and Robeson was offered the role of Joe. He would only have to sing one song, "Ol' Man River," which would be repeated three times as a theme for the show. The producer, Florenz Ziegfeld, expected that Robeson's fame would increase press coverage of the revival. Paul headed back across the Atlantic, and Eslanda planned to join him when she was well enough to travel. As anticipated, Robeson's singing was an "outstanding feature" of the show, which became a sensation among London audiences. A story wired to the *New York Times* reported that a "queue of women had waited all night and all day" to get gallery seats in the Drury Lane Theatre. Some critics were less than enthusiastic about the show, but Robeson's reviews were for the most part better than those of the overall production. His sincere portrayal of a working man on the Mississippi River seemed to elevate what was essentially a melodramatic romance.

Some of the African American reaction to *Show Boat*, however, reflected a continued frustration with the dearth of dignified roles for black actors. J. A. Rogers, writing for the African American newspaper the *Pittsburgh Courier*, especially objected to Robeson's use of the degrading term *nigger* in "Ol' Man River." However, Rogers thoughtfully suspended judgment toward African American artists who worked for the white entertainment establishment until there were black playwrights who were able to produce well-rounded characters that defied conventional stereotypes. It was a constant struggle for Robeson, indeed for minority artists then and still today, to balance the need to make a living with the roles that are available. Like Rogers, and many artists during the Harlem Renaissance, Robeson looked forward to a day when "there will come Negro playwrights of great power," as he commented in a 1924 interview. He especially longed to participate in "a great play about Haiti . . . written by a Negro, and acted by Negroes." Once Robeson was established as an acclaimed and politically motivated artist, in the years to come, he was far more selective about the roles he accepted and eventually rejected film and much of the theater world in favor of the concert stage, where he was in complete control of the presentation.

In May 1928, Eslanda left young Paul with her mother and made the journey to London. Upon her arrival, the Robesons settled into a flat across from Regents Park. They reconnected with Lawrence Brown, who had been left behind upon Paul's hasty departure from their last European tour. Robeson's stunning popularity in *Show Boat* left audiences clamoring to see more of him on the concert stage. In July, Brown and Robeson gave a recital to an excited full house at Drury Lane Theatre, who demanded numerous encores. Reviews were laudatory, and a critic for the *Daily Telegraph* appreciated the "simplicity and sincerity" of the music, especially since those were "two virtues" that were "conspicuously absent from our contemporary art." When Paul was not enchanting audiences, the Robesons delighted in the London art and social scene. They heard Feodor Chaliapin sing *Faust* and saw Igor Stravinsky himself conduct *Firebird*; they watched Learie Constantine play cricket and listened to Marian Anderson regale a crowd. Both Robesons felt quite comfortable in England, where the people certainly admired Paul, and Mrs. Goode joined them with Paul Jr. in the autumn of 1928.

After *Show Boat* closed early in 1929, Robeson and Brown headed out for several European concert dates in the spring. In Vienna, the audience fell "under the spell" of Robeson's interpretation of African American folk music. Their reception in Prague and Budapest was similarly warm and encouraging. On this trip, Robeson's interest in folk music from these regions was piqued as he began to uncover connections between European folk songs and the songs of his people. This curiosity blossomed into a lifetime of study and performance of folk music from around the world. In the years to come, Robeson's remarkable affinity for learning languages facilitated his investigation of this music as well as his recitals of folk songs in their native tongues. Upon returning from the continent, Robeson thrilled in a concert that sold out London's prestigious Royal Albert Hall with one of the largest crowds ever gathered there. He was now in an exclusive echelon of artists. Nevertheless, Robeson's celebrity status could not circumvent the color line that, while not as virulent as segregation in the United States, did rear an ugly face at times. When the Robesons were refused service in the Savoy Hotel's dining room, the incident made headlines in the fall of 1929. Robert S. Abbott, publisher of the African American newspaper the *Chicago Defender*, had also recently had difficulty securing hotel accommodations in London. The minority population used the opportunity to speak out against racial discrimination in the city, and a minister of Parliament promised to raise the issue in the House of Commons. In the end, the incident brought some attention to a trend that was all too common in the capital of the British Empire, as most Indians, Africans, and West Indians in the metropolis already knew. This was a community that Robeson would get to know much better in the 1930s.

In the autumn of 1929, the Robesons sailed back to New York, and Paul prepared to undertake a North American concert tour, which commenced at Carnegie Hall in New York. Crowds flocked to purchase tickets in anticipation of the famed artist's return to the United States. Two shows at the venerated theater in Manhattan sold out so quickly that, as the *New York Times* reported, a thousand would-be concertgoers had to be turned away. It was a triumph that Robeson's focus on interpreting African American spirituals and folk music was clearly still beloved despite his extended absence. Audiences at each stop on the two-month tour across the United States and Canada seemed to be enraptured by Robeson and his music. A "thrilled" reviewer in Pittsburgh was torn over what aspect of Robeson was most impressive: "his voice, his bearing, his personality, his repose, [or] his engaging air." This critic found Robeson's interpretation of "Didn't It Rain" to be so arresting that he asserted, "All of us thought it certainly did rain, while he was singing it." A reviewer in Toronto perhaps summarized the overall reception of this tour by proclaiming, "If you wanted to define eloquence, you would say—'Hear Paul Robeson sing!'" This reflective critic concluded that "a voice like his is worth waiting ten years to hear, and an art like this comes once in a generation." In December, he closed the year with a series of concerts at the Town Hall in New York before journeying again overseas to sing and fulfill an engagement to play in Shakespeare's *Othello*.

During the twenties, Robeson honed his natural artistic talents and discovered that his gifts resonated deeply with audiences in many countries. The extent to which people responded in such rhapsodies to his performances held a certain wonder for Robeson. While he was the toast of London, he commented in a 1928 interview that "there is something within me that all my life has caused me to succeed whenever I appeared before the public far beyond what my experience, training or knowledge deserved." Jotting some ideas in a diary in 1929, Robeson observed that "by chance" some people have the "power to create beauty." Though not usually overtly religious, Robeson did attribute this power to create beauty, with which he was certainly blessed, as having a divine origin. He recognized this as a purpose in his life, and it gave an underpinning to his personal strength that sustained him through difficult periods. Indeed, the trajectory of Robeson's life through this decade was uncannily designed as if by a higher power. He settled in Harlem at the precise time that a historic cultural movement was flourishing, which helped nudge him toward public performance. In addition, he had met and married Eslanda, who perceived his gifts and was willing to devote herself to the advancement of his career. By the end of the decade, the artistic renaissance in Harlem was waning, and the effects of the depression gripped the neighborhood. However, Robeson's career, though rooted in the African American community, would now grow to global dimensions as he spent much of the 1930s abroad. He left the country in 1929 to prepare to play one of Shakespeare's only African characters, and it was during the next decade that Africa and its colonized people came to play a significant role in his political beliefs.

3

WORLD CITIZEN

Paul Robeson sailed across the Atlantic Ocean for England in 1930 on the cusp of what would be a rather turbulent decade. The United States, and indeed much of the Western world, was beginning to experience the effects of economic depression. The stock market crash in New York in the autumn of 1929 signaled the approaching contraction of an economy that was bloated from speculation. In the early thirties, stock prices were still sliding down as unemployment edged upward. Banks in the industrialized world were going out of business; hundreds failed in the United States alone. Germany defaulted on its World War I reparations to France and Britain, which meant these countries had difficulty paying their war debts to American banks. In cities across America, sidewalks were crowded by breadlines, and urban shelters swelled with newly homeless families. Farmers packed their children and a few possessions into trucks and headed west, away from the devastating dust bowl that ravaged the plains.

The 1932 presidential election swept Franklin D. Roosevelt into office on a platform that promised a "new deal" for the economically distressed population. Rebuffing his predecessor Herbert Hoover's largely hands-off approach to the crisis, Roosevelt's administration passed a nearly unprecedented amount of legislation to bolster the beleaguered capitalist system. Banks were reassessed, new regulatory bodies were formed, and some of the most expansive public works programs in U.S. history were undertaken to strengthen infrastructure and create much-needed jobs. The president's vigorous and socially conscious wife, Eleanor, traveled widely to observe firsthand the problems wrought by the Depression and to advise her husband. Interestingly, rather than squelch public protest, the economic crisis inspired a spirit of rebellion that fueled increased labor militancy. Groups such as the emergent U.S. Communist Party and the newly created Congress of Industrial Organizations (CIO) tried to harness the growing fury with the unpredictability and inequality of the capitalist system. The Communist Party's popular front policy, inaugurated in 1935, enabled the group to participate in broad coalitions with liberals and New Dealers to push for progressive social change. Tactics such as spontaneous sit-down strikes and the general strike alerted employers and political leaders that many workers did not want to return to business as usual but instead demanded broad economic security and a more equitable distribution of the nation's wealth.

In the neighborhood of Harlem, which had fostered Robeson's acting and singing career, the artistic energy that had fed the renaissance of the 1920s was ebbing. Many black intellectuals shifted their focus to the contemporary economic crisis. Working-class Harlemites felt the economic downturn acutely. While the national jobless rate peaked at around 25 percent, unemployment among African Americans in Harlem was nearly twice as high. Even so, African American families in Harlem were still charged more for rent than white families. Probably half of the married women in Harlem worked as domestic laborers and, thus, were not eligible for New Deal programs such as Social Security. To make matters worse, the repeal of the prohibition of alcohol in the early 1930s sounded the death knell for many of the informal speakeasies and small theaters that had enlivened the nightlife of the previous decade and provided employment. Frustration with social and economic conditions exploded in the 1935 Harlem riot, which caused considerable damage and left several people dead.

In the 1930s, the U.S. Communist Party was the only national political party that made a serious attempt to break racial barriers by organizing in African American communities and working to eliminate racial prejudice within their own membership. The Communist Party USA (CPUSA), for example, supported "Don't Buy Where You Can't Work" campaigns in Harlem, endeavored to unionize sharecroppers in the South, and used its legal arm, the International Labor Defense (ILD), to raise consciousness about the nine black youths who were wrongfully accused of rape in Scottsboro, Alabama. The Communist ideology was appealing to some African

Americans given the circumstances of the Depression and continued racial discrimination. Some of the black intelligentsia, including W.E.B. Du Bois, Langston Hughes, Claude McKay, and Paul Robeson, traveled to the Soviet Union in the 1930s to explore the Soviet approach to race relations. They were also attracted to the Marxist critique of capitalism as well as the anticolonial and antifascist positions embedded in Communist philosophy.

Robeson spent much of the decade of the 1930s away from the United States, so his political consciousness developed primarily through his travel and independent study. For example, his appreciation for Marxism grew through reading Marx in the original German. His dogged antifascism was cemented when he visited the front of the Spanish civil war. His anticolonial stance took root through his interaction with people from the African diaspora in London and his personal study of African languages and culture. Robeson wrote in his memoir that during those years abroad he had "witnessed the rise of fascism." The Nazi Party secured power in Germany, Benito Mussolini expanded Italy's empire by invading sovereign Ethiopia, and Spain became embroiled in a bloody struggle that was ultimately won by Francisco Franco. The Western powers, Robeson reflected, were "calm and unmoving in the face of the agony of Ethiopia and Spain." However, he simultaneously observed in Britain the mobilization of the "common people" who "rallied for anti-fascist action." The 1930s, then, were a pivotal decade in Robeson's life. His stature as a world citizen was solidified as he gave concerts in new places and expanded his repertoire to include folk music from several countries. It was African culture and the goal of colonial independence that animated much of his writing, and he tried, with varying degrees of success, to integrate his study of Africa into his film career. He became increasingly vocal about global political issues and made more appearances at political events as he consciously chose to affiliate with working people in the struggle against fascism. For Robeson, the decade opened with several European concert engagements and his first portrayal of an African character in London, the heart of the British Empire.

Robeson's artistic career kept him buzzing around Europe in the early months of 1930 before rehearsals started for the *Othello* production in London. On his tour of Britain, audiences came to hear Robeson sing a program of mostly African American spirituals. While some critics wished that he would expand his repertoire, others were satisfied that Robeson continued "sticking to the music that he best understands and loves." Crowds favorably received Robeson as he traveled through Central Europe in cities including Prague, Dresden, Vienna, and Bucharest. Following the concert tour, Paul and Eslanda journeyed to the mountains of Switzerland to participate in the making of a silent film called *Borderline*. The residents of Territet, where the film was shot, thronged along the sidewalks and poked their heads through open windows for fleeting glimpses of the tall American actor strolling through their town. Paul headlined a small cast that also featured Eslanda. Written and directed by Kenneth Macpherson, the avant-garde film hinged on an obscure plot in which Robeson's character resided in a boardinghouse in a bucolic Swiss village. His calm life, however, was upended by a series of events following the arrival of his girlfriend, who was played by Eslanda. For the viewer, some of the scenes were confused by Macpherson's rather frantic cuts and references to ambiguous metaphors. (In 2006, the art house film was digitally restored by the British Film Institute and overdubbed with a jazz score that melded well with the black-and-white imagery and enhanced the film's accessibility.) The project was mostly a bit of fun for the Robesons, who understood that *Borderline* would probably not be widely released. They were instead anticipating the more serious acting challenge for Paul that was soon approaching.

Before heading to London to undertake the role of Shakespeare's noble Moor, the Robesons stopped in Berlin, where Paul was scheduled to do two performances of *The Emperor Jones* with director James Light from the old Provincetown group. The German people embraced Robeson, and the Robesons enjoyed visiting the city. However, as biographer Martin Duberman has pointed out, 1930 was a turning point in German politics, as Nazi Party rallies were springing up across the country and the party grew to be one of the largest in the nation. While Robeson did not often comment publicly on contemporary political developments in the early 1930s, he was most likely aware of the transitioning political situation in Europe. A few years later, he would have a very different experience in Berlin that starkly illustrated the hardening of the political climate in Germany. These travels nurtured Robeson's growing political consciousness and helped motivate him to speak out against fascism more vigorously later in the decade.

Back in London, which was home for the Robesons for much of the 1930s, Paul began preparing for his Shakespearean debut on the professional stage. *Othello* was a play with which Robeson was quite familiar. In his memoir, he fondly recalled that an English teacher, Miss Miller, had coached him in the role for a high school performance. On that occasion he had been "nervous and scared" as he "struggled through his lines" while being "mindful" that his father was listening carefully to his diction from the audience. For the 1930 revival, Robeson studied the play thoroughly to help stave off any trepidation he felt about tackling Shakespeare in England before the tough London theater critics. He had some concern about mastering the language of the Bard, knowing that the reviewers would be listening intently for his American accent. Robeson solved this issue by examining the play in its original seventeenth-century spelling and then approaching the pronunciation as he would any foreign dialect. Robeson was conversant in multiple languages, and this remarkable facility for languages helped him master Shakespeare's dialogue.

He also honed his interpretation of the character Othello while considering the text of the play. Though the famed African American actor Ira Aldridge had played the Moor in the 1830s, very few dark-skinned actors had portrayed Othello in London. In 1930 there was still considerable debate among literary critics as to Othello's racial identity. The racial overtones in some of the reviews of Robeson's performance suggested that the idea of a black Othello was far from universally welcomed. Robeson, however, consciously emphasized Othello's African origin as well as the importance of race in the play in interviews for the revival. For example, he thoughtfully pointed out that Othello had been portrayed as a dark-skinned African during Shakespeare's time in the early 1600s. It was not until the early 1800s, following the rise of African enslavement and theories of African inferiority, that Othello was more commonly played with lighter skin as a character with an Arab or Mediterranean identity. Even in 1930, some reviewers were reluctant to see the noble Othello portrayed as a dark-skinned African. Robeson's insistence on interpreting Othello as a noble African was an early example of the fusion between his emerging political consciousness and his artistic work. Even though he was still growing as an actor, Robeson's Othello was nevertheless vital to the stage history of the play because he restored the dark-skinned Othello that Shakespeare had intended to the British theater in the twentieth century.

Unfortunately, the *Othello* revival of 1930 was not in Robeson's hands alone. While his performance was historic and the female supporting cast of Peggy Ashcroft and Sybil Thorndike flourished, the overall production was mediocre at best. The major deficiencies of the production can be attributed to the producer/director team of Ellen Van Volkenburg and Maurice Browne, who also played what the critics labeled a completely ineffectual Iago. Reviewers condemned nearly every major decision they made for the revival. For instance, critics did not fail to observe that the lighting was too dim, the show was too long, the "fussy" sets were bulky, a superfluous dance number bored the crowd, and Robeson's costumes were ill suited for his role as a noble military leader. Probably the most unfortunate mistake was Van Volkenburg's seemingly indiscriminate cutting of Shakespeare's script. This not only impeded the audience's full experience with the drama but also hindered Robeson's performance, since he had studied the text closely.

Eslanda recounted the anxious weeks before the May premiere in her diary. She pegged Browne and Van Volkenburg as "hopeless amateurs" that made Paul "wild with nerves" over his Shakespearean debut. Robeson remarked in an interview that he had hoped to have had more "real guidance" through the play. Though guidance was not forthcoming from the production team, Robeson did get support from Max Montesole, an experienced cast member, as well as James Light, who was in town. Peggy Ashcroft also came by for informal rehearsals at the Robeson's home, which Eslanda characterized as a "boarding house" prior to the opening. Despite the troubles with the production, Robeson's acting matured during this encounter with Shakespeare. The reviews of Robeson were mixed and riddled with racial stereotyping, but many critics found reasons to praise his performance. Most critics found his voice to be a strong asset, but his lack of experience prevented some reviewers from fully endorsing his interpretation. While a handful of those reporting on the play found that Robeson's race added "a certain verisimilitude" to the plot, others could only see "a flat-footed negro with a prognathous jaw." One attentive critic commented that Robeson possessed the power necessary for the role of Othello but he had yet to develop the requisite "control and discipline." This observation summed up the

1930 revival rather well. Even though his performance was embraced by many, it was clear that there was room for growth and improvement. The production was a learning experience for Robeson, and by the 1940s, when he played Othello on Broadway, his acting had matured enough for him to truly inhabit the role.

Even as Robeson's professional life was progressing, his personal life was becoming unsettled. Around the same time that *Othello* opened in May 1930, Eslanda's biography of her thirty-two-year-old husband, *Paul Robeson Negro*, was published. The book received positive reviews in many of the major London newspapers. It probably also helped generate publicity for the *Othello* revival and vice versa. The review in the *Times* noted that both the author and subject's "racial pride" and "enthusiasm for negro culture" were "very deeply expressed." However, the personal implications of the book for Robeson were troubling. Eslanda's portrayal of Paul emphasized her own critiques of his character and, in the words of Paul Robeson Jr., "invented" other faults as well. While not apparent to outsiders, much of the book was misleading and served, in part, as a platform for Eslanda to air her grievances about their marriage. Eslanda presented Paul as being affable and genial in public but also as lazy, unfocused, indecisive, and having a "child-like" simplicity. The book expressed that she did not believe that he was ambitious enough about his career. These allegations angered Paul, who preferred to keep his personal life private, and they stood in stark contrast to his dignified public persona. Against his flaws, Eslanda portrayed herself as conscientious and efficient. She even invented conversations between the couple on the subject of infidelity. Coincidentally, around the time that the book came out Eslanda discovered a letter that revealed Paul's brief relationship with Peggy Ashcroft. She was incensed.

The book helped to reveal some of the primary fault lines in the Robesons' marriage, which were underscored by fundamental differences in their personalities and needs. Paul Robeson Jr. maintained that his mother viewed the marital relationship as "a kind of ownership," but his father strongly rejected the notion of any kind of confinement. In a letter to Essie, Paul disclosed that their relationship left him feeling "spiritually starved" at times. Though he loved her, he recognized that they were very "different in temperament." Their different temperaments had led Eslanda to become antagonistic, as illustrated by her publishing this biography, while Paul, on the other hand, became more disconnected from their relationship. These differences would surface again in the near future, but for the moment, Paul focused on work. Eslanda set about planning renovations on an apartment for them in the center of London while Paul Jr. was sent to live in Switzerland with Mrs. Goode.

Though the affair with Peggy Ashcroft had been short-lived, Paul's involvement with another woman, Yolande Jackson, became more intense around the summer of 1930. This news caused Eslanda to suffer a nervous collapse that triggered a partial paralysis in her face. Her recovery took several months. During that time, Paul and Eslanda worked to reach an amicable living arrangement. They considered divorcing, and Paul contemplated marrying Yolande Jackson. Both of them wavered on the issue of divorce, which they pondered several times over the next two years. As in many marriages, the emotional dynamics between the Robesons were complicated. They needed each other's companionship and support, but in different ways: Eslanda wanted to build her whole world around her husband, whereas Paul craved more independence.

In January 1931 Paul headed overseas for an extended concert tour across the United States with Lawrence Brown. He noted to a newspaper reporter that though he was an American singer, he was not known widely outside of New York. Now he wanted to sing "from one end of America to the other." His program included African American spirituals as well as folk songs from Europe. Concert halls were mostly full, according to the reviews, and many audiences stood and requested numerous encores, which Robeson generously granted. Some reviewers preferred the spirituals to the German lieder and other songs from abroad. Several critics were duly impressed that Robeson's enunciation was as clear in other languages as it was when he was singing in English. One writer elegantly summarized that Robeson's "supremacy lies in the fact that he regards song as part of life rather than as an ornament to it." During this period, Robeson became good friends with Robert Rockmore, who he had met when he did *All God's Chillun Got Wings* with the Provincetown Players. Rockmore was an entertainment lawyer and began acting as Robeson's manager over the course of the next few years.

In May 1931, Robeson was back in London for a production of Eugene O'Neill's play *The Hairy Ape*, to be directed by James Light with Rockmore as one of the producers. The play explored class boundaries and social divisions in modern life through the character of Yank, played by Robeson. Yank was a stoker on an ocean liner who felt secure as a cog in the machinery of the mighty vessel until an insult from a passenger upended his sense of identity. Robeson's role was originally written for a white actor, and some of the critics later viewed Robeson's assumption of the role as a mistake in casting. The part, nevertheless, was physically demanding, and the run of the production was cut short when Robeson ended up in a hospital bed with a case of laryngitis. Through much of the year Paul and Eslanda were living separately, though Paul and Lawrence Brown would sometimes rehearse in the central London flat on Buckingham Street. In the autumn of 1931, the Robesons again discussed divorce as Paul still vacillated about marrying Yolande Jackson. The tumult in Robeson's private life seemed to take a toll, and in November a concert at Albert Hall had to be canceled because he was sick with flu. However, the Robeson family spent Christmas Day together in London with Paul Jr. and Mrs. Goode visiting from Europe. Relations between Paul and Eslanda were friendly for the holiday, even though Paul was still involved with Yolande. Late in December, Paul sailed for another concert tour in the United States.

The program for Robeson's 1932 U.S. concert tour contained familiar spirituals, such as "Nobody Knows the Trouble I've Seen" and "Joshua Fit de Battle of Jericho," as well as music from Russia and Europe, including Alexander Kipnis Gretchaninoff's "The Captive" and Modest Petrovich Mussorgsky's "Silent Room." The tour closed in New York in March with two enthusiastically received concerts at Town Hall. In the spring, Robeson joined a revival of *Show Boat* in New York. At this time he was again considering divorce, and proceedings began, although they would not be carried through. *Show Boat* opened in May to madly glowing reviews. Robeson had been part of the cast in London in 1928, so this was the first opportunity for audiences on the other side of the Atlantic to see him play the role of Joe. But hearing Robeson was the real treat for the crowd. They went wild, and the show had to be momentarily stopped after he sang Jerome Kerns's "Ol' Man River." The musical ran for several months, and during that time Robeson was swamped with profitable offers. Accolades were abundant as his career continued to blossom. In June Robeson returned to his alma mater, Rutgers University, to receive an honorary master of arts degree.

While Robeson was in New York, the rumor mill had been speculating about a possible separation between Paul and Eslanda. His relationship with Yolande Jackson was at times erratic, and by late 1932 it had finally run its course. Ultimately, Paul and Eslanda did not divorce, and the issue was not seriously raised again after their reconciliation that year. Their partnership endured for decades and held fast even if one, or the other, had a discrete affair. Eslanda began focusing more on continuing her intellectual develop-ment in the 1930s, which helped her to create an independent identity. Interestingly, Paul and Eslanda both became more politically conscious as the decade progressed. They both studied Africa, with Paul concentrating on language and culture and Eslanda delving into anthropology. Both part-ners remained dedicated to the advancement of Paul's career while, as Paul Robeson Jr. summarized, Eslanda stopped trying to own Paul and he ceased to dispute her status as Mrs. Paul Robeson. With his personal life stabilized, Robeson could now fully dedicate himself to his artistry. He also undertook an assiduous study of languages, music, and culture in the coming years.

Early in 1933 Robeson agreed to revisit the role of Jim Harris in a Lon-don production of Eugene O'Neill's *All God's Chillun Got Wings*. A young, dedicated actress named Flora Robson, who lived near the Robeson's Buck-ingham Street apartment, played the role of Ella, and Andre Van Gyseghem directed. The revival opened in March and ran for a couple of months at the Embassy Theatre, which was known for hosting material that was on the cutting edge. The play's theme of interracial marriage did not cause the sensation that it had in New York, and it gave the actors a unique opportu-nity to probe the emotional and spiritual depths of their characters. Robeson and Robson's theatrical collaboration was quite fruitful. This production was perhaps the first time Robeson participated in an onstage partnership in which the emotional turmoil of the characterizations was more gripping than the text of the play. The reviewers praised both performances, noting that Robson was more technically accomplished but Robeson's interpreta-tion of Jim was "intensely moving." Indeed, Robeson was still developing as a professional actor. He had thus far relied mostly on instinct to guide him onstage and would continue to refine his theatrical skills over the years.

In May 1933, Robeson headed to New York to return to the role of Brutus Jones for the film version of *The Emperor Jones*. While the medium of film had become familiar to audiences by the 1930s, movies with sound, or "talkies," were only a few years old. This was Robeson's first chance to reach a larger audience through film with his best asset, his voice, intact. Perhaps even more significant was the fact that this was the first time an African American actor headlined in a major motion picture. DuBose Heyward penned the screenplay, based on O'Neill's play, J. Rosamond Johnson wrote the score, and Fredi Washington played Jones's love interest. Robeson was paid a salary for the weeks of filming, and a jungle was constructed in a film studio in Astoria, Queens, because he refused to shoot in the South. However, Robeson was compromised in other ways. The film's dominant theme was primitivism, which was portrayed as the link between African Americans and their forebears. Robeson even used the term *nigger* more than once, which rankled the film's black critics.

Embedded in the *Jones* project were several of the fundamental problems with film that would plague Robeson until the early 1940s when he broke with the industry completely. Images of African Americans onscreen seemed to be afflicted with possible contradictions, and Brutus Jones was no different. Was it meaningful for audiences to see a black lead even if his character had, as Jeffrey Stewart has observed, absorbed colonialism's ethics of abusing the weak? Did the mental collapse of Jones as he descended back to savagery arouse sympathy or revulsion? Did the film simply portray black people as irrational, superstitious, and criminal, or was it a cautionary tale to warn blacks not to mimic their oppressors? As primarily a psychological character study, *The Emperor Jones* did not offer much direct commentary on the social or political oppression of people of African descent, though Jones's character could be viewed as a product of that exploitation. Robeson hoped that film could be a vehicle to bring greater exposure to the rich culture of the African diaspora. However, it was a constant struggle for him to improve the content of scripts and dissuade producers from relying on denigrating images of people of color. Film financers were often hesitant because they worried about losing potential Southern audiences.

Critical reception of *Jones* in the mainstream press was almost uniformly congratulatory. Reviewers recognized Robeson's onscreen debut as an African American leading man and professed the film to be "satisfying and absorbing." Black critics, predictably, were more reserved. Most appreciated Robeson's acting but denounced the use of demeaning stereotypes as "damaging propaganda against the Negro." Robeson later acknowledged that the film had not been successful because the order of the scenes had been altered (the film was told chronologically and the play had been conveyed through flashbacks). Additionally, the drums had not been engaged onscreen as they had been onstage. All in all, the film project showed Robeson that actors have little control in that medium. Toward the end of the decade, he publicly declared his frustration with the industry and tried to negotiate contracts that gave him more power over a film's content.

The early 1930s was a time of intense intellectual growth for Robeson, and as he reflected more on political and social issues, he gradually became more vocal. Back in London, following the filming of *The Emperor Jones*, Robeson expressed his desire to make a film about Africa. His interest in the continent also motivated him to enroll in the School of Oriental and African Studies at London University in early 1933, where he explored African and Asian linguistic families. (Eslanda had also registered for anthropology coursework there.) Robeson was pleased to discover connections between African dialects and the speech patterns of African Americans. He listened to African folk music on the gramophone and read voraciously. Robeson believed that black Americans were detached from their cultural heritage and felt strongly that Africa held the key to the future for people of the diaspora. London was an important center of education and the circulation of ideas for people from the Caribbean and parts of Africa that were colonized by the British. Through international groups such as the League of Coloured Peoples and the West African Students' Union, Robeson became acquainted with students, intellectuals, and future leaders of postcolonial Africa such as Jomo Kenyatta, Nnamdi Azikiwe, and C. L. R. James. In his memoir he recalled that it was in London that he "discovered Africa" and that he felt "as one" with his African friends. Paul and Eslanda became honorary members of the West African Students' Union. At a meeting of the League of Coloured Peoples, Robeson emphasized his connection with Africa and noted that his personal success had only fortified his commitment to breaking down further racial barriers. His identification with Africa solidified as the decade progressed. For a 1934 piece on what he wanted out of life, Robeson declared that in his art he wanted "to carry always this central idea: to be African." He concluded, "Multitudes of men have died for less worthy ideas; [this] is even more eminently worth living for."

As Robeson ruminated on African culture, he began writing more and articulating his ideas in interviews. The themes in his writing revealed a critique of Western culture and civilization. Robeson urged people of African descent to rediscover the hidden history and art of Africa. He maintained that the West had become overintellectualized and had lost much of its spirituality in the quest for rationality. Links to Africa had been suppressed through the pressure to assimilate to European culture. As a result, African Americans were largely unaware of African history, music, art, and language. People of African descent, however, should not seek to emulate Western art forms but should look for inspiration from their African roots, which contain the gift of intuition, a great capacity for spirituality, and deep wells of emotion. Robeson argued that African civilization was not barbarous but was equal to Western civilization, even though it was culturally different. Singing and dancing, for example, were not divorced from life but were ingrained in daily living in Africa. This cultural heritage was valuable, and such cultural differences should be honored. Also central to Robeson's position was the necessity of full self-determination for all people of African descent in order that they might develop their cultural gifts. A few other intellectuals were reaching similar conclusions around this time. For example, Robeson corresponded with Columbia University anthropologist Melville Herskovits, whose 1941 book, *The Myth of the Negro Past*, made an important contribution by reconstructing the cultural history of African Americans.

Robeson's beliefs, however, could not be easily labeled as nationalistic even though he was not an assimilationist. He did not advocate a literal "back to Africa" movement as suggested by nationalist leader Marcus Garvey in the 1920s. Robeson insisted that no matter where he lived geographically he could still "think and feel as an African." While he maintained that black people should have equal political rights, this did not necessarily mean that they needed to completely assimilate and relinquish their unique ethnic heritage. While much of the racial theory in the early twentieth century exploited racial difference as evidence of innate inferiority, Robeson made the opposite claim. The unique and complex cultural heritage of African people was, in his view, proof of their inherent equality. In later years, Robeson's position would grow to encompass folk culture from around the world. While still identifying with Africa, he contended that the shared humanity among all men was best evidenced through global folk culture. He frequently made this case from the concert stage by singing a folk melody from one country, in its original language, and linking it with an African American spiritual, work song, or other folk song. There existed, Robeson believed, a kinship among all people, especially the laboring classes whose cultural forms were born out of their common experiences. Cultural distinctions, rather than dividing people, could be the basis of international solidarity. Robeson's internationalism became more politicized after his visit to the front of the Spanish Civil War in the late 1930s, and defending folk culture was intrinsic to the strong antifascist position he developed.

In 1934, Robeson signed on to a film project with African themes that was called *Sanders of the River*. He hoped this would fulfill his intention of making a film that introduced audiences to the African music and culture that he had been exploring so passionately. Though the film had some promising elements, these were ultimately overshadowed by its imperialistic message. The film was a creation of the producer/director team of Alexander and Zolton Korda. Zolton had collected reels of footage of indigenous African music and dance from the continent that would be woven into the plotline. Robeson was excited by the prospect that these images would get a wide viewership. Additionally, many Africans were hired as extras for the film, including Jomo Kenyatta, who later became a leader of the anticolonial movement in East Africa. Robeson made many friends while practicing their languages, and he generally relished the company of the Africans while on the London set.

The script, however, had a glaring procolonial bias that emphasized the need for a British presence, personified in the noble patriarch Commissioner Sanders, to civilize the primitive, childlike Africans. Robeson's character, Bosambo, represented the submissive, loyal, indigenous leadership that was cultivated by the British and fundamental to the success of their colonial system. The fur-skin loincloth that served as his costume made his character come across less as a dignified leader and more as a caricature. In the end, the unfortunate glorification of colonialism overshadowed the footage of indigenous culture from the continent, and black critics lambasted the film. In response, Robeson pointed out that the imperialist message of the film had been added after shooting and during the editing process. However, the script was replete with patronizing language that clearly established the colonial bias early in the film. For instance, Sanders was described as having been "father and mother" to the people of the river who "enjoyed their primitive paradise" under his "just rule." To his credit, Robeson later admitted publicly that "all of the attacks against me and the film were correct." He also refused other projects that were offered to him by the producer.

Robeson's chief concern was for people of the diaspora to know that he was trying to use film to honestly portray African culture. He stated that "nothing would hurt me more than to have the African natives think that I have betrayed them." Having started the project with good intentions, the final product was commercially successful but a source of personal embarrassment. His son's biography noted that Robeson was so "mortified" while watching *Sanders* at the London premiere in 1935 that he quietly exited the theater and went back to their apartment to mull over his response to the film. By 1938, he described the film as having been a "total loss." Yet Robeson's experience with *Sanders of the River* demonstrated that it would be more difficult than he had initially predicted to wed his growing cultural awareness with his film career. He would aim to proceed more cautiously in the future.

An interesting offer came to Robeson in 1934, which provided what would be a life-changing opportunity to visit the Soviet Union. Soviet director Sergei Eisenstein greatly admired the hero of the Haitian revolution Toussaint L'Ouverture and wanted Robeson to collaborate on a film honoring that historic struggle. This was exactly the kind of project that Robeson was yearning to undertake. He had discussed Soviet politics with acquaintances in England, including Emma Goldman, and wanted to learn more about Russian folk culture. A visit to the Soviet Union was definitely in order. In December, Robeson set off for Moscow with Eslanda and Marie Seton, a British friend and writer who had contacts in the Soviet Union. (She later published a biography of Robeson in the 1950s.) On the journey east, the group had an extended layover in Berlin. Paul and Eslanda had enjoyed their previous visit to the city, but the atmosphere had changed and now it felt more repressive. The dark-skinned visitors seemed conspicuous to passersby at the train station. At one point, Eslanda went to check on their luggage, leaving Paul and Marie behind. The sight of a black man and a white woman together instigated angry glares, and they were soon approached by several men in uniform. Robeson quickly recognized the possible rumblings of a lynch mob and warned Marie to show no fear. Fortunately, the tense situation soon diffused and the men retreated. Eslanda returned, and luckily their train pulled into the station. It was a memorable day, however, and an ugly illustration of the intensifying fascist climate in Germany that was marked, in Robeson's words, by "hatred, fear and suspicion."

In stark contrast, there was a hearty welcome for the three travelers in Moscow that was cheerfully led by Eisenstein. Paul enchanted everyone they met with his Russian language skills and soon felt that "this is home." Eslanda was reunited with her two brothers, John and Frank Goode, who were part of a small community of African Americans who were sympathetic to the Soviet experiment and had relocated. Reporters clamored for comments from the film star, who wisely directed his remarks toward cultural themes rather than broaching politics, as Eisenstein had advised. The Robesons stayed at the well-appointed National Hotel adjacent to Red Square for their whirlwind two-week visit. Discussions with Eisenstein and tours of civic institutions such as hospitals and factories filled their days, while elaborate dinners, elegant receptions, opera, and theater shows consumed their evenings. They spent Christmas Eve dining and dancing at the home of the Soviet foreign minister. The Russian people wholeheartedly adored Robeson. They clasped his hand on the street, delighted in his informal singing, and made him feel not just welcomed but truly embraced. Children on a snowy playground were entranced with the tall, dark stranger who spoke their language, and they nicknamed him "black Grandfather Frost" according to Paul Jr.'s account.

The impact of this first exchange of goodwill between Robeson and the people of the Soviet Union was tremendous. Robeson would refer to it for much of the rest of his life as the first time he had been able to "breathe freely" and walk "secure and free" as an equal with full human dignity. He discerned from the frank testimony of the Goode brothers that he was not being treated well simply because of his celebrity but because racial prejudice was practically nonexistent in the country. Robeson was impressed that the Soviet constitution outlawed racial discrimination and that the Soviet people expressed an understanding of the oppression of both Africans and African Americans. Eslanda was heartened by the care she observed in hospitals and child care centers. Perhaps caught up in the spirit of the moment, Robeson might have at times overstated his enthusiasm for the Soviet system that, after all, did have serious faults of which he was aware. During his visit, for example, he declared several times that he intended to move to the Soviet Union. However, the fact that the culture of minority groups was respected at places such as the Technical and Theater School of the National Minorities (which he visited) was profoundly moving to Robeson. Experiencing life without the burden of racial discrimination was deeply affecting, despite the underlying realities of Stalin's authoritarian leadership.

While in Moscow, Robeson spent time with William Patterson, an African American lawyer, whom he had known back in Harlem in the 1920s. Patterson was in Moscow temporarily while convalescing from illness. He had become a dedicated member of the U.S. Communist Party and was working with their International Labor Defense to secure the release of the Scottsboro boys. These nine black youths had been wrongfully accused of rape and were sentenced to death in Alabama. Patterson urged Robeson to return to the United States and join the struggle for African American rights. At this time, however, Robeson was neither interested in joining a political organization nor in moving back to the States. He was, on the other hand, considering relocating his son to the Soviet Union. Since the black expatriate community seemed at ease in their new home and had attested to the lack of racial prejudice, both Paul and Eslanda thought it could be beneficial for his son to be educated in such an environment. Robeson had felt the stigma of being one of a few black students at a school in the racially charged United States, and he hoped that his namesake could forge a more positive set of memories. The Robesons rounded out their journey with a few days in Leningrad and then returned to London by way of Scandinavia (not Germany). All in all, the trip had been quite significant. While he was not yet animated by any specific political ideology, Robeson would begin leaning toward left-wing ideas and reading more about theorists such as Karl Marx. Martin Duberman has interestingly surmised that Robeson's negative experience in Berlin, a day of "horror" as he later called it, being followed so closely by a very warm experience in the Soviet Union perhaps helped to fashion Nazi fascism and Soviet communism as two opposing binaries in his mind. In future years, though he never officially joined the Communist Party, the Soviet Union always remained dear to Robeson while staunch antifascism framed his political outlook.

Upon returning to England in early 1935, Robeson took off on a heartily received concert tour of the British Isles with his regular accompanist Lawrence Brown. The tour began with a show at Albert Hall in London. Crowds thronged to hear him throughout the United Kingdom. People sat on steps and stood for two hours hoping to get a seat in the Sheffield City Hall. In one seaport town, seats to hear Robeson were at such a premium that the chairs that an opening quartet had used were immediately sold to concertgoers when the musicians left the stage. The program for the tour included African American spirituals such as "Go Down Moses" and "Deep River" as well as Russian songs like Alexander Gretchaninoff's "Homeland Mine" and "The Laborer's Plaint" by Alexander Kopyloff. "Short'nin' Bread" was also thrown in for fun. As usual, Robeson accommodated numerous encores that were requested by audience members even if they were songs that had already been part of the program, such as "Water Boy." "Ol' Man River" from *Show Boat* was also a favorite request. His generosity and sincerity was not lost on the reviewers. One critic summed up the reception of the tour well when he observed, "Robeson is one of the few artists who can duplicate their programmes [*sic*] year after year with renewed success." His celebrity status in Britain clearly had not been diminished by his recent time in the Soviet Union.

Robeson teamed up again with director Andre Van Gyseghem in May 1935 for the play *Stevedore*, which had been well received in New York the previous year. The script by Paul Peters and George Sklar touched upon several themes that were important to Robeson, including civil rights and working-class unity. As one reviewer noticed, "Paul Robeson is evidently looking around for a play" that will "give dramatic conviction to the cause of coloured [*sic*] races." *Stevedore*'s plot focused on a dockworker named Lonnie Thompson, played by Robeson, who was falsely accused of rape but roused his fellow laborers to stand up against their common oppressor and was shot dead during the uprising. Numerous extras were hired as stevedores, and even Lawrence Brown made an appearance in which he proved to be, in one reporter's view, "a fine emotional actor." The production opened at the Embassy Theatre, but notices were for the most part uncomplimentary. Most critics felt the play was little more than "obvious propaganda," though they praised Robeson and looked forward to him undertaking a more "suitable" role. The production's run was short-lived, and Robeson then concentrated on a summer concert tour as well as continuing his intellectual endeavors.

Later that year, Eslanda helped secure a lucrative deal for Paul to reprise the role of Joe in the film version of *Show Boat*. In September they sailed across the Atlantic and were bound for Hollywood. Once in the United States, Robeson first partnered with Lawrence Brown for several concerts in New York and other selected cities. The Robesons also visited young Paul, who was then living with his grandmother in western Massachusetts. By this time, nearing the age of eight, Paul Jr. had been separated from his parents for much of his life and had resided in several countries under the watchful eye of Mrs. Goode. Though he excelled in athletics and spoke two languages, he was having a tough time. Paul Robeson Jr. recalled that his father promised to arrange for him to move into the London flat when they returned to England the following spring.

In California, the Robesons temporarily settled in a Pasadena apartment for the two-month shooting of *Show Boat*. Eslanda explored the sets on the Universal studio during the days while Paul worked. James Whale directed the lavish musical, which had been so successful onstage in both New York and London. The role of Joe, however, did not push beyond common stereotypes of black characters, as black critics of the film did not hesitate to emphasize. Joe and his wife, Queenie, played by Hattie McDaniel in the film, were laborers on a southern riverboat and were essentially observers to the plot, which centered on the escapades of the white characters. Joe was predictably loyal and was chided for being lazy and shiftless. He seemed to understand the stratification of southern society when he sang about it in "Ol' Man River," but Joe did not question his subservient position. Still, *Show Boat* was an important vehicle for Robeson's career. It provided vital income that allowed him to undertake less profitable but more meaningful roles, and it elevated his celebrity status so that he could afford to be more selective about the offers he accepted in the future. Of course, the song "Ol' Man River" from the production was immortalized by Robeson and widely beloved. Following *Show Boat*, offers from Hollywood were abundant. However, Robeson preferred to return to England where he believed there was a better chance for undertaking substantial projects.

In January 1936 Robeson traveled back to Britain and set off on a concert tour that was characteristically well received. Significant world events were also taking shape around this time. Robeson was asked to comment on the recent purges in the Soviet Union, but he did not condemn Joseph Stalin's crackdown. According to his son, Robeson "harbored grave doubts about internal Soviet politics." Yet he made no mention of these publicly. Robeson chose instead to maintain solidarity with the Soviet Union because of its positions against racism and colonialism. He held fast to this stance through the Second World War and even into the repressive days of the early Cold War. Additionally, the rise of fascist leader Benito Mussolini in Italy had direct implications in Africa. Mussolini appealed to Italian nationalism by promising to invade Ethiopia, where they had been previously defeated. Ethiopia was a crucial symbol of independence on the continent that had been colonized and exploited by Europe since the nineteenth century. Italy's rapid and brutal defeat of sovereign Ethiopia in 1936 roused the indignation of people throughout the African diaspora. Unfortunately, it did not rouse any Western powers, which remained silent before Emperor Haile Selassie's ardent plea for assistance to the League of Nations. It was clear that fascist forces were on the move. In an interview in early 1936, Robeson noted that his sympathy was with the Ethiopians. He stressed that Ethiopia should be left to "work out her own problems" and that the Ethiopians could get along without "the kind of 'civilizing' that European nations do with bombs and machine guns." Robeson's next theater project also indirectly commented on the Italian invasion of Ethiopia.

In the spring of 1936 Robeson joined forces with West Indian C. L. R. James on a play about Toussaint L'Ouverture that was written by James. The film with Sergei Eisenstein never came to fruition, so this was Robeson's only opportunity to portray a leader of the rebellion that formed the only free black republic in the Western hemisphere in 1804. Though the play with James was on a relatively small scale it gave Robeson the rare opportunity to merge his anticolonial beliefs with his artistic career. Additionally, Robeson was able to form a friendship with James, who was a significant figure in left-wing, anticolonial political circles in London. James, a writer and engaging speaker, departed from his home in Trinidad in 1932 and remained industrious throughout the decade, publishing political theory as well as biography and fiction. His 1938 landmark chronicle of the Haitian revolution, *The Black Jacobins*, marked a crucial turning point in the writing of Caribbean history. Drawing on data from Caribbean and European archives, James's compelling narrative presented the black insurrectionists as heroic figures. The timing of his work was also conscious. Anna Grimshaw has pointed out that in the wake of the Ethiopian defeat, James wanted to demonstrate that the people of the diaspora had a revolutionary tradition of their own. He hoped his work could illustrate "how the African revolution would develop." By looking to Toussaint and avoiding his mistakes, a new anticolonial struggle could be born out of the present crisis. James wanted his ideas to reach as wide an audience as possible, so he fashioned the historical narrative first into a play. This piece engaged Robeson's long-held desire to do "a great play about Haiti" that was "written by a Negro" and "acted by Negroes."

The Stage Society in London mounted *Toussaint Louverture* for a brief run at the Westminster Theatre. Unfortunately, James was not as adept a playwright as he was a scholar. Although "written from the heart," most critics found his script to be dull, unimaginative, or "unevenly written." It seemed that although James knew the facts, he did not know how to "marshal them for stage effect." Robeson's performance, on the other hand, was nearly unanimously applauded. Accolades such as *noble*, *dignified*, and *thoughtful* were not in short supply in the notices. One enthusiastic reviewer concluded that Robeson was "one of the most impressive actors alive." The reviewer for *The Keys*, the journal of the League of Coloured Peoples, welcomed seeing Robeson finally in a play that was "worthy of his powers." Several critics also noted the political significance of Robeson as Toussaint L'Ouverture. One commented that Robeson had "found a hero after his own heart," and another remarked that this historic black character was surely "a great pleasure" for Robeson to portray. A particularly attentive reviewer linked the play directly to the context of the Ethiopian invasion. It was noteworthy, he wrote, to see a play in which a black man "pleads for his people" at a time when Italy was "crushing out Abyssinia with gas bombs, aeroplanes and tanks." Though the script was not perfect, James's overall message had gotten through.

In his continuing search for meaningful film projects that addressed African themes, Robeson agreed to star in several British films in 1936. First up was *Song of Freedom*, which costarred Elisabeth Welch. Directed by J. Elder Wills and produced by British Lion Films, the movie was based on a piece by Claude Wallace and Dorothy Holloway called *The Kingdom of Zinga*. Robeson played a dockworker, John Zinga, whose vocal talent was discovered by a manager when he was singing on the street with his fellow laborers. Upon pursuing a concert career, a series of events led to Zinga's discovery that he was the long-lost heir of a tribe in Africa. Zinga and his wife traveled to Africa and were initially rejected by the tribe until Zinga revealed that he knew their sacred song of freedom. While not terribly profound, the film was refreshing for Robeson. The black lead character was not a shiftless stereotype but a believable person who was honorable, sincere, and talented. Likewise, his wife was intelligent and supportive. John Zinga, moreover, shared with Robeson a personal identification with Africa and a desire to connect with the place of his ancestors. The film further portrayed the idea of reconnecting with Africa as being possible, perhaps even fruitful. When it was released, *Song of Freedom* was especially appreciated by black critics, and Langston Hughes reported to Eslanda that Harlem enjoyed the film.

Following a brief vacation in the Soviet Union, Robeson returned to England to begin shooting another British film, *King Solomon's Mines*. Largely an adventure tale, this film was based on H. Rider Haggard's novel. Umbopa, played by Robeson, was an African chief disguised as a servant who assisted some white treasure hunters, saved his throne, and sang his way into the proverbial sunset. It lacked the imperialist implications of *Sanders of the River* but was no great favorite of critics, who found that it also lacked substance. While Paul was hard at work making films relating to Africa, Eslanda and young Paul embarked on a journey across the continent. The pair sailed to South Africa in May 1936 and then spent three months making their way northward by land. Max Yergan, an African American who had worked for many years with the YMCA in South Africa, helped with arrangements and introductions. Yergan was becoming politicized by the deteriorating conditions he observed for black South Africans, and he became a close associate of the Robesons for many years. While her visa underscored that Eslanda's trip was for anthropological field research, it also had political undertones. Yergan helped her meet key black South African leaders who opposed the burgeoning apartheid system. She also saw the conditions of that country's infamous mines and visited the black townships outside of Cape Town. A travelogue of Eslanda and Paul Jr.'s adventure was published as *African Journey* in 1945. In it, she argued fervently against the prevailing theories of African inferiority.

Robeson's busy year included filming for another cinematic project with British Lion Films titled *Big Fella*. This movie again featured Robeson with Elisabeth Welch and was directed by J. Elder Wills. It was based on Claude McKay's novel *Banjo* and was Robeson's sole attempt at a comedic role. Set in Marseilles, France, the plot followed Robeson and two of his fellow dockworkers, one played capably by Lawrence Brown, who struck up a friendship with a boy who ran away from his well-heeled parents and their swanky yacht. Eslanda was also featured as the owner of the café where Robeson and his chums socialized after work.

Paul Robeson (center) in the film Big Fella *from British Lion Films. Lawrence Brown, Robeson's long-time accompanist, is on the far right; Eslanda Robeson is to the left of Robeson. Photographs and Prints Division, Schomburg Center for Research in Black Culture, The New York Public Library, Astor, Lenox, and Tilden Foundations.*

The film was basically frivolous, but Robeson made certain that his character, Joe, was not portrayed as indolent. He was to be comedic but not foolish. While they both had a penchant for singing informally on the docks, unlike his namesake in *Show Boat*, this Joe was hardworking, trustworthy, and was his own man, not a servant. Overall, these British film projects helped solidify Robeson's position as a film star. Though not always successful, he persistently strove to convey African themes and dignified black characters.

Somehow Robeson also managed to squeeze in a concert tour of the Soviet Union in the fall of 1936. In October, he sang twelve concerts with Lawrence Brown in four major cities: Moscow, Leningrad, Kiev, and Odessa. The concerts were broadcast over the national radio, so Robeson's voice reached a vast audience far beyond the concert halls where he performed. The Russian audiences responded quite warmly to Robeson's performances as well as to his selections of folk music. Even though he sang African American spirituals in English, Robeson first explained their content to the crowd in Russian. His facility with their language and dignified interpretations sealed the endearing relationship between Robeson and the Russian people. In a radio broadcast, he revealed that he felt "a tremendous bond of sympathy and mutual understanding" when singing the songs of his people before the Russian people. While there, Paul and Eslanda enrolled their son in a Russian school, as they had considered on their first visit to the country. While it was labeled public, the school was more like an exclusive private school. Paul Robeson Jr. wrote that Stalin's daughter and Foreign Minister Molotov's son attended the school, along with the children of other high-ranking officials. Even though he did not speak the language initially, with some extra Russian tutoring, he soon felt like "one of the group." He later recalled that Russians from "all walks of life" were "friendly" in a "natural and spontaneous fashion." As his parents had hoped, Paul Jr. settled into a convivial environment in a way that would not have been possible for a young black student in the United States. However, his stay in the Soviet Union was curtailed by the purges of suspected spies in the coming year. Due to the repressive political climate in the Soviet Union and the winds of war that were blowing across Europe, Paul and Eslanda moved young Paul back to England in the autumn of 1937 and enrolled him in a school for Soviet children in London.

In January 1937, Robeson was at work on another British film project. Shooting for *Jericho* was done in Egypt, so Paul and Eslanda set off for Cairo only four days after they returned to London from the Soviet Union. Largely an action film, *Jericho* was considered by some to be one of Robeson's better films, perhaps even his best. Robeson's character, Jericho Jackson, defied stereotypes as a purely heroic lead. In an interesting reversal of the common cinematic trend of the laughable black sidekick, the comic foil, played by Wallace Ford, was white. The film's plot opened in World War I with Jackson on a ship full of troops that was torpedoed. While trying to rescue several trapped men, Jackson accidentally killed an officer. Jackson escaped to avoid a death sentence by a court martial and ended up in North Africa, where he became a leader of a desert tribe. However, a captain pursued Jackson for years and finally tracked him down and found him living peacefully with his beautiful wife, played by a real-life African princess, and his family. At the close of the film, Jackson decided to return with the captain to face the consequences of his actions from so long ago. But the captain had a last-minute change of heart after observing the wise, dignified Jackson and the loyalty of his new kinship network. Rather than turning Jackson over to the authorities, the captain left Jackson to continue in his role as a noble African leader. Unlike with past projects, Robeson maintained considerable control over this script. Jackson was originally slated to die tragically at the end, but Robeson helped influence a triumphant conclusion. While not primarily a character study, the film portrayed Jericho Jackson as strong, noble, and intelligent. He was not a complex character, but he was a natural leader who possessed a conscience. The film did make use of Robeson's voice by having him break into song at several unexpected intervals. But the scene of Robeson singing solo atop a sand dune was rather elegant and memorable. The images of the great salt caravan across the desert further evoked the grandeur of an ancient civilization.

For the filming of *Jericho*, Paul Robeson was in Africa for the first time! The Robesons thoroughly relished visiting the historically rich city of Cairo. The Egyptians, while still technically under British rule, had practiced a unique measure of political autonomy since 1922. Seeing Africans undertake a degree of self-determination was exciting for Robeson. Much of the film was shot outside of the city in the desert. One day Robeson and a few others, including actor Henry Wilcoxon, explored the great pyramid at

Giza. With the help of a guide, they ventured into the dimly lit tomb at the center of the majestic, ancient structure. Everyone fell silent when Robeson hummed a few notes, which echoed through the chamber. Stepping into the center of the ageless geometric space, Robeson began to sing "O Isis und Osiris" from Mozart's opera *The Magic Flute*. According to Robeson biographers, Wilcoxon remembered tears streaming down the cheeks of all who were present. No one could summon any words, so the group traveled back to the city in an enraptured quiet. Though *Jericho* was not a big success commercially and the critics' reviews were somewhat tepid, the project had been personally fulfilling for Robeson. He had traveled to Africa and seen some of its ancient glory for himself while satisfying his aim to portray an honorable black lead character in film.

Back in England in the spring of 1937, Robeson began moving in a more politicized direction. From this point forward, he began speaking out against fascism and colonialism and using his celebrity to raise money at benefits. He contributed $1,500 to the fledgling International Committee on African Affairs that was led by Max Yergan, who had now relocated to New York. The organization soon changed its name to the Council on African Affairs, and Robeson served as its chairman for many years. Until its dissolution in 1955, the Council was one of the only groups in the United States that consistently provided reliable news about events on the continent and lobbied for African independence. Robeson was also attracted to the fundamental tenants of socialism including, as his son has noted, control of the economy by the workforce rather than the employers and production based on need rather than maximum profit. In his 1958 memoir, Robeson underscored his "deep conviction" that socialism represented an "economically, socially, culturally, and ethically" superior system to that based on "production for private profit." He read Marx and Lenin in their original languages and became acquainted with leaders in the British Labour and Communist parties as well as dignitaries from the Soviet Union. Robeson linked the provisions of Article 123 and chapter X of the Soviet Constitution to the continued oppression of his people. Whereas Western authorities were oppressing people throughout the African diaspora, the Soviet Union had decreed that any "establishment of direct or indirect privileges" based upon "race or nationality" would be "punishable by law." In Robeson's view, this act placed the Soviet Union in opposition to global racial exploitation. It further positioned the Soviet Union as a protector of national culture. He was in "100 hundred percent agreement" with the Communist Party's anticolonial position. And Robeson believed that the Soviet Union could be a "bulwark" against fascism.

This was especially crucial to Robeson in light of the recent and unsettling spread of fascism. Since Ethiopia had been defeated by the Italian fascists, Robeson turned his attention to Spain, where the Republican forces were, in his words, "defending" society against "the ravages of the fascist hordes." Spain was divided by civil war as Francisco Franco's fascist army attempted to overthrow the Republican government. Robeson pointed out that victory for Franco would mean that the "poor, landless and disfranchised" would remain "poor, landless and disfranchised." None of the Western powers (England, France, the United States) rallied to support the antifascist cause in Spain. Robeson was grieved at the West's lack of concern but was heartened by the Soviet Union's call for a "united front" against fascism. Volunteers from around the world were mobilized under the aegis of the united front and traveled to Spain to defend democratic principles. Robeson strongly believed that "all lovers of peace" should join forces against fascism, which he described as "the new slavery." Oppressed groups should especially take heed in Robeson's view because a fascist conquest in Spain would only worsen the conditions for all oppressed people.

During the summer of 1937, the war in Spain was escalating. General Franco was supported by both Germany and Italy, while the Republicans depended on volunteers from abroad and help from the Soviet Union. During the Robesons' vacation in the Soviet Union, a rally was being planned in London to raise money to support Spanish refugee children. Robeson had initially planned to record a statement from Moscow to be broadcast via radio for the rally. When he learned that his message could be jammed by the Germans, he hurried to appear in person. The Royal Albert Hall was crowded with thousands of people on the night of June 24, 1937. Robeson sang for the audience, and his historic speech signaled a profound turning point in his public career. Though Robeson had commented previously on political issues, the Albert Hall speech succinctly, but clearly, framed his view of the artist's role in society. The true artist had a duty, a responsibility, to serve humanity. "Like every true artist," Robeson opened, he had "longed to see his talent contributing in an unmistakably clear manner to the cause

Paul Robeson's grave at Ferncliff Cemetery in Hartsdale, New York. Photo by author.

of humanity." No one could "stand above the conflict" against fascism, and there could be "no impartial observers." Therefore, "the artist, the scientist, the writer is challenged" and "must decide NOW where he stands." The role of the artist was particularly crucial in Robeson's view because "fascism fights to destroy the culture which society has created" through "pain and suffering" as well as "desperate toil" but "with unconquerable will and lofty vision." All of "progressive and democratic mankind" must fight "to save this cultural heritage" and to "prevent a war of unimaginable atrocity from engulfing the world." The most memorable, and often quoted, part of the speech positioned Robeson firmly in the antifascist camp: "The artist must take sides. He must elect to fight for freedom or for slavery. I have made my choice. I had no alternative." These words stood as public testimony of his conscious decision to be a politically motivated artist for the rest of his career. They were the words emblazoned onto his grave marker.

For Robeson, the war in Spain was indicative of a broader struggle against the forces of reaction that fuel fascism. He correctly predicted a global conflict of "unimaginable atrocity" in the wake of the Spanish struggle. His antifascism was firmly rooted in his analysis of colonialism and racial discrimination. Robeson stressed in the Albert Hall speech, "the history of the capitalist era is characterized by the degradation of my people," and he believed that full rights and recognition of human dignity for people in the African diaspora could never occur if the fascist powers were not defeated. Following his powerful speech, Robeson sang "Ol' Man River." However, he purposely altered the closing lines of the song to make them more politically evocative. He changed "I gets weary and sick of tryin' / I'm tired of livin' and scared of dyin'" to "I keeps laughin' instead of cryin' / I must keep fightin' until I'm dyin'." The effect on the audience must have been captivating. Perhaps more than any other single moment, this night illustrated Robeson's maturation into a political advocate. He would further take ownership of the song "Ol' Man River" as his career progressed. He also changed the line "get a little drunk and land in jail" to "show a little grit and land in jail." Robeson nudged this piece away from being a simple ballad of a dockworker into a more politically charged hymn that mirrored his own development into a determined artist and activist.

Robeson's appearance was the highlight of the rally at Albert Hall, which raised thousands of dollars for the Spanish Republican cause. Throughout 1937, Robeson performed at benefits for Spain and made more appearances at political events. His political engagement was becoming an important priority in his career. Late in the year, Robeson decided that he needed to visit Spain to observe the situation personally. Eslanda initially opposed the dangerous idea of journeying to the front lines of the civil war. But once she saw that Paul was determined to make the trip with or without her, she undertook the careful planning necessary for such a venture. The Spanish ambassador helped the Robesons secure visas, and they disembarked from London in January 1938. They traveled by train through France to the Spanish border, where a car and a military escort met them. Captain Fernando Castillo, according to Eslanda's diary, was their official guide and escort. They all seemed to hit it off immediately. The Robesons visited several villages and towns in Republican territory, including Madrid, where they were not far from the front and could hear gunfire at night. A Cuban reporter, Nicolas Guillen, who interviewed Robeson in Spain, found him at a hotel "blockaded by a crowd of people" who were "hanging on his most insignificant gestures." Guillen carefully described Robeson's interaction with the crowd: He paid attention to everyone while smiling and posing repeatedly for photographs. An expression of happiness always played across Robeson's face as he spoke passionately and moved with the "elasticity of an athlete." Guillen recorded that Robeson came to Spain because of his "devotion to democracy" and because he believed it was "dishonorable" as an artist to place himself "on a plane above the masses . . . since we artists owe everything to the masses." He stressed that as a member of an oppressed race, he "could not live if fascism triumphed in the world." The visit to Spain, then, solidified the political stance that he had articulated in the Albert Hall speech.

A highlight early in the trip to Spain was meeting an African American volunteer on a road near a hospital that was "thronged" with wounded and convalescing soldiers. Eslanda recorded in her diary that the black soldier "stopped dead" when he looked in the car and recognized Robeson. Soon the car was surrounded by English, American, and Canadian volunteers who were astonished and thrilled to see Robeson. At the training camp for the International Brigade, the Robesons met African American volunteers from places like St. Louis and Baltimore, who would soon be sent to the front lines. The Abraham Lincoln Brigade was comprised of volunteers from the United States and was, significantly, a desegregated unit. Paul sang for the men who "stomped and applauded" after each number.

In Madrid, where they ran into poet Langston Hughes, the streets were barricaded and sandbagged. One morning, a shell exploded near the palace of the premier, where the Robesons had breakfasted. Despite the dire circumstances, Paul was impressed by the courage and warmth of the people who were "energetically working for victory." They liked to playfully call him "Pablito," and he even indulged a group of neighborhood boys in a game of football. People across Spain heard Robeson sing in a nighttime radio broadcast from Madrid. They were delighted when he sang to them in their language. Eslanda's diary noted that it was "rather sad" departing from Madrid, as they had "come to love it." Later in his memoir, Paul wrote that the visit to Spain had been "a major turning point" in his life. He was especially touched by the courage of volunteers such as Oliver Law, a black soldier from Chicago, who had ascended to the top of the ranks in the Lincoln Brigade only to die on the front at Brunete. Robeson wanted to make a film that told the story of the international volunteers like Law, but it never came to fruition. At least he had gotten to sing with his "whole heart and soul" for the "gallant fighters of the International Brigade."

In spite of the efforts by the volunteer soldiers and its steadfast citizens, the strength of Republican Spain was waning. By the autumn of 1938, the Republican forces were on the defensive, and the International Brigade was disbanded. Franco took Barcelona and Madrid early in 1939 and declared victory that spring. Meanwhile, fascists were also on the move across Europe and in the Pacific. Hitler's Germany had occupied the Rhineland in 1936, Japan invaded China the following year, and the Germans annexed Austria in the spring of 1938. In September of 1938, the Munich Agreement sacrificed Czechoslovakia in a vain attempt to appease Hitler. Of this period, Robeson remarked in his memoir that "a quiet serenity prevailed" in the "great country houses" of England as the ruling classes held onto Prime Minister Chamberlain's "umbrella of appeasement." However, he noted that the perspective of the "common people" was not obscured by Chamberlain's position. They clearly read the portents in the sky that pointed toward the need to form antifascist coalitions. Just months after Franco's triumph in Spain, Hitler invaded Poland, and war was declared by France and Britain.

Upon returning from Spain in early 1938, Eslanda decided that the family should move from their central London flat to a larger house with a garden in Highgate near Hampstead Heath. Although Paul preferred the design of the Buckingham Street apartment, the new home did have more room for entertaining, which he enjoyed. People such as Max Yergan, singer Marian Anderson, and Indian anticolonial activist Jawaharlal Nehru stopped through to call upon the Robesons. At a welcome rally for Nehru in London in June 1938, Robeson spoke of the connection between the struggle in India and all anticolonial movements.

That summer, Robeson also became involved with the Unity Theatre group in London. The group was left-leaning and aimed to mount politically oriented productions. Political theater was also alive and well in the United States during this time due, in part, to the money allocated to the arts through the Federal Theater Project under the auspices of the New Deal's Works Progress Administration. It was not surprising, then, that the Unity troupe chose to revive an American play, *Plant in the Sun*, which advocated for labor organizing. The production was directed by Herbert Marshall, who was acquainted with Robeson and knew that he was searching for material that complemented his political outlook. The plot focused on an interracial sit-down strike in a candy factory. Robeson was glad to join the cast of mostly amateurs to play an Irishman who helped organize the strike. He was not financially remunerated for his participation in the play, for Robeson had reached a point in his career where he could volunteer to participate in endeavors that excited him. "Joining Unity Theatre," Robeson commented in an interview, "means identifying myself with the working class." Additionally, it gave him the opportunity to "act in plays that say something I want to say." He felt that playing a role written as an Irishman could underscore the need for working-class solidarity. In playing that part, he felt he could give it a "special but not unrepresentative negro flavor."

Following the run of *Plant in the Sun*, Robeson set off with Lawrence Brown for a concert tour across Britain. The performances were quite well received. For example, in Glasgow a line a quarter of a mile long had formed outside the concert hall by 4:30 p.m., even though the doors did not open until 7:00 p.m. It seemed that rather than alienating audiences, Robeson's more outspoken political advocacy was widely embraced. The concert program included African American spirituals as well as Russian and Spanish folk songs. Additionally, back in London Robeson made a series of low-cost appearances at popular cinemas so that working people and retired pensioners who could not afford to attend a show at a major concert hall could hear him sing in person. As the year drew to a close, Robeson kept performing at benefits for Spain even as the Republican cause dimmed.

As the political situation in Europe deteriorated, the Robesons began to consider returning to the United States in 1939. That spring, as Spain fell to the fascists, Robeson and Brown performed several concerts across Scandinavia in Oslo, Copenhagen, and Stockholm. The enthusiasm of the crowds was tremendous. By this time, Robeson's political reputation was well known and the concerts of folk music, including songs of the Spanish civil war, turned into virtual antifascist rallies. He then traveled to the States where his business manager, Robert Rockmore, was concerned Robeson's audience might be dwindling. Robeson stayed for several weeks giving concerts and performing in a brief revival of *The Emperor Jones* (without the word *nigger* this time). He appeared at an event for the NAACP and gave interviews for the black press to reinvigorate his image in his home country given his long absence. Robeson also solidified new political connections in the United States to the dismay of some older friends in the art world, who felt he had left them behind. Robeson looked up Langston Hughes and visited the left-leaning Harlem Suitcase Theater. He contacted Angelo Herndon, an African American Communist who had been arrested in Atlanta for labor organizing, and met with Herndon's lawyer Ben Davis, who would become a close friend and leader in the U.S. Communist Party. By 1939, the Communist Party had a considerable presence in Harlem. The party had promoted strategies such as rent strikes and "Don't Buy Where You Can't Work" campaigns throughout the Depression. With varying degrees of success, the CPUSA had also promoted interracial cooperation and had outlawed racial chauvinism within the organization. The party had formed political and cultural coalitions with liberals to promote a united front against fascism. It was these progressive-minded political circles that Robeson would join when he moved back from England at the end of the year.

There was, however, one more British film that Robeson wanted to undertake before returning to the United States. Shooting for *The Proud Valley* was slated to begin in the summer even as war seemed imminent. In August, the Soviet Union signed a nonaggression treaty with Hitler, which instigated anti-Soviet sentiment throughout the West. Robeson, however, viewed the pact as the inevitable result of the West's lack of support for Spain and continued appeasement of Hitler. Having already forfeited Czechoslovakia, France and Britain hoped Hitler would continue to march eastward. But Stalin wanted to secure their borders. Nevertheless, the tenuous Nazi-Soviet agreement folded when Hitler invaded the Soviet Union in 1941.

Back in London, Eslanda hurried to pack the Robesons' belongings so they could sail as soon as Paul finished with his latest film project. *The Proud Valley* was set in the contemporary moment and focused on a group of hardworking miners in Wales. The screenplay was based on a story by Herbert Marshall from the Unity Theatre, and the film was directed by Pen Tennyson. Robeson's character, David Goliath, turned up in a village looking for work just as the local choir was rehearsing for the annual Eisteddfod music festival. Naturally, the locals arranged a job for Goliath so he could join their singing group in time for the festival. The film underscored the need for labor solidarity through the friendship forged between Goliath and the miners. Ultimately, Goliath sacrificed himself so that the mine could be reopened and the village could fully participate in the mobilization for the war. The script and character both appealed to Robeson, and he was determined to carry out the project even though Hitler invaded Poland and England declared war while the shooting was underway.

The exterior scenes had been filmed in Wales, where Robeson stayed with the families of actual miners. The interior scenes were shot in a London studio. At this time, mobilization for the war had dramatically changed the face of London: blackouts were mandated, gas masks were distributed, rationing was underway, and antiaircraft blimps filled the skies. Filming wrapped up on September 25 and, after seeing a rough cut of the film, the Robesons set sail into the dangerous waters of the Atlantic on an American ship three days later. It was a harried exit that was compounded by safety concerns over the German naval presence. However, Paul and Eslanda were happy with *The Proud Valley*, and Paul was glad to be returning home. He felt that he "must be among the Negro people during the great crisis that was looming." Robeson wanted to "be part of their struggles" and "bring them a message about Africa" that would encourage unity between African Americans and their "struggling kinfolk in the colonies."

4

PEOPLE'S ARTIST

In October 1939 Paul and Eslanda Robeson arrived at New York harbor to once again make their home in Harlem after having been away from the United States for much of the decade. Signs of the war had recently permeated Britain, but isolationist sentiment in America was still fairly widespread. The Nazi-Soviet Pact, signed that summer, had unsettled the European Allies. Newspapers in the United States wanted to know where Robeson stood politically. To the curious reporters assembled at the port, Robeson stressed the antifascist position he had developed. The journalists wondered whether he had become a Communist. While he did support the right of the Soviet Union to defend its borders, he emphasized that his focus was on the need to defeat race prejudice and colonialism. Over the next few weeks, Robeson gave more interviews to facilitate his transition back into the American cultural scene.

Soon, the family settled into two apartments at 555 Edgecombe Avenue in the exclusive Sugar Hill neighborhood. Paul and Eslanda shared a spacious flat for working and entertaining while Paul Jr. and Mrs. Goode settled in an upstairs apartment. Harlem began to feel like home again for Paul. He sometimes visited and even sang occasionally with the choir at Mother AME Zion church where his brother Ben was pastor. The Robesons were now big celebrities among Harlemites, and it did not take them long to reenter the social scene. Intellectuals, artists, and civil rights leaders wanted to mingle with Paul or be invited to one of the parties hosted by Eslanda. NAACP leader Walter White and his wife were practically neighbors on Edgecombe

Avenue. Newer acquaintances such as Max Yergan and W. Alphaeus Hunton, of the Council on African Affairs, and Ben Davis, a leader in the Communist Party, illustrated the Robesons' progressive political activity. Attorney and family friend Bob Rockmore continued to help manage Paul's career. Robeson also renewed his intimate relationship with Freda Diamond, which lasted for many years. Interestingly, she also became a good friend of the whole Robeson family.

Robeson's return home was quickly cemented by what became a historic radio broadcast. A CBS radio program called "The Pursuit of Happiness" hired Robeson to perform a patriotic song recently written by composer Earl Robinson and lyricist John Latouche. The piece, originally called "The Ballad of Uncle Sam," represented the progressive spirit of labor solidarity that was on the rise during the New Deal era. "Ballad for Americans," as it

Paul Robeson rehearses "Ballad for Americans" with the CIO chorus; Lawrence Brown is at the piano. This popular song remained in his repertoire in the 1940s after the live broadcast in 1939. Daily Worker/Daily World Photographs Collection, Tamiment Library, New York University.

was renamed, contained a message of ethnic unity and religious tolerance that resonated with Robeson's antifascist values. For the radio performance, Robeson received the nearly unprecedented sum of $1,000, which was indicative of his artistic stature. On November 5, the broadcast of the eleven-minute performance aired live. The ovation that thundered from the audience of six hundred gathered in the studio went on for several minutes after the song ended. The phone lines at CBS were tied up for hours, and letters poured into the mailroom for days afterward. The radio performance was repeated on New Year's Day, and Robeson's recording was a popular seller. He also added the number to some of his concerts in the early 1940s.

The synergy of Robeson's voice and the ballad's celebration of freedom and liberty clearly touched people across the United States. The circumstances of the economic depression and the winds of fascist war overseas made the moment ripe for Robinson and Latouche's collaboration with Robeson. An African American vocalist offering this tribute to democratic principles imbued the song with additional depth. Though discrimination persisted, Paul Robeson singing "Ballad for Americans" made the realization of racial equality seem attainable.

Having solidified his position with audiences in the United States, Robeson undertook several projects in 1940. He narrated an independently produced documentary about labor and civil rights called *Native Land*. The film's content coalesced with Robeson's political consciousness, but it would not be released for a couple of years due to funding constraints. A more commercially viable piece was rooted in African American folk culture. In *John Henry*, Robeson brought to life the black folk legend whose feats of strength were passed down in oral tales. Eslanda worried that the play was overly focused on John Henry's physique and reinforced the notion of black intellectual inferiority. But the production could give Paul a chance to further reconnect with American audiences. The working-class protagonist was appealing, and he felt confident in the score written by Jacques Wolfe. According to most reviewers, the music and acting were fine but the script did not succeed in conveying John Henry's character, and the direction contained "lapses." Overall, Robeson maintained a "truly heroic presence," but he could not overcome the "ineptness of his material." After performances in Philadelphia, Boston, and New York, the play closed with little fanfare.

Still, the brief run of *John Henry* brought Robeson back to the American stage and reinforced his place as, in the words of *Collier's* magazine, "America's Number One Negro Entertainer." An honorary doctorate from Hamilton College in Clinton, New York, also underscored Robeson's prominence. At the ceremony, Robeson read from "Ballad for Americans" and commented that he looked forward to a future in which one combined human culture would reflect the cultures of the diverse people of the world. As Robeson biographer Martin Duberman has thoughtfully observed, "Acknowledgement from the mainstream did not deflect Robeson from his commitment to the margins." Robeson was not content simply with the blessings of fame and financial reward. He continued to focus on using his art and his celebrity to raise consciousness about racial justice and freedom for marginalized and oppressed people.

While his overall popularity was high, some of Robeson's artistic efforts still met mixed reviews. For example, when *The Proud Valley* opened African American labor leader A. Philip Randolph was critical of the film after Walter White invited him and other prominent members of the community to a private screening. Randolph felt the film stressed the inferiority of people of color. He also worried that the film would harm interracial labor relations because, for example, Robeson's character was excluded from consulting management along with the white workers. These criticisms notwithstanding, *The Proud Valley* was a film that remained particularly dear to Robeson. The relationship that he formed with the miners in the Rhondda Valley of Wales during the making of the movie affected him deeply. He would refer to this later as the time when he "first understood the struggle of white and Negro [labor] together." Robeson's close affinity with Welsh folk music and the camaraderie he felt with the working people of Wales lasted for many years and helped sustain him even in the most repressive days of the Cold War. In the view of a few critics, like Randolph, *The Proud Valley* had not underscored themes of cooperation and camaraderie. Even so, the connection established between Robeson and the people of that proud Rhondda Valley did exemplify true interracial solidarity.

In the spring and summer of 1940, Robeson set off on a major American concert tour that was received eagerly by sizeable crowds. Thousands, even tens of thousands, packed venues from Lewisohn Stadium in New York to Grant Park in Chicago to the Hollywood Bowl in Los Angeles. A highlight of the program at these shows was Robeson's interpretation of "Ballad for Americans," which audiences craved whether with full choral and orchestral accompaniment or just with Robeson and Lawrence Brown on piano. The ugly reality of segregation was a constant reminder of racial injustice, however. Despite his celebrity status, for instance, Robeson had trouble obtaining hotel accommodations in Los Angeles. The Beverly Wilshire agreed to sell him a room only if he registered under another name. Robeson, thus, made a point of spending a couple of hours each day in the lobby to help break down the racial barrier for other traveling artists.

As Robeson took to the concert stage, significant events animated the global geopolitical stage. The Soviet Union had invaded Finland in November 1939, and the Fins were forced to cede part of their border by the spring of 1940. These moves stirred the ire of some Americans, but Robeson did not denounce the Soviet Union. Meanwhile, Germany maneuvered across substantial portions of Europe. By that summer, Hitler's army had invaded and occupied Denmark, Norway, Luxembourg, the Netherlands, and Belgium. France was divided in June, with the northern part of the country occupied by the Germans, while the south was ruled by the cooperating Vichy government. The Soviets also took possession of the Baltic States, and Germany set its sights on invading Britain. The Battle of Britain began in earnest in July, but the Nazis were repelled by October, making the air war with England their first major defeat. Some Americans sympathized with Britain. However, most were hesitant about getting involved in another European conflict, as illustrated by the neutrality acts passed by Congress in the mid-1930s. Congress did offer subsequent support for the Allies by supplying weapons on a cash and carry basis in late 1939. Many on the political left in the United States actively spoke out against the war during the period of the Nazi-Soviet pact. Given the Soviet Union's alliance with Germany and its aggressive securing of borders, Robeson concentrated mostly on music during his 1940 concerts.

In the autumn, Robeson and Lawrence Brown were joined on tour by Bob Rockmore's wife, Clara, who was an accomplished musician. Clara was a proficient player of the theremin, an electronic instrument named for its inventor, who was a Russian physicist. On this instrument an otherworldly sound is generated by the position of the musician's hands in an electromagnetic field. Some reviewers were flummoxed by the "curious device" but conceded that audiences liked its music. Mrs. Rockmore toured with Robeson and Brown for several seasons in the 1940s and become close friends, but not lovers, with Robeson. Traveling was sometimes complicated for the interracial trio and was eye-opening for Rockmore, who was white. Their party was, for example, refused service at an upscale restaurant in San Francisco one night following a concert. As she got to know Robeson better, Rockmore was surprised at the juxtaposition between Robeson's intense anger at the discrimination directed at his race as a whole and the way he could brush off a personal insult. The program for these concerts included an array of African American spirituals and Russian songs performed by Robeson, along with some Bach and Tchaikovsky from Rockmore as well as Brown and Robeson's version of "Ballad for Americans." Rockmore, as a classically schooled violinist, believed that Robeson was sometimes too concerned about not having had enough technical training. In her view, there would always be people with good voices, but they would not have "as much heart" as Robeson.

Robeson continued touring in early 1941. He often performed at colleges and universities that were outside major urban areas, which helped reinforce his growing image as a people's artist. He also performed at benefits to aid China, which had been invaded and occupied by the Japanese. Japan had aligned itself with the fascist powers of Europe the previous fall with the signing of the Tripartite Pact. In April, Robeson was scheduled to perform at a Chinese benefit in Washington, D.C., at Constitution Hall. The Daughters of the American Revolution, however, blocked his appearance just as they had canceled a concert by black vocalist Marian Anderson a couple of years earlier. After some controversy, the China Aid Council teamed up with the local National Negro Congress and filled the Uline Arena with Robeson as headliner. Around this time, Robeson also urged black workers to join the Congress of Industrial Organizations (CIO), which was a left-wing labor union that had been created from a split in the American Federation of Labor (AFL) in 1935. The CIO contained active Communist Party members, as well as other labor organizers, and it was one of the only groups willing to recruit black workers on a desegregated basis. At a May 1941 rally in Detroit, Robeson urged black autoworkers to affiliate with the United Auto Workers, a CIO union. This was indicative of Robeson's strong belief in the power of interracial labor solidarity. "The best way my race can win justice," he summarized, "is by sticking together in progressive labor unions." For years to come, he maintained that progressive change could be wrought through a broad coalition of the working classes. That spring, Robeson also supported the movement to free Earl Browder. Browder was a leader of the U.S. Communist Party who had been imprisoned purportedly for passport violations but was released in 1942. Paul and Eslanda had met Browder in war-ravaged Spain and, thus, Robeson connected Browder firmly with the global cause of antifascism. Robeson's involvement with campaigns such as these solidified his affiliation with progressive and left-wing political circles. Not surprisingly, it was around this time that the FBI started its file on Robeson.

While Paul was on tour, Eslanda had been overseeing renovations on a sizeable family home in Enfield, Connecticut, that sat on a couple of acres of land. In the early summer of 1941, Mrs. Goode, Paul Jr., and Essie moved into the country house named "The Beeches." Eslanda tackled decorating the new estate, but she came to realize that this would probably not be Paul's full-time residence. Although she had not been flourishing in New York, the city was the center of Paul's artistic and political life. He considered New York to be home, and he was not thrilled at the idea of living with Eslanda's mother. Essie worked hard to transform the property, which was only about three hours from Harlem, into a comfortable refuge from the urban environment. Paul's son has some fond memories of spending time with his father at The Beeches. Robeson guided his namesake through the family's extensive reading library. He taught Paul Jr. to consider various games and sports, such as billiards, chess, football, and basketball, analytically and to enjoy learning and playing simultaneously. The small Connecticut community was always pleased when Robeson turned up for events at the local high school where Paul Jr. attended. Ultimately, Paul did spend time in Enfield but often stayed with friends in the city. The country home became more of a space for Eslanda to cultivate an independent life by working on her own studies and her writing and speaking engagements.

In June 1941, Germany invaded the Soviet Union, which had significant consequences for left-wing politics in the United States. The Communist Party dramatically reversed the noninterventionist stance it had maintained during the period of the Nazi-Soviet Pact. This abrupt change in policy caused some to lose respect for the Communist Party but, overall, it meant that liberals, progressives, and Communists could work together under the umbrella of antifascism. For Robeson, this meant that his sympathetic view of the Soviet Union was now in step with mainstream sentiments, which considered Hitler to be the prime enemy in Europe. The Soviets could now be seen as victims of German aggression. Importantly, they were also one of the main forces preventing a fascist takeover of Europe. Aid for Russia became a focal point for left-wing activists and sympathizers. After the bombing of Pearl Harbor in December and the U.S. declaration of war, support for the Soviet Union, a vital European ally, was entirely suitable and generally accepted. Robeson became actively involved in benefits for Russian war relief, especially in the fall and winter of 1941 when the situation looked particularly dire. By December, the Germans were driven away from Moscow, but many brutal days of fighting lay ahead. Robeson insisted defiantly in press statements that "Hitler will meet defeat in Russia."

During his 1941 to 1942 season tour Robeson used his concerts to advocate for antifascist support. In addition, he appeared at dinners, benefits, fund-raisers, and rallies to call for aid to the Allied mission. He scheduled some of his concerts at black colleges in the South to engage more closely with the African American community and to highlight the link between the antifascist war and civil rights. Robeson urged African American men to enlist in the armed forces, but he wanted to see their "full participation" in the war effort. This scale of participation was prevented because black men were excluded from many military jobs and black women were often barred from helping in auxiliary services. Robeson knew that the Roosevelt administration needed to be nudged to back full civil rights for African Americans. Though FDR did not desegregate the military, he did create the Fair Employment Practices Commission (FEPC) in 1941 as part of Executive Order 8802, which outlawed racial discrimination in defense industry jobs. Critics maintained that Roosevelt only issued this order because of A. Philip Randolph's call for a massive march in Washington to protest employment discrimination. Regrettably, the FEPC did not have much authority to mandate change, though it could document contemporary circumstances.

Roosevelt ultimately felt his hands were tied because of the segregationist wing of the Democratic Party. He never took a strong stand on civil rights for fear of alienating the powerful southern politicians whose congressional support he needed. Nevertheless, Roosevelt was popular among many

African Americans because of his appointment of African American activist Mary McLeod Bethune to the National Youth Administration, and his wife, Eleanor, was known as a defender of civil and human rights. Given this complicated political situation, Robeson was careful to connect the war against fascism abroad with the need for civil rights enforcement at home. Unlike the Communist Party, which concentrated mainly on the war overseas, Robeson consciously related his antifascist message to the need for domestic racial justice. Toward the end of the war, he also stressed independence for colonized people as a necessary goal for the peace process. Robeson's values were reflected in his concerts, as he avoided segregated venues. While touring in 1942, Robeson conducted a performance in Kansas City under protest because the audience was segregated. He called off a show in Santa Fe when the local hotel canceled his reservation and the local concert organizer attempted to justify the hotel's discriminatory policy.

In the early 1940s Robeson strengthened relationships with a couple of left-wing African American activist groups. He became acquainted with the young people of the Southern Negro Youth Congress (SNYC) when he appeared at their annual conference at Tuskegee University. This grassroots organization campaigned for civil rights and maintained an international, anticolonial perspective, in part, because several founding members were actively involved with the Communist Party. Robeson formed enduring relationships with several SNYC members, including Louis Burnham and James and Esther Jackson. Hundreds of delegates from all over the South attended this meeting, which passed resolutions in support of the war effort as well as civil rights for African Americans. Robeson also served as chairman of the Council on African Affairs, which he had helped form in the late 1930s. Max Yergan, who had joined Robeson at the SNYC event, was executive director of the Council. While not a mass organization, it was an informational and lobbyist group that provided news of the African continent to people in the United States. Obtaining accurate and recent news from Africa was problematic at this time. The Council was almost alone in this mission, which was accomplished through its newsletters, press releases, and events. The group grew in the early 1940s, especially after W. Alphaeus Hunton was added as educational director in 1943. Hunton tirelessly wrote articles and maintained copious correspondence with African contacts. Hunton, Yergan, and Robeson, the core leadership of the group, all shared a left-wing, Pan-African perspective. They believed that people of African descent, whether in Africa or the Americas, shared a common oppression and could work together for full freedom. Because of its anticolonial sympathies, they considered the Soviet Union to be an ally in this cause. These groups supported the war mobilization largely because they saw possibilities for progressive change embedded in the antifascist rhetoric of the Allies.

In the midst of his concertizing and support for the Allies, Robeson still found time for his acting career. In 1942, *Tales of Manhattan*, a film that Robeson had shot the previous year, was released. It was a Hollywood film with an all-star cast that included Ginger Rogers, Rita Hayworth, Charles Laughton, Edward G. Robinson, and Ethel Waters, who played a sharecropper opposite Robeson. The film consisted of a series of sketches about an evening coat as it impacted the lives of different owners until finally dropping from an airplane, its pockets brimming with money, into the lives of the poor sharecroppers. Even though the film offered Robeson a chance to illustrate the plight of black Southern poverty, he did not have full script control. Robeson suggested changes that were not incorporated, and the black characters turned out like stock, hallelujah-singing caricatures. The result was not only disappointing to Robeson; it was highly criticized in the black press. Robeson's reputation as an advocate for racial justice was blemished. Black reviewers decried the oversimplified portrayals of the black roles and the use of dialogue that was "of the minstrel show variety." Nell Dodson, in the progressive *People's Voice* newspaper from Harlem, pointed out that more was expected of Robeson, who had recently demanded equal rights in Kansas City.

To his credit, Robeson admitted the film was insulting and took action. He acknowledged publicly that portraying a black person "singing his way to glory" was "very offensive" to the community because it was reminiscent of "the old plantation tradition." In a press conference, he explained that the film's producers had been unwilling to revise the film because they were concerned about alienating Southern audiences. Robeson also confirmed that he would picket the film and had turned down subsequent film offers. His frustration with the dearth of dignified roles and substantial themes had been building for years. Robeson had ended a hiatus from film work to appear in *Tales*, which had proven to be a mistake. Realizing that the movie industry was more focused on profits than content, Robeson courageously suspended his film career, which meant that *Tales of Manhattan* was the final film in which Robeson starred. His standing as an advocate for his people's culture would not again be tarnished as a result of demeaning images in the cinema. Fortunately, this hullabaloo would ultimately be overshadowed by Robeson's interpretation of a much weightier African character in the early 1940s.

Since his debut as Othello in 1930, Robeson had wanted to revisit the role. The London production had suffered from serious flaws, and Robeson had now matured as a politically motivated actor. In the early 1940s, Robeson and director Margaret Webster shared the goal of mounting a revival of Shakespeare's play for the Broadway stage. Webster came from a British family who lived and breathed theater. Her parents, Dame May Whitty and Ben Webster, were acting icons. Webster spent her early years performing Shakespeare in repertoire around Britain with contemporary actors such as John Gielgud and Laurence Olivier. By the 1940s, Margaret Webster had been identified by *New York Times* critic Brooks Atkinson as "the finest director of Shakespeare this town ever had." She aimed to bring Shakespeare's words to life for audiences and had done so in her productions of *Richard II*, *Macbeth*, and *Twelfth Night*. Though she had seen Robeson in 1930 and "thought him very bad," Webster believed he had potential. However, she and Robeson approached the theater from very different backgrounds. Webster's perspective came from more formal British theater training, while Robeson tackled Shakespeare from textual study, instinct, and method acting strategies. This was, at times, a source of tension backstage. Still, Robeson and Webster both agreed on the fundamental significance of portraying Othello as a black African character. In her commentary on the play, Webster asserted the centrality of Othello's race to understanding the plot. "The difference in race between Othello and every other character in the play," she observed, "is, indeed, the heart of the matter." Robeson also emphasized the importance of acknowledging Othello's African identity as he had in 1930. "This play is about minority groups," he noted in an interview, "It concerns a blackamoor who tried to find equality among whites. It's right up my alley."

Once Webster and Robeson began looking for funding and cast members, they met resistance. Producing an *Othello* revival with an interracial cast had never been done in New York. An actor friend of Webster's, who turned down the part of Iago, remarked that the "public would never go for it." Financial backing did eventually materialize, and the Theatre Guild came on board as producers. Two promising actors, José Ferrer and Uta Hagen, who were then married, were selected to play Iago and Desdemona. Webster decided to play the other principle role, Emilia, herself. The Brattle Theatre in Cambridge, Massachusetts, hosted the premiere in the summer of 1942. The production did not debut in New York because no theater would agree to sponsor this play with a black lead actor and white cast. Webster condensed the action of the play but did not sacrifice the poetry in the process. José Ferrer's Iago was a "swift" and "mercurial" foil to Robeson's tall and sturdy Othello. The intended effect was to build tension until the explosive final act provided a catharsis for the audience.

The opening at the Brattle became a huge event as people began talking about a black actor playing Othello with a white Desdemona. A capacity crowd crammed the theater seats on the warm August night. In fact, the temperature mandated that Robeson's Moorish robes had to be wrung out between scenes. At the closing curtain, the eager cheers and fervent stamping of feet signaled that the production had truly touched those present. Critics also praised the show, calling Robeson's portrayal "heroic and convincing" and proclaiming that Webster's "special faculty for direction" made for "vivid" drama. Reviewers found a black Othello and a white Desdemona to be "electric," and many believed this lent "credibility and intensity" to the passion of the play. Black and left-wing critics were especially excited by the prospects of Robeson's Othello. A reviewer for the African American *Pittsburgh Courier* newspaper felt that Robeson's interpretation had aided a "leap" in black artistry to the "highest pinnacle of the profession." Ralph Warner, writing for the *Sunday Worker*, believed that the interracial production represented a move toward the "democratization of our theater." Now that brilliant reviews were rolling off the presses, New York theaters, which had "refused to touch the idea with a twenty foot pole" in Webster's words, were now tripping over each other to offer the production a home on Broadway. Due to Robeson's concert schedule, however, *Othello* would not move to Broadway until the 1943 season.

In the autumn of 1942, Robeson's calendar was filled with political events. He spoke out for labor unity, saluted the armed forces at rallies, and praised the courage of African Americans in the South who continued to support the war effort despite continued discrimination. At a mass meeting sponsored by the Council on African Affairs in September, Robeson strongly backed the anticolonial movement in India. He encouraged the U.S. government to espouse the fight for freedom in this British colony. Robeson connected the need for independence in Africa with the anticolonial campaign in India. He hoped that the present war would be a war for global colonial liberation. In October, he disembarked with Lawrence Brown and Clara Rockmore on an extended U.S. concert tour that lasted until the following April. He was by now, in the words of one reviewer, "the greatest singing-actor of the day." Opening before a desegregated audience in New Orleans, Robeson commented on the need to fight for the African American community in places that were the most oppressed. He admired the "dignity and courage" of his people down South and predicted that "nothing the future brings can defeat a people who have come through three hundred years of slavery . . . with heads high and eyes clear and straight." Racial violence during the war years was not uncommon. Riots occurred in numerous cities across the country, especially in places such as Mobile, Alabama, where white workers resented the presence of black workers in defense industry jobs. Robeson's desegregated concerts, then, represented unique spaces where progressive values surmounted racial antagonism.

During these years, the realities of the war were never far from the minds of the people. However, neither blue illumination at outdoor shows nor a ban on pleasure driving seemed to dampen the spirits of concertgoers. In his concerts, Robeson maintained selections of African American spirituals, folk music, and Russian songs in his program. One stop during the tour was for a recital at Abraham Lincoln High School in Brooklyn, New York, where the students had voted Robeson to be the most outstanding American of the year. Record crowds in many cities and towns heard his singing as well as his calls for support for the Soviet Union. One reporter summarized that freedom, equality, and Russia have a "great ambassador" in Robeson. At a rally in Madison Square Garden for the Congress of American-Soviet Friendship, Robeson emphasized his antifascist stance and paid tribute to the dedication of the Red Army. As Robeson's tour traversed the United States, Soviet Allies clashed with the Germans at Stalingrad, U.S. and British troops faced off against the Axis in northern Africa, and American soldiers curtailed Japanese expansion in the Pacific by island hopping.

In the spring of 1943, Robeson retreated to Enfield to rest and spend some time with his wife and son. He also needed to prepare for *Othello* rehearsals, which were slated to begin in the summer. Paul Robeson Jr. recalled that his father began conditioning himself for the physical demands of playing Othello nightly by working out at the YMCA, running laps, and playing basketball. He also made time to appear at a Labor for Victory rally at Yankee Stadium with Mayor LaGuardia and other labor leaders. In June Robeson received another honorary degree, this time from Morehouse College in Atlanta. In conferring the doctor of humane letters, President Benjamin Mays honored Robeson's efforts to "dignify and popularize the folk-songs composed by the oppressed peoples of the earth." As a champion of the cause of the common man, Robeson could truly be called "the people's artist." Mays's comments illustrated contemporary perceptions of Robeson as an artist as well as an advocate for oppressed and colonized people around the world. Robeson himself summarized in an interview that he considered art to be "a social weapon." Yet not everyone was impressed with Robeson's increased public presence during the war. Because of his outspoken support for the Soviet allies, director J. Edgar Hoover, who was known to target civil rights activists, suspected that Robeson was a Communist, possibly even a spy for the Soviet Union. The FBI, thus, stepped up its surveillance of Robeson during this period.

Othello was scheduled to open on Broadway in October, but the production would be previewed first in New Haven, Boston, and Philadelphia in September. About six weeks of rehearsals were planned prior to the first curtain. There was some tumult backstage when Webster and the Theatre Guild tried to replace Uta Hagen and José Ferrer because they were, in Webster's view, "over-rating their financial worth." Robeson, however, insisted that they remain in the cast and, according to Webster's letters, threatened to leave the production. There was also friction between Robeson and Webster backstage due to their different theatrical approaches. Robeson was more focused on the internal. He observed, "What makes me a great artist is the emotion I've got." For example, he used the memory of racism on the football field from his Rutgers days to conjure Othello's rage. Webster, in contrast, concentrated more on the external and had trouble relating to Konstantin Stanislavski's strategies, such as emotion memory. She found Robeson's performances to be uneven and undependable and complained about directing him in correspondence with her parents. Years later, Webster admitted that if she had been more of a method director, she might have had a more fruitful collaboration with Robeson. Despite this tension, Robeson got along well with rest of the cast and crew. Fellow cast members remember his warmth and generosity. He made a point of learning everyone's name and leaving his dressing room door open to encourage interaction. Behind the scenes, Robeson and Uta Hagen carried on a love affair during the Broadway engagement and subsequent U.S. tour.

Paul Robeson Jr. remembered the whole family, Eslanda and Mrs. Goode, brother Ben with his wife and daughters, sister Marian with her husband and daughter, even the housekeeper from The Beeches, Cecelia, traveling to New Haven for the *Othello* preview. Initial reviews showed that audiences and critics were still moved by the production, as they had been the previous summer. When the show opened on Broadway at the Shubert Theatre, the cast celebrated afterward at Freda Diamond's apartment. And there was much to celebrate. The night had been a triumph, and Webster recalled it as the most exhilarating opening night she had ever experienced. After plentiful curtain calls, the audience screamed until she made a little closing speech. She explained to her parents that "it was just one of those nights" when "magic happened." The notices, by and large, were glowing. Critics enjoyed the characterizations by the principle actors, the set, and costumes, and many felt the condensed action increased the pathos of the play. Robeson was praised by most reviewers and won an award from *Billboard* magazine for outstanding lead performance. He was also honored by the American Academy of Arts and Letters for his diction onstage.

Most importantly, numerous reviewers noted the significance of a black actor playing this African leading role for the first time. It was a "victory for democracy" and a "tribute to art that transcends racial boundaries" to see an interracial cast in a Shakespearean play on Broadway. Robeson had successfully broken a racial barrier at the highest level of an almost all-white profession. Reporters in the black press believed Robeson's pioneering performance would open the way for more black actors on Broadway. In addition to race relations, the production shed light on the current global conflict. In an article on the play, Robeson connected *Othello*'s themes to the present circumstances of World War II. He noted how audiences found the play to be "painfully immediate." Just as "Othello's world was breaking

Paul Robeson as Othello on Broadway. Library of Congress, Prints and Photographs Division, FSA/OWI Collection, LC-USW331-054944-ZC.

asunder," Robeson pointed out, "we stand at the end of one period in human history and before the entrance of a new." Still, he hoped that this could be "the final war" that would solve the issues of human poverty and equality "once and for all."

The *Othello* revival played in New York for a record 296 performances during the 1943 to 1944 season. The troupe then traveled across the country from September 1944 to April 1945 and finally closed the show in New York. Robeson, and the rest of the cast, refused to perform in segregated venues, so the tour did not stop in the South. Theaters in the North and Midwest, where segregation was the norm, were desegregated for the *Othello* shows. The play was extremely popular and attracted diverse audiences. For instance, Robeson recollected that the opening in Detroit was unique in that many of the seats were taken by black and white autoworkers who sat alongside wealthy theater regulars. The play was Robeson's main focus during these months, but he also made political appearances even while portraying Shakespeare's Moor up to seven times a week. Significant world events that could not be ignored were unfolding as *Othello* meandered from from city to city. The Red Army was marching west toward Berlin even as a second front was inaugurated by the Allied landing in France. Italy was invaded, and the Japanese faced the United States in the Philippine Islands. By the time the play closed, the United States was mourning the death of President Roosevelt and the war was winding down.

Robeson's political appearances during the *Othello* run included an address on African Americans in the War at the New York Herald Tribune Forum on current problems in November 1943. In his speech, he stressed the need to defeat fascism, and he underscored issues such as economic insecurity, disfranchisement, and segregation as impediments to full African American participation in the war effort. In December 1943, Robeson contributed to a meeting with baseball commissioner Kenesaw Mountain Landis on the issue of integrating black players into the Major Leagues. Interestingly, at this session Robeson cited his warm reception in *Othello* as evidence of progress in the fight against racial segregation. (Two years later, Jackie Robinson joined the Brooklyn Dodgers farm team in Montreal.)

He also found time to socialize while the play was in New York. Robeson's son remembered seeing his father play Othello several times. Afterward, the pair would go to the fashionable nightspot Café Society to eat a late supper and hear some music. Musicians such as Hazel Scott, Teddy Wilson, and Lena Horne would stop by their table to chat between sets. One night Robeson hushed the noisy crowd to better hear a young Sarah Vaughan sing at the microphone. In April 1944, the Council on African Affairs hosted a benefit on the occasion of Robeson's forty-sixth birthday. A multitude of entertainers and activists paid tribute to Robeson, and around twelve thousand people attended the tremendous event at the 17th Regiment Armory. Police were called to handle the crowd of thousands more who failed to get inside. Adam Clayton Powell Jr., who was soon to be the congressman for Harlem, observed that the venue reminded one that Robeson was a warrior for humanity. Mary McLeod Bethune, of the National Council of Negro Women, labeled Robeson "the tallest tree of our forest." A message from Vice President Henry A. Wallace noted that Robeson expressed "the aspirations of the common man" more than any other artist in U.S. history. Performers for the evening's entertainment included Count Basie, Duke Ellington, and Mary Lou Williams. This event illustrated the high esteem in which Robeson was held. However, the fact that FBI agents reported on the event foreshadowed the suspicion of left-wing sympathizers that engulfed postwar politics.

That same month, Robeson participated in another event sponsored by the Council. It was a conference on the future of colonies in Africa that was attended by activists and scholars as well as future leaders such as Kwame Nkrumah. Nkrumah was studying in the United States and went on to become the first prime minister of the independent nation of Ghana and a vital proponent of Pan-African unity. This meeting was an early attempt to initiate an international dialogue on postwar Africa. In this way, it was an important precursor to the Pan-African Congress that convened in Manchester, England, after the war. Robeson's address opened the conference. In it, he stressed the importance of international cooperation following the war. The Allies should not look upon Africa's resources as "the jack-pot of World War II" but should consider the welfare of the continent's people in postwar planning. "Winning the peace," Robeson maintained, was just as imperative as "winning the war." Later that year, the Council on African Affairs forwarded a set of resolutions to the president and secretary of state that urged them to remember the contributions of African troops in the war effort at the preliminary United Nations meetings at Dumbarton Oaks in

Washington, D.C. International collaboration leading toward full democratic rights for colonized people, the Council pointed out, should be part of the U.S. government's postwar vision. Robeson, when speaking independently or as chairman of the Council on African Affairs, insisted that freedom for colonized people must be an outcome of the war against fascism.

In the autumn of 1944, while on tour with *Othello*, Robeson endorsed Roosevelt's unprecedented fourth campaign for the presidency. While he had never fully backed civil rights for African Americans or an antilynching law, Roosevelt's New Deal reforms were widely viewed in the black community as progressive. It was during the Roosevelt years that most African American voters switched from being faithful Republicans, the historic party of Abraham Lincoln, to being loyal Democrats. Eslanda, who also publicly supported Roosevelt's campaign, received an appreciative letter from Eleanor Roosevelt for her efforts. In April 1945, the *Othello* troupe was in Chicago. Essie and some friends from New York traveled to Illinois for the show and to celebrate Paul's birthday. However, the nation was soon mourning the untimely death of FDR. Few but those close to him had been aware of the extent of Roosevelt's frailty during his final campaign. It was a difficult leadership transition since Roosevelt had been in the White House since 1933 and was much beloved. This was further compounded by the fact that his successor, Harry S. Truman, was not well known nationally and was largely untested in the realm of international affairs. He had been added to the Democratic ticket in 1944 as a replacement for Henry A. Wallace, who had long served Roosevelt. The April 12 performance of *Othello* in Chicago was dedicated to the memory of Roosevelt. Robeson gave a poignant tribute to the deceased president after that night's curtain. Victory for the Allies was only a few months away, but the United States faced the complexities of peace negotiations with an untried leader at the helm.

Support for the rights of people in the African diaspora was high on Robeson's priority list in the spring and summer of 1945. That spring, delegates from fifty countries signed the charter that formed the United Nations. The idea of an international cooperative body went back to the creation of the League of Nations after the First World War. Many activists viewed the drafting of the UN charter as an important opportunity to advocate for minority rights. The Council on African Affairs, as well as other organizations such as the NAACP, lobbied on behalf of oppressed people. The Council focused its argument on freedom for all colonized people, especially in Africa. Their argument was based on the democratic rhetoric espoused by the Allies throughout the war. For example, the Atlantic Charter, which was the first statement of principles from the United States and Great Britain, had declared the right of freedom for occupied people. It was only logical, noted the Council, that this promise be maintained for those who had long been occupied by European colonizers. In addition to supporting Council statements, Robeson wrote articles, editorials, and sent telegrams reminding leaders to support independence for the colonized. In a *People's Voice* article, he observed that colonized people who joined the antifascist effort now anticipated "a new order of justice and equal opportunity." When the U.S. delegation dragged its feet on supporting the right of independence for African colonies, opting instead for a program of UN trusteeship, Robeson wired the group and urged them to "support the principle of full freedom." In another published message Robeson urged readers that "the colonial peoples' struggle against imperialism is also *our* struggle." Unfortunately, the U.S. government was disinclined to share Robeson's position, as would become increasingly clear in the American votes in the UN over the coming years.

Robeson also advocated publicly for African American rights after the war. Like most civil rights activists, Robeson believed the antifascist war would spur momentum in defeating injustice back in the United States. A campaign calling for a "Double Victory," meaning victory over fascism abroad and manifestations of fascism at home, had been widely adopted in the black community. As the war overseas ended, it was vital to make sure the issue of black rights stayed in the national dialogue. In June 1945, twenty thousand people packed Madison Square Garden for a Negro Freedom Rally. Artists and civil rights leaders called for continuation of the Fair Employment Practices Commission as well as an end to discrimination and "Hitlerism" in the United States. Robeson sang "Let My People Go" as well as "Ol' Man River" and assured the crowd that "Jim crow will go . . . and we won't get discouraged."

Later in the summer, Robeson and Lawrence Brown joined the first interracial United Service Organizations (USO) tour for two months in Europe. Across three countries, Robeson sang for "rapt" and "spellbound" gatherings of soldiers. A writer in *Stars and Stripes* remarked, "Once you hear Robeson you don't forget him." The small concert unit with which Robeson and Brown traveled never missed an engagement and made a point of visiting out-of-the-way units that probably had not seen much entertainment. The Associated Negro Press reported that Robeson's appearances especially boosted the morale of black troops "who needed it badly." The tour also had a downside, however. Paul Robeson Jr. wrote that his father was "startled by the ferocity" of the anti-Soviet sentiment he overheard from some of the generals he encountered in Germany. The relationship between the United States and Britain with the Soviet Union was already beginning to break down. The views of these military men were perhaps an indication of the anti-Communist fervor that soon gripped the United States.

In 1945, the NAACP, the preeminent civil rights organization in the United States, paid tribute to Robeson's artistry and advocacy by selecting him for their highest honor, the Spingarn Medal. The accompanying citation, as reported in the Associated Negro Press, read: "For his distinguished achievements in the theatre and on the concert stage as well as for his active concern for the rights of the common man of every race, color, religion and nationality." This summarized Robeson's career well, particularly his tireless efforts through the war years. At the gala banquet in New York in September, Robeson's comments reflected the transitioning postwar political climate. The decorous crowd of several hundred at the Biltmore Hotel was "shocked" by the passionate remarks that he had not submitted to anyone prior to the event. Robeson emphasized that the people of colonized Africa and Asia "want to realize the promises [of democracy] made to them." He held up the Soviet Union as a model for employing its people and eliminating racial discrimination. Finally, he decried the emerging hostility between the former allies and encouraged "the creation of a world" where all people "can live in peace and harmony" and "resources can be used for the good of all." Paul Robeson Jr. has thoughtfully observed that the audience was dismayed because many of them either endorsed anti-Soviet sentiments or were afraid to challenge them. The FBI got a report on the function and continued to keep a close eye on Robeson. As the mood of the nation transitioned, Robeson's kinship with the Russian people would arouse suspicion and even come under attack.

The gradual disintegration of the U.S.-Soviet relationship was accompanied by a crisis in the U.S. Communist Party. Earl Browder had been reforming the party during the war years by encouraging its members to participate in progressive coalitions that were pushing for labor rights and social change. "Browderism" suggested that socialism and capitalism could coexist. Hardliners, like William Z. Foster, worried that the party should be maintaining a more revolutionary doctrine. When Browder was denounced by French theorist Jacques Duclos, Foster seized the opportunity to take control of the CPUSA and to oust Browder. As President Truman abandoned Roosevelt's internationalist approach in foreign relations, Foster believed that Truman's more conservative policies needed to be directly challenged. The struggle within the Communist Party had caused upheaval among its membership, but ultimately Foster won. The party then began moving in a more radical direction as the political climate in the United States was becoming more antiradical and anti-Soviet. As historian Robin Kelley explained, "On the eve of the greatest red scare in American history, Foster marched his party directly into the eye of the storm." Though he was not a member, Robeson was friends with some leaders in the CPUSA, like Foster, and was close to Councilman Ben Davis in New York. This ensured that Robeson would be the focus of more FBI attention. Phone taps followed many of his conversations, his mail was monitored, and informants reported on his movements as well as his public appearances.

In this dispiriting political environment, Robeson disembarked for an extended U.S. concert tour for the 1945 to 1946 season. Capacity crowds packed auditoriums to hear Robeson and Brown perform their familiar repertoire. Most reviewers found Robeson "now back in his old field [and] stronger than ever." Not surprisingly, he also made time for political appearances such as Ben Davis's reelection campaign. At a meeting of American rabbis at the Jewish Institute, Robeson regretted that "the unity of the three major powers" was being "dangerously assailed." In March 1946, the rupture in the relationship between the former allies seemed irreparable when former British prime minister Winston Churchill famously envisioned an "iron curtain" descending across Europe. His implicit incitement of war was alarming to many, especially on the political left. Even more unsettling was the fact that Truman's presence on the stage during Churchill's speech seemed to give it his tacit approval. Council on African Affairs leaders Robeson and Max Yergan quickly drafted a letter of protest to the president. A primary concern for the Council was the defense of imperialism outlined in

Churchill's speech, which would seriously undermine the cause of colonial freedom. Robeson also criticized the speech at public appearances as his tour wrapped up in the spring. At a mass meeting in California, he denounced what he viewed as the development of Churchill's "Anglo-Saxon world domination" plan. Though Churchill's speech accelerated the advancement of Cold War animosity, Robeson was not alone in questioning what looked like preparation for a war with the Soviets. Hundreds of delegates to a Win the Peace conference elected Robeson to cochair their group. His comments at this meeting continued to focus on his worry that dependency in Africa would continue by way of a "kind of benevolent Anglo-American imperialism." For Robeson, then, the looming Cold War caused unease because of Western militancy toward the Soviet Union and the possibility of the continued domination of Africa.

In May, Robeson took a much-needed break in Connecticut. Eslanda had also been staying busy. She had published a book, *African Journey*, the previous year that was based on her travels in the 1930s and was preparing for a trip to Central Africa for anthropological research. Africa was on Paul's mind in the summer of 1946 when the Council on African Affairs organized a rally at Madison Square Garden for African famine relief. Millions of black South Africans who were segregated onto insufficient plots of land by white supremacist policies were starving. In a letter to the *New York Herald-Tribune*, Robeson carefully explained African economic and political realities that were not widely known in the United States. He then underscored the injustice of continued colonialism. "The right of self-determination," Robeson pointed out, was "written into" the UN Charter. Unfortunately, there was too often "a large discrepancy" in implementing this pledge. In his remarks at the mass meeting of fifteen thousand in June, Robeson connected the oppression of African Americans, West Indians, and Africans. The forces of "progress and democracy," he warned, were in a race against "forces of imperialism and reaction." Getting tough with Russia would only stymie the advancement of colonial people toward independence. Only a "total peace" would mean "total freedom" for all oppressed people around the world.

Robeson was also moved to speak out against the increasing racial violence that followed World War II in the United States. In addition to a riot in Columbia, Tennessee, and a vicious lynching in Monroe, Georgia, over fifty black Americans were murdered between June 1945 and September 1946. Returning black veterans were often targeted because they were viewed as potentially threatening to the segregation system. Robeson and veteran activist W. E. B. Du Bois called for a mass meeting to inaugurate a crusade against lynching. The NAACP leadership was irritated by this new campaign, which they viewed as being in competition with their antiviolence movement. However, Du Bois cogently pointed out that no one organization could have a monopoly on "the fight against mob law."

The American Crusade to End Lynching sponsored a mass rally in Washington, D.C., and Robeson led a delegation to discuss the issue with Truman in September 1946. About three thousand people turned out to hear Robeson read a new Emancipation Proclamation at the Lincoln Memorial. Robeson told the crowd that despite the elimination of enslavement, the oppression of African Americans had not ended. According to newspaper accounts, "sparks flew" when Robeson confronted Truman about backing lynching legislation. Truman felt that a statement against lynching was not politically expedient at the moment. If the government would not take action against racial violence, Robeson cautioned the president, "The Negroes would." Taking strong exception, Truman retorted that this sounded like a threat. Some accounts have Truman "shaking his fist" at Robeson. Robeson then calmly remarked that he was simply commenting on the frustrated mood in the black community. At a press conference following the meeting with the president, reporters quizzed Robeson on whether he was a Communist. Robeson stressed that he was antifascist but reminded them that the Communist Party shared his position against lynching. Truman, in the end, never took a strong stand against racial violence, and no law was ever passed by Congress to outlaw lynching.

In October, Robeson was again queried on his political affiliation when he was called to testify before the Joint Fact-Finding Committee on Un-American Activities in California, which was also called the Tenney Committee after its chairman. The committee was akin to the more well-known House of Un-American Activities Committee (HUAC) in Washington that subpoenaed Robeson ten years later. Tenney's group interrogated Robeson on his travel to the Soviet Union and his organizational affiliations. Significantly, this was the only time Robeson commented directly on his political party membership while under oath. He described his politics as antifascist and independent but not Communist. However, he made certain to point out that the Communist Party was a legal political entity that anyone had the constitutional right to join.

In subsequent years, Robeson eschewed the question of his political party membership. He instead continued to stress that the CPUSA was a legal party and that democratic freedom meant having the right to vote one's conscience in the ballot booth without fear of recrimination. This was a courageous stand to take during the Cold War when it would have been easier to simply deny party membership. Robeson chose the more difficult path of elevating constitutional freedoms during a time when the Bill of Rights was being disregarded in favor of anticommunism. Interestingly, his testimony before the Tenney Committee turned into something of a philosophical discussion on racial oppression and political economy that ended amicably. The aggression and enmity of the Red Scare were not yet entrenched. But they soon would be. Indicative of the hardening of Cold War politics was the forced resignation of Henry A. Wallace from Truman's cabinet as Secretary of Commerce in the autumn of 1946. A staunch New Dealer, Wallace had served FDR as Secretary of Agriculture from 1933 to 1940, through the Depression, and as Vice President from 1941 to 1945. As a proponent of peace and diplomatic relations with the Soviet Union, Wallace had criticized Truman's policies. This political scuffle would lead Wallace to run for president on a third-party ticket in the 1948 election.

Early in 1947, during his annual U.S. concert tour, Robeson made a surprising announcement. Through the tour, accompanist Lawrence Brown remembered Robeson being in a poor mood. According to his son, it "distressed" Robeson to make large paychecks singing formal concerts while his people were suffering. At a stop in St. Louis, Robeson joined a picket line with the local Civil Rights Congress to protest segregation at a local theater. The next day at a press conference he stated that he was going to take a two-year hiatus from the formal concert arena. Instead he would "talk up and down the nation against hatred and prejudice." At a Council on African Affairs event in April, he explained that he would be giving his time "in the forefront" of the struggle. But he was still an artist. "I will function as an artist," he told the crowd, "but I give of my talents to the people." During this period, controversy stirred in some cities where Robeson was scheduled to perform. A wheel spun off a car carrying Robeson, which possibly indicated an attempt on his life had been made. J. Edgar Hoover took a fresh look at his FBI file, and mainstream newspapers became more critical of Robeson.

That April, there was difficulty securing a venue for a planned Robeson appearance in Peoria, Illinois. The city council denied use of the city hall because the HUAC had recently denounced Robeson, and hundreds of others, as a supporter of the Communist Party and therefore "un-American." Progressives in the local community protested this denial of the freedom of speech but ultimately to no avail. By the time Robeson arrived, the specter of violence loomed over the town. Robeson was spirited from the train station by armed union men who aimed to protect him from racist reactionaries. He was taken to the black community where he held a peaceful meeting in the home of a local union leader. Not long after the Peoria affair, trouble arose in Albany, New York. The mayor pressured the board of education to cancel a Robeson event at a local high school. However, the black sponsors of the event took the matter to court as a free-speech violation. The New York State Supreme Court ruled that the board could not call off the event but mandated that Robeson could not make a speech at the appearance. Yet they could not stop him from singing. And sing he did to a packed house of over one thousand. Struggles such as these became more common for Robeson in the late 1940s. Though racists and right-wing reactionaries moved against him, as in Peoria and Albany, Robeson was typically welcomed by black communities and progressive groups. Robeson's hiatus from formal concerts gave him more time to collaborate with groups such as the Council on African Affairs, the Civil Rights Congress (a left-wing group that offered legal counsel to wrongfully accused minorities), and the Progressive Citizens of America (the organization that mobilized for the Wallace presidential campaign).

A government exhibition illustrated well the complexities of civil rights and political dissent in the late 1940s. Beginning in the autumn of 1947, an exhibit called the Freedom Train wound its way across the country via railroad. Over 3 million visitors saw its cargo in cities and towns from coast to coast. The train carried precious historical documents that celebrated democratic freedoms, including the Declaration of Independence and the Gettysburg Address. Significantly, when the National Archives proposed including documents such as the Wagner Act (which guaranteed the right of workers to unionize) and the Fourteenth and Fifteenth Amendments (which guaranteed citizenship and voting rights for former slaves), they were excluded. Historian Eric Foner has pointed out that no documents relating to social legislation from the twentieth century boarded the Freedom Train. This was indeed a conspicuous omission. In his poem of the same name, Langston Hughes wondered, "When it stops in Mississippi, will it be made plain / Everybody's got a right to board the Freedom Train?" Paul Robeson famously recorded the poem and read it at appearances during this time period. Ironically, while the exhibit avoided directly acknowledging provocative issues like black disfranchisement, the organizers refused to stop in towns where viewing would be segregated. At the same time, the FBI was monitoring the exhibit and collecting data on anyone who issued a complaint about its content. The legacy of the Freedom Train, then, was rather mixed with regard to civil rights. In a similar way, the politics of the era were sometimes incongruous. Even as the Truman administration inched toward civil rights protections, such as desegregating the military, political dissent became more dangerous.

By late 1947, the course of U.S. foreign policy and domestic policy was increasingly leaning toward anticommunism. Containment, or containing the influence of the Soviet Union, was at the heart of the Truman Doctrine. In calling for aid to Greece and Turkey, Truman set a precedent for American support of anti-Communist groups no matter how undemocratic they happened to be. Aid to rebuild Western Europe through the Marshall Plan further divided the globe into two spheres: Communist and anti-Communist. With defense as a top priority, loyalty oaths were required for federal employees, and the National Security Act created, among other groups, the Central Intelligence Agency. The political left was marginalized when the Taft-Hartley Act, passed over Truman's veto, weakened the power of labor unions. Fear of Communist infiltration was propagated by campaigns such the HUAC investigation of Hollywood.

Robeson responded to these developments by focusing more ardently on political activity. He labeled Taft-Hartley "the death of the trade union movement." The working classes in Europe viewed the Marshall Plan to be a takeover by "American Big Business," Robeson observed. It further enabled U.S. capital to help bolster European empires at the expense of freedom for colonized people. Robeson questioned the constitutional authority of HUAC because its southern members, such as fervent segregationist John

Paul Robeson at a Madison Square Garden rally for Henry A. Wallace, who is second from right, next to his wife. Daily Worker/Daily World Photographs Collection, Tamiment Library, New York University.

Rankin, remained in office only because the black population was robbed of the right to vote. Robeson and other progressives encouraged Henry A. Wallace, who was also troubled by the country's political direction, to launch a challenge to Truman in the 1948 election. In December 1947, Wallace formally announced his candidacy under the auspices of the Progressive Party. Robeson campaigned doggedly for the progressive candidate until the November election.

The Progressives expanded on "New Deal traditions," in Robeson's words, and emphasized peace in an increasingly militaristic political climate. Their platform advocated, for example, an amendment against gender discrimination, health care for all citizens, and peaceful use of atomic energy. It endorsed reparations for interned Japanese Americans. The Truman Doctrine and the Marshall Plan would be repealed. Wallace also called for complete racial equality socially and politically. He refused to speak before segregated audiences, which was a new precedent for a presidential candidate. The Progressive Party also nominated more black candidates for state offices than the two major parties. These positions appealed to many black voters. The Progressive Party's stand for more diplomatic relations with the Soviet Union attracted a variety of concerned liberals and union members as well as members of the Communist Party. However, these issues proved to be thorny for the party. Truman and the Democrats easily exploited Wallace's collaboration with Communist Party members by painting the coalition with a suspicious red veneer. Additionally, international events undermined Wallace's peaceful foreign policy perspective. When Stalin obstructed access to western sectors of Berlin in the summer, airlifting supplies proved to be a successful strategy to avoid the blockade. These events, and others like the coup in Czechoslovakia, highlighted Soviet aggression and made containment more appealing to many voters. With regard to civil rights, Truman's timely maneuver to desegregate the military in July was enough to persuade a number of black voters to stick with the party of FDR. Many in the civil rights establishment, including the NAACP, saw the dangers of colluding with the left-leaning Progressives and backed Truman.

Nevertheless, Robeson witnessed firsthand the courage of many activists as he campaigned for Wallace. He was moved by the bravery of progressives, especially in the South where the party was often targeted by extremists. The Klan was a continuous menace. Progressive supporters had their lives threatened and crosses burned on their lawns. Yet, they bravely showed up for rallies and offered protection (sometimes armed) for Robeson's appearances. On Election Day, the Progressive Party lost dreadfully in the four-way presidential race. They proved to be less popular than even the resolutely segregationist Dixiecrats, who had split from the Democratic Party. Robeson had been heartened by the interaction he had with working people across the country during the campaign. However, the decisive Progressive loss was a bitter pill for many on the political left. Not only were their positions increasingly marginalized, but Truman's policies now had a mandate from the American people.

During the Progressive campaign, other events illustrated the Cold War political climate. Robeson testified before a U.S. Senate committee in opposition to the proposed Mundt-Nixon bill. The law required members of the

Communist Party and organizations considered to be "communist-fronts" to register with the federal government. Robeson argued that this measure was tantamount to "complete subordination of the rights of individuals to the state." Still, these measures were included in the McCarran Internal Security Act that was passed in 1950. In the summer of 1948, the FBI raided the offices of the Communist Party and indicted twelve party leaders under provisions of the Smith Act for conspiring to advocate the overthrow of the federal government. Their trial and ensuing appeals were drawn out for years. Robeson and W. E. B. Du Bois viewed this indictment as a move that threatened the rights of all minority groups. In the charged anti-Communist environment, however, few except devoted Progressive activists deigned to share their perspective.

Also that year, a vitriolic dispute led to a split in the Council on African Affairs. Max Yergan, with whom Robeson had collaborated since the late 1930s, began to backpedal from the Council's progressive positions on anticolonialism in Africa after Attorney General Tom Clark labeled the group subversive. Ultimately, Yergan departed, along with many of the organization's members, who were either nervous about left-wing affiliations or fed up with the bile between the leaders. Alphaeus Hunton, Doxey Wilkerson, and other Council stalwarts remained, as did Du Bois. Yergan went on to disavow his progressive past completely and become a conservative commentator on Africa in the mainstream press. According to Paul Robeson Jr.'s biography, Yergan had even acted as an FBI informant while he was executive director of the Council. In a similar vein, Du Bois was asked to leave the NAACP in 1948, which he had helped found in 1910, because of his left-wing political views. Robeson offered Du Bois office space with the Council, diminished though it was. The two men found in each other a consistent ally during these difficult times.

With the Progressive campaign finished, Robeson decided to return to the concert arena for the 1948 to 1949 season. A management company booked engagements for him, but local organizers wanted to be assured that his program would be musical, not political. He stuck to his traditional repertoire of folk songs and spirituals, and early results were positive. Auditoriums sold out, and reviewers reported "toes were tapping" through the shows. Appearances were booked in Trinidad and Jamaica, where the torrent of affection for Robeson must have been palpable. When he realized that most islanders could not afford tickets, Robeson sang a free concert in Kingston where tens of thousands packed an outdoor venue. Connecting with people from the African diaspora touched Robeson deeply. The trip to the West Indies made him feel as if he had drawn his "first breath of fresh air in many years." It was exhilarating for him to "see what it will be like when Negroes are free in their own land." He felt that these people were on the "road to freedom" and was moved to observe the workers "walking erect and proud." Even more meaningful was his reception as a people's artist. He explained, "They called to me: 'Hello, Paul. We know you've been fighting for us.'" Robeson's reputation as a political advocate was not embraced back home, however. Upon arriving in Enfield for a holiday vacation, he was told that all of his concert dates in the spring had been canceled. Pressure was being brought to bear on any venue or radio station that worked with Robeson. It seemed that the doors of the American entertainment industry had been summarily closed to him.

Since the U.S. tour was canceled, Robeson traveled across the Atlantic for a four-month concert tour of Europe early in 1949. The tour began in England where he received a hearty welcome. The sold-out shows illustrated that the British love for Robeson was undiminished. He also appeared at political events in London. At a conference of two thousand people, he criticized the South African government's repressive regime. The Council on African Affairs had focused on raising consciousness about the situation of black South Africans for years. In 1948, the Malan administration, a U.S. ally in the Cold War, began institutionalizing the strictures of the infamous apartheid system. Following Robeson's public condemnation of their policies, his records were banned from the radio in South Africa. The same group that had sponsored the London meeting, the Coordinating Committee for Colonial Peoples, asked Robeson to appear at an upcoming peace conference in Paris in April. They wanted the conference delegates to know that the colonized world was focused on maintaining peace and achieving self-government.

In the spring of 1949 Communists in China were making headway in the civil war, and the North Atlantic Treaty Organization (NATO), a Cold War Western alliance, was being created. Against this backdrop of heightening tensions, a congress with close to two thousand delegates from around the world convened in Paris. Notables such as Pablo Picasso and scientist J. D.

Bernal attended. W. E. B. Du Bois, who was becoming very involved in the nascent global peace movement, was part of the delegation from the United States. He wrote eloquently of the event in a Council press release, in which he emphasized the anticolonial resolutions adopted at the meeting. Du Bois was clearly moved by the conference, at which he felt the "outpouring for peace was extraordinary." After Robeson took the stage, an intense ovation preceded his brief, improvised address. He also sang several songs to the delight of the audience. Though his remarks were not substantially different from those of Du Bois or most of the other presenters, they had profound consequences for Robeson's career in the United States.

The principle trouble arose from the Associated Press account of Robeson's appearance, which misquoted him. The AP dispatch quoted Robeson as saying, "'It is unthinkable' that American Negroes 'would go to war on behalf of those who have oppressed us for generations' against a country 'which in one generation has raised our people to the full dignity of mankind.'" His actual address stressed that people in colonial territories wanted "a decent life" that included "programs of human emancipation." African Americans, he observed, desired an equitable distribution of wealth that reflected their contributions to building the United States. Further, they were "determined to fight for peace" and did not want war with the Soviet Union or anybody else. Newspapers in the United States seized on the AP misquote and lashed out against Robeson as unpatriotic. Only a few progressive papers, like the *Daily Worker* and *National Guardian*, verified Robeson's true statement. Biographer Martin Duberman reflected that even if Robeson had made those comments in the AP account, it would have hardly been the first time a black leader questioned whether African Americans should fight for a country that did not protect their civil rights. This debate had been waged since the American Revolution.

Scores of reporters, commentators, and public figures, however, used the erroneous address to denounce Robeson as traitorous. Numerous civil rights activists either volunteered or were pressured into criticizing Robeson. Congressman Adam Clayton Powell Jr. and Mary McLeod Bethune, who had participated in events sponsored by the Council on African Affairs, denied that Robeson was qualified to speak for black Americans. Roy Wilkins, of the NAACP, distanced the mainstream civil rights establishment from Robeson, noting that he did not "represent any American Negroes."

The NAACP's Walter White was more cautious in remarking that white America should "abstain" from denouncing Robeson until "the United States cleanses itself of its own racial sins." Du Bois stood out as a defender of Robeson and of his stand for peace. Du Bois insisted that "no lying distortion and twisting of our prostituted press" could conceal the "heartbreaking significance" of the peace congress.

Robeson traveled to his next bookings in Scandinavia after the Paris meeting. He was largely unaware of the vitriol against him that was making headlines in the United States until Alphaeus Hunton reached Robeson by phone and explained the extent of the negative press back home. Robeson then tried to clarify his Paris statement at a press conference in Copenhagen. He pointed out that his remarks had emphasized the need for peace, but this had little impact. Robeson was now not in a hurry to return to the United States, so he extended his concert tour to Prague, Warsaw, and Moscow. In these cities, people greeted Robeson in the streets, brought flowers to his hotel, and offered heartfelt ovations to his singing. In Moscow, Robeson participated in a celebration of the birth of the beloved Russian poet of African lineage, Alexander Pushkin. On this visit Robeson was unsettled that he could not locate some of his Jewish friends. This was an unfortunate consequence of Stalin's purge of Jewish intellectuals the previous year. He made inquiries and finally got to see his friend Itzik Feffer, who had been arrested and imprisoned. At his last show in Moscow, Robeson commented in Russian on the important ties between the Jewish people in the United States and the Soviet Union and mentioned his personal friendship with Feffer and others. In a demonstration of solidarity, he then sang the song of the Warsaw ghetto, "Zog Nit Keynmol," in Yiddish before a visibly affected crowd. Upon returning to the United States, Robeson did not comment publicly on the Soviet purges. He felt that doing so would only provide additional fodder for the right wing, which was already stoking anti-Soviet panic.

Robeson arrived back in New York in June where several friends, and a small cadre of police officers, greeted him at the airport. FBI agents oversaw a thorough customs search of his luggage. At a press conference, he pointed out that there was no hysteria overseas like there was in America. A big day was soon approaching, which included a public event, a welcome-home rally for Robeson, and a private event, his son's wedding. Paul Jr. had met Marilyn Greenberg while the couple was studying at Cornell University.

They wanted a small, private event at a friend's apartment. However, an aggressive all-white crowd gathered in front of the building alongside their police escort. Reporters swarmed around the couple as they made their way into the front door, which angered the father of the groom. Following the ceremony, the family again had to face the hostile throng as well as the reporters. Racist handmade signs jeered the young African American groom and his Jewish bride. This event underscored Paul's broader concerns about his family's safety. Paul's brother Ben suggested the use of a bodyguard when he was outside of Harlem. Paul also secured a temporary bodyguard for his son and new daughter-in-law and advised the interracial couple to avoid lingering in white neighborhoods given this vicious climate. Eslanda was firm in her decision to stay in Enfield, though it was isolated. At least her neighbor was a keen hunter and could help fend off marauders with his rifle.

At the rally that afternoon, Robeson addressed an enthusiastic crowd of five thousand at Rockland Palace in Harlem. As demonstrated by the turnout, Robeson maintained a solid following in the black community and among progressives in New York. Rather than distancing himself from the Associated Press account of his Paris remarks, Robeson's speech clarified his political perspective. He emphasized the connection between people from across the African diaspora, asserting, "I'm not ashamed of my African origin. I'm proud of it." People of the diaspora shared a struggle against the forces of white supremacy. In Robeson's view, getting involved in another foreign war would prevent progress against discrimination in the United States and colonialism in Africa. Ensuring peace, according to Robeson, was the best way to work toward full freedom and liberation. He stressed, "We do not want to die in vain any more on foreign battlefields for Wall Street and the greedy supporters of domestic fascism. If we must die, let it be in Mississippi or Georgia! Let it be wherever we are lynched and deprived of our rights as human beings!" The Council on African Affairs published the speech as a pamphlet in response to the "campaign of vituperation against Robeson."

The campaign against Robeson, however, continued that summer. The HUAC launched an investigation into Communist infiltration of minority groups. Numerous leaders from the black community testified and some, such as Alvin Stokes and Manning Johnson, disparaged Robeson, calling him a Communist who wanted to become a "Black Stalin" in the United

States. Other leaders, such as Charles S. Johnson and Lester Granger, were a little more circumspect. Granger, for example, was not exactly a Robeson supporter but suggested that the HUAC consider investigating vigilante groups like the Klan, which were a clear threat to democracy. The committee's celebrity witness was baseball star Jackie Robinson, who appeared under some pressure. His highly publicized move to the Major League Brooklyn Dodgers had been influenced by Robeson's meeting with the baseball commissioner to push for integration. While he admitted that racial discrimination was not a Communist hoax, Robinson told the committee that Robeson's Paris statement sounded "silly."

This was offered as damning evidence against Robeson by the mainstream press. The *New York Times* ran a headline avowing, "Jackie Robinson Disputes Robeson." The black press, on the other hand, was divided. The *Amsterdam News*, for example, sided with Robinson, but the *Afro-American* made certain to point out that Robeson was as loyal as any American. Progressive papers such as the *Daily Worker* and the *California Eagle* fervently defended Robeson, pointing out that Robinson might not have been the first African American in the Major Leagues if not for Robeson's pioneering efforts in civil rights and sports. Robeson tried to stay out of the fray but remarked to the *Daily Worker* that HUAC's strategy of compelling loyalty testimony was an "insult to the entire Negro people." In hindsight, Robinson wrote in his autobiography that he had "increased respect" for Robeson, who he believed had genuinely tried to help his people.

Despite the hostility against him, Robeson continued his political activity. He was a fixture in Harlem speaking for progressive unions, groups such as the Civil Rights Congress, and for freedom for the leaders of the Communist Party. In September, he planned to travel to the small town of Peekskill in Westchester County, New York, to perform an annual outdoor benefit concert. The area was a popular vacation spot for people from the city. Yet some of the locals resented the presence of these outsiders. It did not help the tension that many of the seasonal residents were left-wing sympathizers and some were Jewish. The recent press against Robeson had raised the ire of conservative groups and right-wing reactionaries who were determined to disrupt the concert. In fact, the concert did not occur at all. Instead there was a violent attack against the outsiders, the perceived Red infiltrators. After blocking the road to effectively trap the concert attendees, groups of irate roving men fanned out to attack them with rocks and vicious insults as they attempted to make their way to the venue. Windows were broken out of cars, and suspect individuals were physically attacked. Police standing by did little or nothing to stop the fracas. Around a dozen Robeson backers ended up in the hospital. Expletives hurled by the offenders ranged from antiradical and anti-Semitic to anti-Robeson. Several witnesses remembered a cross burning visibly on a nearby hill, which illustrated the racist intent of the mob. Fortunately, Robeson never made it to the Lakeland Acres picnic grounds because the car he was in got caught in the resulting traffic jam. Shocked and disturbed, he spent the night in Ossining at the Rockmore's house before the heading back to New York City the next morning. His unease focused mainly on the people who had been put into harm's way for supporting him.

People from across the political spectrum weighed in on the alarming events at Peekskill. Some staunch anti-Communists shrugged, and a few headlines asserted that Robeson had asked for this. But many of those who did not fully agree with Robeson's politics decried the vicious assault of a peaceful concert crowd. Those on the political left viewed Peekskill as a harbinger of the extent to which anti-Communist hysteria had seized the nation. At a rally in Harlem just days after the melee, Robeson assured the three thousand people at the Golden Gate Ballroom that he was loyal to America's "true traditions" of those who tried to free his people rather than enslave them. "We're all fighting together," he reminded the crowd, "for the freedom not only of the Negro people but of an America which . . . our children can be proud of." A committee of concerned citizens was quickly formed and another concert was planned as an answer to the violence. A couple of progressive unions offered to help with security.

The second concert was held on the grounds of Hollow Brook country club. Thousands of union men arrived early to organize security for the over twenty thousand people who attended the concert. They rooted out a sniper's nest in the hills surrounding the grounds. Meanwhile, an antagonistic crowd gathered to protest the concert near the entrance of the hollow. They waved homemade placards proclaiming, among other sentiments, that Hitler had not finished the job on the Jews and commies. The show started in the early afternoon. Pete Seeger sang, and Lawrence Brown accompanied

Paul Robeson, flanked by union men, performing in Peekskill, New York, in 1949. Daily Worker/Daily World Photographs Collection, Tamiment Library, New York University.

Robeson when he performed. A throng of union men encircled the stage to protect Robeson.

He sang several selections from his repertoire and opted not to make a speech. The concert remained peaceful, but as people began to leave the grounds, they ran into hostile protesters. Again, cars were charged, and people were violently assaulted. Buses were pummeled by rocks as glass shards scattered on the men, women, and children inside. Concertgoers and union men were trapped in the hollow and left at the mercy of the venomous attackers. Some witnesses saw police chitchatting with the locals, while others saw officers joining the brawl, which continued until well after midnight.

Repercussions from Peekskill continued for quite some time. Effigies of Robeson were displayed in several towns. Litigation was pursued but was ultimately unsuccessful for Robeson and his supporters. The leaders of the Communist Party who were on trial moved for a mistrial, arguing that they could not get a fair hearing in light of widespread anti-Communist sentiment. The motion was quickly denied. Comments about Peekskill made it all the way to the floor of the U.S. House of Representatives, where Representative Javits from New York denounced the carnage as a violation of the right of free speech. This incited Representative Rankin from Mississippi to condemn Robeson. And the back-and-forth continued. Robeson responded by embarking on a six-city follow-up concert tour sponsored by the Council on African Affairs. Louise Thompson Patterson, who organized the tour, noted that city officials made it as difficult as possible for Robeson to perform. On the other hand, people in local black communities offered to help with security and opened their hotels and their churches to support Robeson. The concerts were all peaceful and well attended. Patterson believed the tour showed that there were people who were ready to "accept a challenge" to back Robeson.

Following Peekskill, judgments for and against Robeson became more entrenched. For those on the right, he represented the Communist menace that was threatening America. Robeson became, for those more to the left, a heroic figure and a symbol of bravery in the face of right-wing vitriol. Robeson and other Progressives wondered where the next Peekskill might occur. Not surprisingly, the leaders of the Communist Party were convicted in the autumn of 1949. Although they were released on bail by the appeals court, this verdict reinforced the antiradical political mood. As the 1940s drew to a close, Robeson focused on the future. Rather than back away from the increasingly hostile political climate, he considered how he might strengthen his base of support in Harlem. He also spoke of traveling to another world peace conference. As it turned out, his energies would be focused on fighting for the right to travel internationally for much of the next decade.

5

COLD WARRIOR

By 1950 FBI surveillance of Paul Robeson was continuous. He could even recognize the agents in plain clothes who tailed him, according to Martin Duberman, but did not let on so as to avoid distressing his friends. The previous year, the Soviet Union had tested an atomic weapon, and the Communists had won the civil war in China, creating the People's Republic. A Red menace now seemed to be spreading across Asia. Fears of communism also loomed large closer to home. Alger Hiss, who was accused of being a Soviet spy, was convicted of perjury. Senator Joseph McCarthy of Wisconsin claimed to have a list of Communists working in the State Department, which launched his frenzied publicity campaign against Communist infiltration. Many careers were ruined and reputations smeared in the wake of McCarthy's tidal wave of baseless accusations. Despite these indicators of the antagonistic Cold War climate, Robeson remained politically active.

However, opportunities for Robeson to make appearances were limited, especially after Peekskill. He spoke at a convention for the Progressive Party, where he concentrated on the importance of civil rights and the need for unity within the party. In March 1950 Robeson was scheduled to contribute to a Sunday afternoon television program that featured the former First Lady, called "Today with Mrs. Roosevelt," on NBC. Representing the Progressive Party, Robeson was to discuss the position of African Americans in political life with Democrat Adam Clayton Powell Jr. and Perry Howard, a Republican. Robeson's appearance, however, was suddenly canceled, and the program was postponed indefinitely. NBC maintained that Robeson had to be barred from the program because of an "influx" of protest calls against his presence. Robeson said he was "not surprised" that a large company that "practically excludes" African Americans from its workforce "should balk" at a program focused on black people that "professes to present all points of view." Adam Clayton Powell Jr. spoke out against the denial of free speech. Singling out one person's views, Powell objected, was not "in keeping with our American principles." Still, Robeson assured the press that he would continue to make his "voice heard for the complete liberation of colored Americans and all oppressed peoples."

In keeping with that pledge, Robeson visited London briefly in May to address the World Peace Council. Numerous peace groups extended invitations to Robeson during this period. He could not fulfill all of the offers, but if he could not attend, he would often send written greetings or a recorded speech. Twenty thousand people came out for the London rally, where Robeson sang a handful of folk songs and reassured the crowd that fascism was not being resuscitated in the United States. The next month he called in on a meeting of the National Labor Conference for Negro Rights in Chicago. His speech, "Forge Negro-Labor Unity for Peace and Jobs," pointed out that peace was "the over-riding issue of the day." Robeson cogently argued that politicians and commentators in America decried campaigns for peace, colonial freedom, and minority rights because Communists supported these movements. Communists were not the only people interested in these issues, however. "Now I have seen," Robeson advised the audience, "liberty-loving, peace-seeking partisans in many parts of the world." He urged the trade unionists that "the progressive forces in American life, black and white together, [must] stop our government's toboggan ride toward war and destruction." Labor, then, should be at the vanguard of the campaign for peace as well as civil rights, in Robeson's view.

The call for peace was seriously compromised that year when Cold War tensions led to war on the Korean peninsula. Korea had been divided at the 38th parallel after World War II. The North, which shared a border with China, leaned toward communism, while the South was an ally of the capitalist West. When forces from the North invaded the South to unify the country, Truman's containment policy was challenged. The Soviets were supporting the North, and the United States sent troops in the summer of 1950. The drumbeat of war was fed by the anti-Communist frenzy in the

United States, and most rallied behind Truman. Even Henry A. Wallace, a
critic of many of Truman's policies, supported the war in Korea. This issue
split the Progressive Party, which had a substantial faction, including Robeson, who opposed the war. Wallace broke with the party, leaving it to limp
along, an isolated voice for peace in a charged militaristic climate. Robeson
spoke out against the war at a mass meeting sponsored by the Civil Rights
Congress at Madison Square Garden in June. Today the United States sent
troops to Asia, and tomorrow it could be Africa, he warned the crowd.
Robeson reminded black America that the place for them to fight was for
their full freedom here at home.

These remarks, which were not substantially different than the ones he
made in Paris the previous year, perked the ears of the State Department.
Robeson had planned to go to Europe later in the summer, but a stop notice was issued against his passport, leaving him grounded in the United
States. In July the FBI was dispatched to physically collect Robeson's passport. They barged into his son's apartment and the home of friends where
Robeson was known to stay. Robeson agreed to meet with the agents in the
presence of an attorney but did not relinquish his passport. In August the
State Department announced that through its discretionary powers it had
canceled Robeson's passport. All border officials were alerted should he try
to leave the country. The only justification offered was that it was against the
best interests of the United States for Robeson to travel abroad. Robeson
was advised that unless he guaranteed not to speak out about the treatment
of African Americans while he was abroad, he would not be going anywhere.
He assembled a legal team to take the matter to court. Robeson was just
one of many who were denied the right to travel abroad during the Cold
War because of their political beliefs. Citizens involved in the peace movement or other left-wing causes, such as W. E. B. Du Bois, Max Shachtman,
Clark Foreman, and Rockwell Kent, shared a similar fate. Public outcry was
minimal since, like the peace movement itself, the mainstream press largely
shied away from this story. Additionally, Madison Square Garden refused
to rent their facility to the Council on African Affairs, though they had used
it previously, for a rally in support of Robeson's right to travel. It was clear
that Robeson was being further isolated in the public discourse.

To make matters worse, freedom of speech and the right to political dissent were restricted with the passage of the McCarran Internal Security Act

Paul Robeson and W. E. B. Du Bois at the Paris Peace Conference. Reference number 549, W. E. B. Du Bois Papers, Special Collections and University Archives, University of Massachusetts Amherst Libraries.

in the autumn of 1950. The law passed over Truman's veto by a Congress that was increasingly animated by anticommunism. The McCarran bill mandated that organizations labeled as "subversive" must register with the federal government. Members of these suspicious groups could be detained or denied the right to travel.

It was in this repressive climate that Robeson's colleague W. E. B. Du Bois decided to challenge the incumbent, Herbert H. Lehman, in a bid for a U.S. Senate seat from New York on the American Labor Party ticket. Du Bois undertook this campaign, at the age of eighty-two, in order to have a platform from which he could speak about the importance of peace. Like Robeson, he was actively involved in the global peace movement, having attended congresses in New York, Paris, and Moscow. The veteran activist was also a supporter of the Peace Information Center, which was formed to help disseminate news about the worldwide movement in the United States. However, Du Bois was discovering that his chances to speak publicly were "increasingly proscribed" and the opportunities to write for publications were "narrower and narrower," even in the black press. He understood that he did not have "a ghost of a chance" of winning but felt that his message was worthy of attention. Ultimately, Du Bois lost the election but made numerous speeches and broadcasts about his platform, which focused on peace. His final campaign address was to a rally of seventeen thousand but was "nearly blacked out by the press."

Robeson and Du Bois, like much of the political left, were constrained by most of the media, which either ignored or vilified them. In response, Robeson and a group of progressive allies formed the United Freedom Fund, which produced a monthly newspaper called *Freedom*. Its masthead read: "Where one is enslaved, all are in chains!" Louis Burnham, who had been a leader in the Southern Negro Youth Congress that had folded in late 1940s due to Cold War political pressure, edited the paper. Burnham had also been an organizer for the Progressive Party. For *Freedom* newspaper, he managed a gifted team of writers and reporters who covered stories on civil rights and labor struggles, anticolonial campaigns, and the repression of civil liberties. The periodical offered space for Robeson to comment on his activities and to elucidate his political views in his column "Here's My Story" that was cowritten by progressive author Lloyd Brown. Du Bois, Alphaeus Hunton, and Eslanda Robeson contributed articles about Africa. News stories from the West Indies and other parts of the diaspora were also featured. African American history was a common theme in the paper. Writer Alice Childress penned a regular column called "Conversations from Life," which offered pithy and sometimes hilarious glimpses of life through the eyes of a fictional domestic worker. Lorraine Hansberry got her start as a reporter for *Freedom* and went on to become a celebrated playwright, whose credits included *A Raisin in the Sun*.

The first issue of *Freedom* came off the press in late 1950. Robeson clarified the purpose of the paper in his inaugural column. Written in an informal style that would appeal to working people, Robeson began with an anecdote of someone on the street in Harlem asking whether he had been born in Russia. "I laughed, of course," Robeson recounted, but then he carefully explained that "the masters of the press and radio" have convinced Americans that anyone who wants friendship with the Soviet Union and equal rights now "cannot be a 'real' American [but] must have been born in Russia." Robeson reminded the reader of his father's origins in slavery and that he was proud of his African heritage. This was why he called for full freedom for Africans and African Americans. He felt connected to the Soviet Union because it was there that he first experienced the human dignity that had been denied to him in the United States. Robeson was not a Russian, his column pointed out, but a representative of the working classes in progressive America. It was because of such misinformation in the mainstream press that *Freedom* aimed to give a "real voice of the oppressed masses" and act as a "true weapon for all progressive Americans." Despite its laudable goals, *Freedom* suffered from financial insecurity for most of its existence. Maintaining a progressive paper would not be easy in a rigidly conservative, anti-Communist political environment.

As a difficult year closed, Robeson's attorneys filed suit in the U.S. District Court in Washington, D.C., for the return of his passport in December. They argued that denying his right to travel internationally violated Robeson's First Amendment rights to freedom of speech, thought, assembly, and association. Because he earned a substantial portion of his living as an artist by fulfilling engagements abroad, they further maintained that depriving Robeson of a passport violated his right to own and procure property, which was protected by the Fifth Amendment. This was a first step in, what turned out to be, an arduous and lengthy battle between Robeson and the State Department.

Robeson's *Freedom* column in January 1951 celebrated the anniversary of "the month of emancipation." His father, who escaped enslavement, knew firsthand about emancipation. Today, Robeson stressed, celebrating emancipation must mean "refusing to hear any talk of war." Instead, the fight should focus on a free Africa, the right to vote in the South, and "the future of your children." However, Robeson's New Year's message reached a limited audience. The leadership of the black community began the year by lashing out at him. An article by NAACP leader Walter White called "The Strange Case of Paul Robeson" was published in *Ebony* magazine. Though White had known Robeson for many years, the article claimed that Robeson had fallen for Soviet rhetoric and had deserted the African American freedom struggle. Eslanda Robeson shot back with a written response, but *Ebony* refused to print it. The *California Eagle* did publish her essay, which pointed to Robeson's continuous efforts on behalf of civil rights for black Americans and anticolonial freedom.

Around this time, the State Department had been making plans to circulate an article that would tarnish Robeson's reputation in Africa. The White article could have fit the bill. But another piece disparaging Robeson was also printed in the NAACP magazine *Crisis* later in the year. Paul Robeson Jr. has suggested that NAACP leader Roy Wilkins might have colluded with the State Department in publishing the article "Paul Robeson—Lost Shepard" to damage Robeson's reputation. This essay, printed under the pen name Robert Alan, denounced Robeson as a dupe of the Soviets. Anyone who knew Robeson or followed his work certainly understood that he was smart and outspoken. He made up his own mind about issues and was not a victim of Communist machinations. Yet the civil rights establishment had chosen to distance itself from Robeson because he was critical of government policies and condemned the Korean War. In the rigidly divided Cold War climate, the NAACP did not want to be mistaken for being weak on communism. Later in the year the *Amsterdam News*, a black newspaper in New York, left Robeson's name off a list of winners of the NAACP's Spingarn Medal, which he had been awarded in 1945.

Tensions were high even in a Harlem nightclub, the Red Rooster, where Robeson was socializing with friends one evening. Don Newcombe, a black pitcher for the Brooklyn Dodgers, sat down near Robeson with a party. When he recognized that Robeson was nearby, Newcombe snarled that he was joining the army to fight people like Robeson. The two groups almost came to blows. Robeson's birthday in April 1951, on the other hand, brought many supportive greetings from around the world. An article that month in *The Worker Magazine* likened Robeson to a towering oak. Though buffeted by the wind, the oak remained sturdy, even serene. The article pointed to the working-class support for Robeson. It was the porters, waiters, cab drivers, regular working folks, who called out to Robeson on the street: "Keep fighting 'em, Paul" or "Paul, I'm with you." The next month, Robeson happily became a grandfather when Paul Jr. and Marilyn had David Paul Robeson. Ben Robeson christened the baby at Mother AME Zion church in Harlem. For many years it had been Paul's habit to stay with friends in the city. But in the early 1950s he felt it would be beneficial to have a more stable residence, so Paul moved into the parsonage with Ben and his family for a period of time. His room was furnished with a seven-foot bed and a piano. In his memoir, Paul had referred to his boyhood in the black church as "a home in that rock." With Ben's hospitality, the church again acted as "a home in that rock" during a difficult period in Paul's career.

Robeson remained busy in 1951 despite the antagonistic political environment. He backed the legal campaigns for Willie McGee and the Martinsville Seven, who were being defended by the Civil Rights Congress. He sent greetings to the World Peace Congress since he could not attend in person. In his message, he referred to his "house arrest" and placed the struggle for peace within the historic tradition of abolitionism. Like Frederick Douglass, Robeson preferred "living a life of activity in the service of my brethren." Troubling signs of contemporary times, however, cropped up continually. Nationally syndicated columnist Robert Ruark proposed that in a national emergency Robeson "was as worthy of internment as any Jap." A copy of that editorial was clipped and saved in Robeson's FBI file. Robeson, however, was not alone in being buffeted by the winds of Cold War politics. The Supreme Court upheld the convictions of the leaders of the Communist Party under the Smith Act. The venerable W. E. B. Du Bois was indicted for failing to register as a foreign agent for his work with the Peace Information Center. Alphaeus Hunton had to take a forced leave of absence from his work with the Council on African Affairs when he received a six-month jail sentence for refusing to divulge the names of confidential contributors to a bail fund for the Civil Rights Congress of which he was a trustee.

In the spring of 1951 a U.S. District Court refused to order Robeson to surrender his passport, a small victory, but the State Department appealed the decision. When he applied for a passport for a British concert tour, it was summarily denied. In response, a Provisional Committee to Restore Paul Robeson's Passport was created. Lloyd Brown wrote a pamphlet titled "Lift Every Voice for Paul Robeson," which was sold at three cents per copy, and he also encouraged readers to subscribe to *Freedom* newspaper. The pamphlet compared Robeson to Frederick Douglass, who had journeyed to England to speak against slavery in the nineteenth century. Brown suggested that since he promoted full freedom when he traveled abroad, "Robeson is the Douglass of today." However, legal fees were mounting due to the prolonged passport struggle. This was compounded by Robeson's loss of income. His income had plummeted because he was cut off from working abroad and had trouble securing concerts in the United States. Eslanda realized that they would have to cut expenses and should probably start looking for a buyer for the Connecticut home. Additionally, the Internal Revenue Service began looking over Robeson's taxes with increased scrutiny, and even Paul Jr. was denied a passport to attend a World Youth Festival in Berlin.

Robeson planned to undertake a concert tour in the autumn of 1951 to raise money for the United Freedom Fund. Major venues were out of the question, but bookings for Robeson were welcomed in many black churches and union halls. A flyer for a Robeson appearance at a Baptist church in the Washington, D.C., area illustrated the pockets of support that still existed. It urged members to come hear Robeson because "we must never forget Paul." In late 1951 Robeson collaborated with Civil Rights Congress attorney William Patterson on a petition that charged that the U.S. government had fomented a policy of genocide against black Americans. The petition was to be presented before the United Nations, where they hoped it would be taken up for debate by the Human Rights Commission.

The petitioners carefully constructed an argument based on the definition of genocide that was adopted by the 1948 UN conference. Genocide could involve "any intent to destroy, in whole or in part, a national, racial, ethnic or religious group," the petition stressed. The document went on to meticulously recount lynchings and other reported acts of violence that had gone unpunished. Congress had failed to ever take action against lynching, the petition pointed out. Justice had been blocked not only through the court system but also through the deliberate effort to disfranchise black citizens since the late nineteenth century. The United Nations, then, was an alternative outlet through which they could push for justice. "We Charge Genocide" was signed by a few prominent black activists, including Du Bois, Mary Church Terrell, Ben Davis, Charlotta Bass, and Bishop William Walls, but many white liberals and black leaders shied away from the petition's radical stance. Robeson, with a delegation, presented the petition to the UN Secretary General in New York, and Patterson delivered it simultaneously to the General Assembly in Paris. The U.S. delegation to the UN worked behind the scenes to make sure that the petition was never seriously debated, and when Patterson returned to the United States, his passport was promptly revoked. Interestingly, the petition was reprinted in the early 1970s when a group of activists was again considering taking the case to the United Nations.

By 1952 the United States was making little headway in Korea. In his January 1952 *Freedom* column, Robeson lamented the continued bloodshed that left American servicemen dead and had "killed, maimed and rendered homeless a million Koreans." Indeed, the war had devolved to a virtual stalemate. President Truman had relieved General MacArthur of his command the previous year when MacArthur wanted to expand the scope of the war by considering the use of atomic weapons to engage the Chinese. Armistice negotiations had been undertaken but had yet to bear fruit, and the prolonged conflict tarnished Truman's approach to the Cold War in the eyes of some critics. Meanwhile, freedom struggles were developing across Africa.

Black South Africans were organizing mass protests against the most despised restrictions of apartheid law. In an editorial in *Spotlight on Africa*, Robeson pointed out that the Council on African Affairs had been "exposing and campaigning against" that vicious system in South Africa for nearly a decade. He urged strong support for African National Congress' current resistance campaign and reminded readers that white supremacist South Africa was part of Truman's "free world." In east Africa, the Kikuyu had formed an armed guerilla group called Mau Mau to contest the presence of colonial settlers. In Robeson's view, these were freedom fighters who were bravely striving to "take back their native land." The British declared a state of emergency in 1952 and arrested Jomo Kenyatta, a leader of the resistance movement and an old acquaintance of Robeson's.

Robeson continued to tour in 1952, but not without encountering significant obstacles. The year did not begin auspiciously. In January he was turned away at the Canadian border even though travelers did not need a passport to visit the northern U.S. neighbor. According to documents in his FBI file, all ports were notified to prevent Robeson from leaving the country. Robeson was threatened with a hefty fine and/or several years in prison if he violated the order. He had been scheduled to appear at a meeting sponsored by the Mine, Mill and Smelter Workers Union in Vancouver, British Columbia. Instead, he spoke and sang to the convention by long distance over the telephone. The group also considered planning an outdoor concert on the U.S.-Canadian border as a creative solution to circumventing this new travel restriction. Back in the United States, Robeson pressed on through his concert tour. Police in plain clothes and federal government agents could be counted on as regulars at Robeson engagements.

Newspaper coverage in several cities such as Oakland and Milwaukee emphasized that Robeson would be singing and *not* making political speeches. A review of the show in Milwaukee judged Robeson's voice to be "as rich and eloquent as ever," but noted that the thirty-five-hundred seat hall had only about five hundred seats filled. In Chicago, Robeson was finally booked to sing at a park when pressure on local pastors made securing a church venue impossible. Local groups, including the International Longshore and Warehouse Union in Seattle, took court action to defend Robeson's right to perform in the Civil Auditorium there. Robeson was able to sing at Berkeley High School in San Francisco only after a close 3–2 vote by the board of education. This was after the Opera House had denied the booking. Eight hundred people came out to hear Robeson in Denver despite the rancorous local press about him and the presence of anti-Communist protesters outside the city auditorium. One local citizen wondered in a letter to the editor of the *Denver Post* whether "those who would stop Mr. Robeson's songs" were "so afraid that they longer respected the Constitution?" The city of Hartford, Connecticut, paid several thousand dollars for police security so that around eight hundred people could hear Robeson at Weaver High School auditorium. The concert was peaceful and, according to one review, "musically" it was "an immensely worthwhile evening." Robeson was not the only person facing difficulties because of the tour. Paul Robeson Jr. recalled the story of a federal worker who lost his job simply for trying to attend a Robeson concert. A couple of local organizers who helped obtain bookings for Robeson also ended up losing their jobs. All in all, the trying tour was only a moderate financial success. Robeson donated most of his earnings back to *Freedom* newspaper.

There was, however, one historic Robeson concert that year. Because of the arbitrary refusal to let Robeson perform in Canada, a committee organized a concert at Peace Arch Park in Blaine, Washington, on the northern U.S. border in May 1952. Border patrol officials assigned extra men to oversee the possible traffic congestion from the concert. When an estimated thirty thousand Americans and Canadians descended on the park for the free show, the border had to be closed for more than an hour because it was simply overwhelmed. The *Vancouver Sun* wrote that the crowd extended across the border like a blanket so that Robeson's voice could bypass the boundary that he could not cross physically. Robeson sang about a dozen songs and spoke briefly about peace. Significantly, the concert remained unmolested by violence or "heckling squads." The event was a great success in that it cleverly sidestepped the State Department's travel constraint and enabled Canadians to demonstrate their support for Robeson. The FBI remained focused on the event, where they even took video surveillance. Nevertheless, the concert proved to be popular, so Robeson returned in subsequent years to sing at the border.

The passport case continued to wind its way through the courts in 1952. A government brief submitted for a Court of Appeals hearing referred to Robeson as a "political meddler" who could cause a "diplomatic embarrassment" if he was allowed to travel overseas because of his "frank admission that he has been for years extremely active politically in behalf of the independence of the colonial peoples of Africa." In a speech the following year, Robeson struck a humorous chord with the audience after he read that passage aloud. "Now that's just too bad," he teased, "because I'm going to have to continue to meddle." And the crowd responded with laughter and cheers. His memoir approached the issue more seriously. "This attitude of the State Department," Robeson cautioned, "should outrage every decent American." He defended not only his constitutional rights in this matter but also pointed out the importance of a global perspective. "Can we oppose White Supremacy in South Carolina," Robeson asked, "and not oppose the same vicious system in South Africa?" He then affirmed that he would "never cease" speaking out for African freedom "no matter what the State Department or anybody else thinks about it." This was a courageous political stand, but not one that would help him obtain a passport any time soon.

Robeson persisted in finding artistic outlets in the constricted Cold War climate of the early 1950s. Since recording companies were shunning him, Robeson collaborated with his son and Lloyd Brown to create the independent Othello Recording Company. Paul Jr. knew about audio engineering, and Brown acted as secretary-treasurer. This venture enabled Robeson to produce and sell recordings for his progressive and African American fan base. The first album they recorded was *Robeson Sings*, which included six songs. No stores or distributors would advertise a Robeson album, so Othello Recording marketed the record in progressive publications, such as the *National Guardian* and *Freedom*. Some were also sold in black churches. The undertaking was quite successful: around five thousand copies were sold for five dollars each. Over the next few years, Othello Recording produced two more albums and created an archive of Robeson recordings. Before it folded in 1956, the company brought in total earnings of $60,000, and $12,000 in royalties for Robeson, according to Paul Jr.

In the autumn of 1952 Robeson addressed the annual convention of the National Negro Labor Council standing in front of a drawing of Frederick Douglass, who had pioneered a path for black resistance. Robeson placed his remarks in the context of the struggles emerging in South Africa and eastern Africa. Just as those African freedom fighters were taking action, working men and women in the United States should focus their energies on "every whistle stop in this land where the walls of Jim Crow still stand." That fall, Robeson also campaigned for the Progressive Party's presidential candidates. Vincent Hallinan headed the ticket with Charlotta Bass, who was the first African American woman contender for the position of vice president. Robeson pushed the message that the "fight for peace and the fight for equality" were "indivisible" because "preparing for war" meant destroying progress toward civil rights. With Cold War politics in ascendancy, few voters agreed with Robeson. The Progressive Party had an even weaker showing than in 1948, and this turned out to be their last national election. Voters in 1952 overwhelmingly liked "Ike," who won in a landslide as the first Republican president since Herbert Hoover won in 1928. Dwight Eisenhower capitalized on his popularity as a World War II general and promised to get the United States untangled from Korea. He was as good as his word, and an armistice was signed the following year that maintained the 38th parallel between North and South Korea. It seemed that, as detractors like Robeson had predicted, little was accomplished by the war in Korea.

Robeson was awarded the international Stalin Peace Prize by the Soviet Union in late 1952. The honor was something of a mixed blessing. The award was highly respected among international Communists who did not yet know the extent of Stalin's own crimes. For conservatives in the United States, it solidified Robeson's place as a Communist propagandist or, worse, a Soviet stooge. To those who followed the international peace movement, however, this represented an acknowledgement of his continuous advocacy for peace. Not surprisingly, Robeson was not granted a passport to travel to the Soviet Union to receive the award. A ceremony was held instead in Harlem at the Hotel Theresa the following year. W. E. B. Du Bois, himself an active proponent of peace, praised Robeson's efforts on behalf of peace, and writer Howard Fast presented the prize. Robeson considered the award to be "a great honor" and accepted it in the name of the peace movement in the United States. The award came with a cash prize of about twenty-five thousand dollars, which was additionally welcomed.

Just a few months later, in March 1953, Stalin was dead. Nikita Khrushchev took the reins of power, which signaled a shift in Cold War politics. Khrushchev even spoke of the idea of "peaceful coexistence" with the United States. Signs on the domestic front, however, continued to be ominous for those on the political left. It was that year that Julius and Ethel Rosenberg were executed for passing atomic secrets to the Soviet Union. Robeson had spoken out on their behalf at a rally held after the couple was sentenced to death. Many progressives questioned the validity of the case, and the evidence against Ethel was especially flimsy. Their executions, however, starkly illustrated that the Red Scare had not subsided. In addition, Joseph McCarthy had been reelected by Wisconsin voters in the 1952 election, and the following year he gained the chairmanship of the Senate Permanent Subcommittee on Investigations. Though this was usually a fairly unexceptional position, he used the post to continue his relentless, high-profile pursuit of Communist infiltrators. One of the witnesses subpoenaed by McCarthy in 1953 was Eslanda Robeson.

This was a trying year for Eslanda. Her mother's health had been declining for some time, so she had been moved into a nursing home in Massachusetts. Mrs. Goode died in the spring of 1953. The house in Enfield, Connecticut, had sold, so Essie packed, downsized, and moved back to New York that summer. Never one to be idle, however, she became an accredited UN observer and wrote articles for the left-wing *New World Review* as well as other progressive publications. In July, she faced off with Joe McCarthy's committee. With her attorney, Milton Friedman, alongside, Eslanda responded to questions about her books and organizational affiliations. She said that she was "very proud" to be the wife of Paul Robeson but demurred when queried about his Soviet connections. "Why don't you ask him?" she replied. Eslanda invoked both the Fifth and Fifteenth Amendments to avoid self-incrimination. McCarthy disputed her use of the latter as it protected voting rights for African Americans. She then pointed out that the Senate was all white and her people were denied voting rights in many places. When asked whether she knew about any violent conspiracies against the United States, she cogently replied that Communists had not wrought the violence she knew of in the United States. A speech on McCarthyism that she had given at a Civil Rights Congress meeting was called into question. Was the speech for or against McCarthyism, one committee member wanted to know. "I'll give you two guesses," Eslanda retorted. Throughout her testimony, she remained "very cool, deliberate, [and] intelligent" according to Associated Negro Press reporter Alice Dunnigan. Even McCarthy had to concede that she was "charming" and "an intelligent lady."

Paul was very pleased with Eslanda's performance before McCarthy's committee. He was facing his own difficulties that year. He planned another benefit concert tour for *Freedom*, but stamina in local communities to organize bookings for Robeson was waning. The Cold War was beginning to take its toll. Eleven shows were scheduled, mostly in cities with substantial black communities. There were two bright spots in the tour that year. In Philadelphia, Robeson sang in an AME Zion church and was heartened to find out that the bishops had agreed to welcome Paul in their churches nationwide. In August, Robeson returned to the U.S.-Canadian border. An audience of several thousand gathered to hear him sing and speak at Peace Arch Park under the auspices of the Mine, Mill and Smelter Workers Union. His speech at the event was defiant but fairly optimistic. He noted that he could not "act or sing in any sort of decent place" but hoped that he would be able to fulfill invitations to sing at the Eisteddfod festival in Wales and play Othello in England. Robeson spoke as one whose forefathers were from Africa and whose family was rooted "in the soil" of America through their toiling in tobacco and cotton. It was "on their blood" that he argued "a good piece of that American earth belongs to me" and "my children" and "my grandchildren." (He added here that he now had two grandchildren and "boy—they are sharp!") "It seems so simple," he reflected, "that all people should live in full human dignity and in friendship." Robeson promised he would continue "fighting for peace" because there was "no force on earth" that could make him "go backward one-thousandth part of one little inch."

The government was not backing down either. Robeson's passport application to go to the United Kingdom was turned down. The people who worked with the Council on African Affairs and *Freedom* newspaper offered an important support system for Robeson, but pressure was starting to mount in these organizations. The attorney general branded the Council on African Affairs as subversive. The group would have to register with the government according to the McCarran Act and appear before the Subversive Activities Control Board. "This attack on the Council," Robeson commented, was an attempt "to frighten" anyone who was "in any way critical of U.S. policies in Africa." Sadly, this was the beginning of the end for the Council, which soon had to spend more time vying for its existence than disseminating information on Africa. *Freedom* newspaper, meanwhile, was barely staying afloat financially. The group had kept subscription prices low to reach out to working people, but the calls for subscriptions in its pages were becoming more urgent. At least Robeson's personal income was somewhat buoyed by royalties from the British films he had made in the 1930s. Paul's weight had been increasing, so Eslanda encouraged him to close out the year by spending a few weeks focusing on diet and exercise at Howard University's medical center. There he dropped twenty pounds and returned feeling much healthier.

In his January 1954 *Freedom* column, Robeson denounced the militarism wrought by McCarthy-style anticommunism. He wondered what could be done if the tens of millions of dollars invested in military spending were redirected to "vast programs of peace-time construction." Segregated schools could be dramatically improved and housing could be improved for the poor, Robeson suggested. "I have no doubt," he concluded, "that we will beat back McCarthyism and restore our traditional liberties." Robeson was right that Joseph McCarthy's antics could not last. In 1954 he tried to prove that the army had been penetrated by Communists but was censured in the Senate and ended up dying just a few years later. He left behind a legacy of demagoguery that has become synonymous with his name. Robeson's mention of segregated schools was also timely. The court campaign mounted by the NAACP legal team had finally reached the Supreme Court. In the landmark *Brown v. Board of Education* decision of May 1954, the Court overturned a long-standing precedent by ruling that schools separated by race were not constitutional. Robeson was correct in predicting that "sections of the Dixiecrats" were "girding themselves for final struggle." Indeed, the backlash against *Brown* was ferocious in some places, and implementation was excruciatingly slow. After the Court's subsequent ruling vaguely mandated that desegregation should take place "with all deliberate speed," an article in *Freedom* accurately calculated that "the road ahead" was "not going to be an easy one."

That year Robeson also decried the Eisenhower administration's role in overthrowing the elected leaders of Guatemala and Iran. He was angered by the British jailing of Jomo Kenyatta and the move by the mainstream press to discredit the anticolonial movement in Kenya. Robeson's analysis of another anticolonial struggle, against the French in Vietnam, portrayed Ho Chi Minh as "the Toussaint L'Ouverture of Indo-China." These outspoken critiques of Cold War foreign policy probably did not help the passport case that he was still pursuing. In July 1954 Robeson applied for a passport to fulfill engagements in Britain and Europe. Meanwhile, an international movement in support of Robeson's right to travel was growing. The *Daily Worker* reported that messages of support were arriving at the office of the Provisional Committee to Restore Paul Robeson's Passport from Europe, Asia, Africa, the Caribbean, Canada, and South America. A letter from cultural and civic leaders in Johannesburg, South Africa, illustrated the global sentiment. The signers regretted that the U.S. government had deprived the world of Robeson's "wonderful voice" in a "political move." They believed, however, that Robeson represented "the true America" that existed "among ordinary people" and was rooted in a "love of peace." In England, a nationwide "Let Robeson Sing" campaign was created. The group mobilized press coverage and meetings, which were attended by scores of trade unionists and progressives.

In the spring of 1954, a "Salute to Paul Robeson" was held in Harlem. Over a thousand people, including entertainers Thelonious Monk and Pete Seeger as well as progressive writers Lorraine Hansberry and Alice Childress, turned up to back Robeson's passport fight. The support for Robeson was encouraging, but the State Department remained unmoved. They denied Robeson's passport application that summer. His only hope was to sign an affidavit stating that he was not a member of the Communist Party. However, Robeson steadfastly refused to do so arguing that it was a violation of his constitutional rights. He maintained that a citizen should be free to travel regardless of his political views. Robeson hired two new lawyers and pressed on with the fight.

There were some gratifying moments for Robeson in 1954. He performed again at Peace Arch Park that summer. Robeson's international program included spirituals, a folk song from Mexico, and excerpts from Antonin Dvorak and Modest Mussorgsky. The song "Scandalize My Name" was especially salient in the Cold War context. Robeson remarked in a newspaper interview that he was not only a citizen of the United States but also a citizen of the world. In the autumn, the *New World Review* hosted a tribute banquet to Paul and Eslanda, which was attended by about five hundred people. Earl Robinson directed a children's choir that sang for the crowd. Others in attendance included W. E. B. Du Bois, Shirley Graham Du Bois, Alphaeus Hunton, Louis Burnham, Lawrence Brown, and Howard Fast. Rockwell Kent introduced Robeson, who then offered a heartfelt tribute to his wife and her contributions to his development as an artist and a man. He honored the "magnificent heroism" of women in the current struggles for freedom. According to the *Daily Worker* account, the audience was "deeply stirred" by Robeson's words, and some even wept. In her comments on the current political climate, Eslanda reminded the audience that "some people forget that freedom and democracy, understanding and tolerance, peace and coexistence begin at home." Paul Robeson Jr. characterized this as a period in which his parents "revived their partnership." Paul and Eslanda decided to move in together in New York and settled into a brownstone in Harlem at 16 Jumel Terrace. They would both benefit from having a home base in the city and the mutual support of cohabitation.

By the middle of the decade, there were a few hopeful signs that Cold War acrimony was diminishing. Khrushchev was working on political reforms, and Eisenhower believed that diplomatic relations could be initiated. Eisenhower and Khrushchev held a summit in Geneva in 1955, which was the first time Soviet and American leaders had met since the Potsdam Conference ten years earlier. In the United States, McCarthy had been silenced, and free speech was being more openly embraced in some places. Students at the University of Chicago, for example, had defended Robeson's right to sing at their school in 1954 even when the local American Legion protested. The students who sponsored the Robeson appearance stated in their school paper, "We do not believe McCarthyism should be allowed to tell us what artists we can hear and appreciate." They were clearly not alone in their beliefs. A crowd packed Mandel Hall where Robeson performed, and a thousand more people had to be turned away.

Similarly, in early 1955, hundreds of hopeful attendees found that Townsend Harris Auditorium was already full thirty minutes before Robeson's appearance at the City College of New York. Following that concert,

Robeson had lunch in the school cafeteria, where students gathered around for autographs and discussions about current events. Robeson wrote about a visit that year to Swarthmore College in his *Freedom* column. He appreciated being able to both sing and have a dialogue with the students as part of their Forum for Free Speech. One thousand people attended the event, more than the school's entire enrollment, and Robeson concluded that "everyone seemed to enjoy the exercise of free speech on this occasion." An article in the college newspaper stated that in hosting Robeson "the honor was all ours." Even though the audience disagreed with some of his political views, the reporter was glad that Robeson had been given "a warm and generous reception."

In addition to the college appearances, an overflow crowd came out to hear Robeson at a church on Long Island. Robeson spoke before thousands at a May Day rally in Union Square in New York. He also traveled to San Francisco to give a concert in celebration of the United Nations' tenth anniversary. The program Robeson sang with Russian, Hebrew, Chinese, English, and German pieces reflected the diversity of the international forum. Not only was the concert a success but Robeson was also excited by the spirit among the people he encountered in California. He was pleased to sense "a new wind blowing" that was "full of promise" as "more people seem to be shaking off cold war hysteria." The *Daily Worker* reported that around fifteen thousand people made a pilgrimage to Robeson's fourth concert at the U.S.-Canada border at Peace Arch Park in the summer of 1955. At the show, Robeson said he looked forward to a victory in his passport struggle so that he could once again "join with audiences throughout the world in the exchange of national culture."

By this time, Robeson had been battling for his travel rights for five years, but it seemed like a break in his passport case could be in the offing. The U.S. Appeals Court in Washington, D.C., had mandated that passports could no longer be denied for Max Shachtman and Otto Nathan. The ruling referred to traveling as a right. Robeson's case looked especially hopeful since Shachtman was a member of the Independent Socialist League, a group that had been deemed subversive, and his right to travel was being restored. Robeson's attorneys again filed an application with the Passport Division of the State Department. In spite of the recent Appeals Court decision, Robeson's application was again denied. The State Department continued to insist that he sign a non-Communist affidavit as part of the administrative procedure for his application. Robeson's legal team appealed, but the judge ruled that he had not completed the administrative process because he had not signed the affidavit requested. Robeson's lawyers argued that the affidavit was not standard practice and was unconstitutional, but his passport application would not be considered. He was granted the right to travel into Canada, but Robeson could not visit other places where no passport was required. Predictions of a Cold War thaw, it seemed, had been premature.

The left-wing press and much of the black press was critical of the ban against Robeson's right to travel. J. A. Rogers, writing in the *Pittsburgh Courier*, wondered whether the State Department was singling out Robeson because of his race. Robeson suggested in a *Daily Worker* article that the government spend less time prosecuting his passport case and more time prosecuting the groups stirring racial violence in places like Mississippi. Representative Adam Clayton Powell Jr. from Harlem noted that "everyone should be free to travel" and commented publicly on the sentiment that was growing overseas. On a recent trip to Europe, he remarked that people asked about Robeson's right to travel "in every country" he visited. The public sentiment in favor of Robeson's right to travel was important, but the prolonged passport struggle was taking a toll. Because he could not travel to fulfill scores of overseas invitations, Robeson was deprived both financially and professionally. Of course, he had lost significant personal income because of the international travel ban. Additionally, many of his good performing years were partially squandered because he could not make use of his talent to its fullest potential. Still, Robeson's intransigent side would not allow him to simply sign an affidavit that violated his constitutional rights. It was a bold stand that came at a high cost.

The passport struggle meant that Robeson missed out not only on concert and acting engagements but also significant political events. In 1955, two thousand delegates from twenty-nine African and Asian nations met in Bandung, Indonesia. The conference was convened by the leaders of five nations (India, Burma, Pakistan, Ceylon, and Indonesia) to find ways "to cooperate with our Asian and African neighbors to live together in friendship and peaceful coexistence," as Kumar Goshal, the correspondent for *Freedom* newspaper, explained. The historic congress called for an end to

Western colonialism and stressed that many African and Asian countries did not want to be forced into Cold War alliances with either the Soviet Union or the United States. Rather than remaining in a different kind of subjugation, the people of Africa and Asia wanted to determine independently the best course for their nations. Though the conference was significant in that it marked the beginning of the nonalignment movement, it did not receive much favorable press coverage in the United States, nor did the government send an official delegation. The Council on African Affairs dedicated two entire issues of *Spotlight on Africa* to the Bandung conference, which was also covered in depth in *Freedom*. While neither W. E. B. Du Bois nor Robeson could attend, both sent messages to the congress. Kumar Goshal reported that the crowd cheered when their greetings were read to the assembly.

In his written message, Robeson saluted the historic conference. He observed that "the time has come when the colored peoples of the world will no longer allow the great natural wealth of their countries to be . . . expropriated by the Western world." The fact that these African and Asian nations gathered peacefully "to solve their common problems" should "stand as a shining example to the rest of the world," Robeson asserted. He closed with a slight lament, "How I would love to see my brothers from Africa, India, China, [and] Indonesia . . . at Bandung." He knew that "old friends" from his days in London in the 1930s when he first joined the anticolonial movement would be at Bandung. But because the State Department considered Robeson to be a "political meddler" on behalf of colonial Africa, he could not join them.

Unfortunately, Bandung was one of the last major stories covered by *Freedom* newspaper and *Spotlight on Africa*. The cover of the March 1955 issue of *Freedom* exclaimed, "Help! Unless we get immediate help from you, *Freedom* will die." The periodical continued to suffer financially from a lack of subscriptions, and Paul Robeson Jr. noted that both subscribers and distributors of the paper suffered from FBI harassment. The newspaper did not last until the end of the year. Meanwhile, the Council had been defending itself to the Subversive Activities Control Board for a couple of years. The group argued against the allegation that it was a Communist front on the grounds that Communist Party did not direct it, nor had it been created to aid the party. The Council's main objective was to disseminate news about

Africa, which it had undertaken since its founding in 1937. As evidence, the Council supplied examples of their copious correspondence with leaders in Africa as well as copies of their newsletters and other publications on Africa. However, a Council press release from 1953 pointed out that the real issue at stake was the right to advocate for African freedom. Just as advocacy for Africa lay at the heart of Robeson's passport case, it was also central to the Council's Cold War troubles. By the summer of 1955, Alphaeus Hunton pointed out at a meeting of the group's leadership that "continued government harassment" was making it "difficult if not impossible" to continue their work. The Council voted to disband at that meeting. Around this time, Othello Recording Company was also deteriorating financially. The Civil Rights Congress, with which Robeson had worked, folded in 1956. Robeson's progressive organizational networks were collapsing one by one.

To make matters worse, both Paul and Eslanda confronted major health problems in 1955. That autumn, after the disappointing news about his passport, Paul learned that Eslanda had been diagnosed with breast cancer. She had kept this news, at first, to herself as she had done with her illnesses in the past. Paul was surprised to find out only days before she had to undergo a mastectomy. The surgery went well, and after a recovery period Eslanda was back at work writing and observing in the United Nations. Not long after Essie's surgery, Paul began passing blood in his urine, and it was determined that he needed prostate surgery. Both Martin Duberman and Paul Robeson Jr. wrote that Paul faced this operation with considerable trepidation. It had already been a stressful year, and he knew the FBI was probably keeping tabs on his health. In fact, they were maintaining detailed reports about his physical well-being. Robeson decided that he did not want to be in a hospital outside of Harlem, where he felt safer, so he chose an urologist at Sydenham Hospital to undertake the surgery. In case the worst happened, Robeson revised his will before his hospital stay. The surgery was successful, and no cancer was found, but he had to remain hospitalized for several weeks. Recovery was slow going, and Paul Jr. noted that it was a couple of months before his father seemed more like "his normal self."

By early 1956, Robeson was well enough to travel to Canada for a few public engagements. He traveled with Alan Booth, who had been accompanying Robeson on piano for many of his concerts in the 1950s. The Mine, Mill and Smelter Workers convention welcomed Robeson's first appearance outside of the United States in almost six years. He assured the gathering that he would continue to use his art in the freedom struggle for his people. In Toronto, a capacity crowd of over two thousand filled Massey Hall for Robeson's concert. Though he was not quite at full strength, the critics found that his magnetic presence remained compelling, and the audience offered an enthusiastic standing ovation. Robeson remarked to the *Daily Worker*, which was reporting on his return to the concert stage, that "resuming his career as an artist" was still "bound up" with "the matter of getting a passport." He also commented that "far above any personal interests" he was "concerned" about the "critical situation in the South." Regrettably, Robeson found out upon his return from Canada that another appeal in his passport case had been dismissed. His lawyers, however, continued to press his case. The "critical situation" in the South to which Robeson referred had several facets. The vicious murder of African American youngster Emmett Till in Mississippi the previous summer fanned flames of righteous indignation, especially among black young people. Courageous individuals such as Autherine Lucy were challenging segregation in higher education. In Montgomery, Alabama, a bus boycott had gotten underway in December 1955 when activist Rosa Parks decided not to relinquish her seat on a city bus. Local civil rights and religious leaders formed the Montgomery Improvement Association to coordinate the boycott campaign. A new pastor in the city named Martin Luther King Jr. headed the group. Robeson monitored these events closely but maintained a healthy distance. Having been labeled a subversive by the U.S. government, his involvement could possibly endanger the nascent movement. Robeson was thus isolated from the emerging struggles for desegregation enforcement. However, his son observed that he "accepted his role" as a "forerunner rather than a direct participant" in the civil rights campaigns of the era following the *Brown* decision.

Significant international events were also taking shape in 1956. Khrushchev gave a speech at the Twentieth Congress of the Communist Party of the Soviet Union, which revealed the previously hidden extent of Stalin's crimes against the Soviet people. These revelations were circulated among party members internationally and published in the mainstream press. The effect on the Communist Party in the United States was debilitating. The party had already been in some disarray with the prosecution of its leadership and ongoing Cold War repression. News of Stalin's brutality from his successor drove scores of members from the group. Robeson's reaction to the speech was hard to discern. He never commented publicly about Khrushchev's revelations, but he did put in an appearance at the seventy-fifth birthday party for Communist Party leader William Z. Foster that year. Still, whatever his feelings might have been regarding the speech, he kept them to himself.

Around this time, Robeson was becoming increasingly, perhaps even compulsively, focused on musical theory. He spent many hours on the piano at Jumel Terrace teasing out a theory on musical scales. In the spring of 1956 a proposed Canadian concert tour was suddenly canceled. By May, Robeson was displaying worrying signs of depression. He was staying in bed, but not sleeping, and rarely eating. He refused psychiatric help but did take some pills to help him sleep. Toward the end of the month, Robeson was subpoenaed to appear before the infamous HUAC. The timing could hardly have been worse. Milton Friedman, the attorney who had accompanied Eslanda before McCarthy's committee, requested a formal postponement. Robeson's doctors supported the argument that he could not appear for medical reasons. The committee offered to put off Robeson's testimony but only until the second week of June. In the meantime, HUAC inquired whether the FBI could help the committee ascertain whether Robeson left his home between the original subpoena date and the newly scheduled date. If he did leave the house, the committee could cite him for contempt. A note on the memo, in what may be J. Edgar Hoover's handwriting, indicated that the FBI should not be making investigations for the House committee.

HUAC began as a temporary committee during the Depression. Run by Texas representative Martin Dies, HUAC raised questions about a variety of issues but was known for attempting to root out Communist infiltration in New Deal programs. When it became a standing committee in the mid-1940s, HUAC's antiradical program became apparent through its investigations of Alger Hiss and the Hollywood Ten. The committee's views on race were also fairly well known. HUAC, for example, declined investigating the Ku Klux Klan, which chairman Francis Walter did not view as a threat to civil liberties. Walter chaired the session when Paul Robeson testified on June 12, 1956. The topic under investigation was the unauthorized use of U.S. passports, but Robeson faced a wide variety of questions. Robeson was accompanied to Washington, D.C., by his wife, son, Lloyd Brown, and William Patterson. Anxiously waiting for Robeson's name to be called, Paul Jr. remembered his father "slumped" in a chair while the rest of their party, save attorney Milton Friedman, was "numb with fear." As soon as he strode into the committee's chamber, however, Robeson came alive. He was bold, confident, and sharp, even putting the committee members on the defensive during the hour-long session.

When the committee queried whether Robeson had been directed to sign a non-Communist affidavit to accompany his passport application, Robeson was forthright. "Under no conditions," he stressed, would he sign such a document, which he viewed to be "a complete contradiction of the rights of American citizens." The committee pressed Robeson as to whether he was a member of the Communist Party. Robeson first emphasized that it was a legal political entity like the Republican and Democratic parties. When the members pushed for a response, Robeson retorted, "Would you like to come to the ballot box when I vote . . . and see?" Robeson then invoked the Fifth Amendment, interrupted a questioner who inquired further, and told them to "forget it." When HUAC probed as to whether Robeson had ever used the alias "John Thomas," Robeson derided the query as "ridiculous." "My name is Paul Robeson," he defiantly replied, "and anything I have to say or stand for I have said in public all over the world, and that is why I am here today."

Chairman Walter posed a line of inquiry, and Robeson questioned him in return. Referring to the McCarran-Walter Act that tightened immigration law, Robeson pointed out that that he was the author of the bill that was going to "keep all kinds of decent people out of the country." "No, only your kind," Walter replied. Robeson clarified, "Colored people like myself . . ." Walter continued, "We are trying to make it easier to get rid of your kind, too." Robeson invoked the Fifth Amendment when asked about organizational affiliations. When the committee brought up the Council on African Affairs, Robeson highlighted that "the State Department itself" said that he should not be able to travel because he had "struggled for years for the independence of the colonial peoples of Africa." The committee wanted to know about the purpose of many of his journeys abroad. They asked why he did not stay in Russia if that was where he "felt for the first time like a human being." To this, Robeson was very direct: "Because my father was a slave, and my people died to build this country, and I'm going to stay here and have a part of it just like you. And no fascist-minded people will drive me from it. Is that clear?'"

Toward the end of the session, Robeson asserted that the committee members were the real un-Americans and that they "ought to be ashamed of themselves." Flustered, the chairman responded, "Just a minute, this hearing is now adjourned." "You should adjourn this forever," Robeson confirmed. Robeson asked several times throughout the hearing to read his prepared statement into the record as other witnesses had done. His request was denied. The committee probably was not used to dealing with such unflinching witnesses. To every question about the Soviet Union, he had countered with the U.S. record of exploitation against African Americans. Not only did Robeson refuse to succumb to their Red-baiting tactics but also he had questioned the very authority of HUAC. The black press and the left-wing press praised his performance enthusiastically. The *Afro-American* was pleased to hear Robeson call for protection of black citizens, the *Daily Worker* headline cheered Robeson for blasting racism, and the *Pittsburgh Courier* used the opportunity to demand the restoration of Robeson's passport. His triumphant encounter with HUAC boosted Robeson's mood significantly. He was soon tackling several projects, including collaborating on a memoir with Lloyd Brown and formulating his thoughts on musical theory into an article series. Robeson also began once again making public appearances.

In the autumn of 1956, Robeson encountered a hostile crowd when he attended a peace conference hosted by the National Council of American-Soviet Friendship. The protesters were registering their opposition to the Soviet Union's recent crackdown against political dissenters in Hungary. Eisenhower had decided against aiding the anti-Communist rebels or challenging Soviet influence in Eastern Europe. Also that year, Israel, France, and Britain collaborated on an attack against Egypt when Gamal Abdel Nasser tried to nationalize access to the Suez Canal. The Soviets offered assistance to Egypt, and Eisenhower, who had not been consulted before the assault, was irate. The coalition soon pulled out of Egypt. Robeson criticized the incident in Egypt as an indication that Western countries still had imperial goals in Africa. He was also critical of those in the United States who called for aid to the Hungarian rebels but did not advocate civil rights enforcement for African Americans. If the Soviets were violating the freedoms of the Hungarians, Americans needed to clean up their own record on civil rights before condemning anyone else. On the civil rights front, the Montgomery bus boycott concluded in late 1956 with a Supreme Court decision declaring segregation in public transportation to be unconstitutional. The high court, however, refused to hear arguments in Robeson's passport case. Undeterred, Robeson ended the year on a positive note. He was heartened by the emerging civil rights campaigns and forged ahead in the struggle for his right to travel.

By the spring of 1957, the Let Robeson Sing movement in Britain had grown significantly. The group included trade unionists, celebrities, ordinary citizens, and even a few ministers of Parliament from the Labour Party. There were around two hundred representatives from England, Scotland, and Wales who decided there should be a national committee to oversee the campaign. Cedric Belfrage, of the *National Guardian*, was a key organizer in the movement. In May, a connection via trans-Atlantic cable was arranged so that Robeson could sing, from a New York studio, for over a thousand fans in St. Pancras Town Hall in London. This meeting was aimed at urging the U.S. government to allow Robeson to travel. A succession of speakers spoke in favor of Robeson's rights and testified as to the high caliber of his artistry. But the "most thrilling" moments of the gathering occurred when Robeson's own voice regaled the crowd with "My Curly Headed Baby" and other musical selections. Robeson also kept busy performing a series of concerts on an extended visit to California. In the summer of 1957 there was some good news on the passport front. While Robeson still could not travel internationally, he could now visit places where no U.S. passport was required, such as Alaska, Hawaii, Puerto Rico, and Guam.

That year, a Prayer Pilgrimage was held at the Lincoln Memorial in Washington, D.C., to honor the third anniversary of the *Brown* decision and to encourage implementation of the ruling. The program included a line-up of singers and speakers culminating with an oration by Martin Luther King Jr. on voting rights. Ten years previously, Robeson had stood on those steps and called for antilynching legislation. Now, along with his wife and son, Robeson was among the twenty-five thousand people who attended the pilgrimage. Though he was not asked to speak, Robeson demonstrated his solidarity by supporting the campaign. Paul Jr. recalled that his father seemed unruffled by the fact that the organizers had ignored him. And something interesting happened among the people at the gathering. Robeson had "stationed himself" under a tree at the margin of the crowd, his son explained, and an informal receiving line unexpectedly emerged as a "steady stream" of well-wishers came over to greet the veteran activist. This spontaneous event offered an interesting metaphor for Robeson's status in the late 1950s. While much of the civil rights establishment had dissociated itself from Robeson, as illustrated by the distance between him and the leaders on the stage, there was affection for him among the grassroots of the black community.

Later that year, nine black students attempted to desegregate Central High School in Little Rock, Arkansas. Their presence made headlines and stirred the ire of segregationists across the South. In a dramatic display of noncompliance, Governor Orval Faubus called out the National Guard to block the students' access to the school. In Robeson's view, the events in Little Rock were "a symptom of the evils of racism" that "constituted a bold and desperate attack upon constitutional government." Ultimately, President Eisenhower enforced the *Brown* ruling by using national troops to protect the nine students and their right to attend the public high school.

In the autumn of 1957, the popular African American magazine *Ebony* published an interview with Robeson by journalist Carl T. Rowan. The title of the article was "Has Paul Robeson Betrayed the Negro?" and Rowan seemed to conclude overall that he had not. This was an important step toward Robeson's reentry into the mainstream public discourse. In a radio interview discussing the piece, Rowan admitted that he disagreed with Robeson on many topics. However, he also pointed out that when Robeson talked about freedom for black Americans or the right to travel, it was hard not to agree with him. That November, Robeson received an exciting invitation to participate in next year's season at the Shakespeare Memorial Theatre in Stratford-upon-Avon, England. This was the heart of Shakespeare country. General manager Glen Byam Shaw offered Robeson the role of Gower in the play *Pericles*. Robeson temporarily accepted but was not able to fulfill the invitation because of travel restrictions. However, the cases of Rockwell Kent and Walter Briehl were working their way to the Supreme Court, and those decisions could set a precedent for Robeson's right to travel overseas.

The following year, 1958, opened with new promise. Robeson was booked for concert dates in California and Chicago. Two thousand people came out on a drizzly day in Oakland to hear him sing. When there was trouble securing a venue in Pittsburgh, two local churches opened their doors to Robeson. His reception by the black community there was warm and enthusiastic. Appearances in Chicago that spring were equally well received. In April, the occasion of Robeson's sixtieth birthday was celebrated around the world. In an article for the *Sunday Worker*, Eslanda explained how birthday committees popped up in over a dozen countries. Some of the groups held concerts, meetings, or radio programs honoring Robeson. Additionally, telegrams, cards, letters, and gifts filled the mailbox at Jumel Terrace. Telephone calls and cables were still coming in even a week after his birthday. She wrote that "Paul is deeply moved by this extraordinary manifestation of friendship, concert and support." Also heartening was a new record deal from Vanguard Records. When it was released, *The Essential Paul Robeson* was the first commercial recording of Robeson's music in nearly a decade.

Robeson's memoir, *Here I Stand*, cowritten with Lloyd Brown, was also an important part of his resurgence in the late 1950s. The independent Othello Associates, a successor to Othello Recording Company, published the book. Though the mainstream media mostly overlooked it, the book was praised in the progressive press and was widely covered by African American papers. A headline in the *Pittsburgh Courier* excitedly announced: "Paul Robeson States His Case!" The *Afro-American* serialized portions of the book in five successive articles with photos in the spring of 1958. The book was marketed primarily by word of mouth but sold surprisingly well. The New York *Amsterdam News* described the clamor to get copies of Robeson's book as a "scramble." This was an apt observation. The first run of ten thousand copies sold out in six weeks, and another run of twenty-five thousand followed. Prices were kept low (one dollar for a paperback copy) to engage the broadest possible readership. Progressive bookstores, such as the Jefferson Book Shop in New York, carried the book. Union halls and other progressive venues also supported sales of the book. The *Sunday Worker* reported that one energetic railroad worker sold seventy-five copies to his coworkers. The FBI dutifully sent an informant to purchase two copies and followed its distribution closely. By May, about three months after its release, the *Pittsburgh Courier* reported that one hundred thousand copies had been sold.

Part autobiography and part political commentary, *Here I Stand* used portions of Robeson's life story to clarify his political perspective, which had often been distorted and maligned. Robeson declared at the outset in the author's foreword that he was "an American." He then explained the purpose of the book. Speaking "as an American Negro" whose life was "dedicated, first and foremost, to winning full freedom," Robeson sought to elucidate how he reached his "viewpoint to take the stand I have taken." The prologue chronicled his early years in the black community in New Jersey and the important influences of his father and the church.

In the body of the narrative, Robeson traced his political maturation through his years in London in the 1930s that aided the growth of his antifascism and anticolonialism. The Soviet Union, he pointed out, was the place where he first felt "secure and free" as an equal human being. For this reason, he had "warm feelings of friendship for the peoples of that land." He stressed his "deep conviction" that socialism was a system that was "economically, socially, culturally, and ethically superior to a system based on production for private profit." The ten principles adopted at the Bandung conference in 1955 represented Robeson's viewpoint on world affairs. These included respect for human rights, the sovereignty of nations and equality of all races, and settling international disputes by peaceful means and promoting cooperation.

The monograph also included a detailed argument on the right to travel. Robeson emphasized the indivisibility between freedom for African colonies and civil rights for African Americans. The "Negro question," he maintained, was "the crux" of the passport case. The State Department had cited Robeson's advocacy for African independence as not being in the country's best interests. To this, Robeson retorted, "Those who oppose independence for the colonial peoples of Africa are the real un-Americans!" A U.S. attorney had also noted that Robeson had "repeatedly criticized" social conditions faced by African Americans when he traveled overseas. In response, Robeson asserted, "Speaking truth abroad has been of great value to the struggle for Negro rights in America." Robeson was not only concerned about travel restrictions against himself. He regretted that W. E. B. Du Bois, an "architect" of the Pan-African Congress movement, had not been able to attend the historic celebrations when the African nation of Ghana achieved independence in 1957.

Robeson closed by calling for a mass movement for civil rights in the United States. He praised the courage of black persistence in places such as Little Rock and Montgomery. Forging a unity of purpose in the black community was a vital goal, in Robeson's view. Finally, he cautioned that Red-baiting black organizations served "no one but our people's worst enemies." He did believe in socialism but, overall, Robeson demonstrated in his book that full freedom for the people of the African diaspora had been, and continued to be, his first priority.

Perhaps the most potent symbol of Robeson's renaissance was his concert appearance at Carnegie Hall in May 1958. Performing at this prestigious music hall illustrated that Robeson had breached the curtain of domestic Cold War isolation. Paul Robeson was back onstage for his first major concert in New York in over ten years! Once the show was announced, it sold out so quickly that another date was scheduled, which also sold out. In addition, Vanguard Records wanted to make a recording to sell as a concert album. The *New York Times* reviewer remarked that the police officers stationed outside the venue were wholly unnecessary. This notice pointed out the diversity of the show: "Robeson sang, lectured, [and] even danced a tiny bit." A highlight was his recitation of Othello's final monologue, which showed considerable "art and vocal resource." The *Daily Worker* review commented that Robeson was in tune with his times as well as his music. The program included folk songs from many countries, accompanied by Alan Booth on piano, and even poetry from Pablo Neruda. The "magnetism" of the performer's personality cemented "an unsurpassed kinship with his audience." Six encores were necessitated at the second show as the audience "applauded with abandon," according to the *Pittsburgh Courier*. At this show, Robeson noted that it "looked like" he would be "traveling all around soon." Indeed, there was finally a break in the passport case in June 1958.

In a split decision, the Supreme Court ruled in the case of *Kent v. Dulles* that the State Department could not reject a passport application because of a citizen's political beliefs. This decision was in response to the cases of Rockwell Kent and Walter Briehl who were both, like Robeson, requested to sign a non-Communist affidavit in order to obtain a passport. The right to travel, the Court decided, was a liberty that could not be denied without due process. With a new precedent in place, the State Department relented. The arduous eight-year struggle for Robeson's passport, and that of many others including his colleague W. E. B. Du Bois, was finally over. Almost immediately, Paul and Eslanda reserved flights to London. Robeson was flooded with letters of congratulations and invitations for appearances. He wanted to accept Glen Byam Shaw's offer to play Othello in Stratford in the 1959 season. Other travel plans came together over the course of the summer. His son remembered that Robeson faced his departure somewhat ambivalently. Of course, the restoration of his passport was a triumph, but now he felt obligated to visit all of the people around the world who had helped secure his right to travel. This was happening just as the black freedom movement was gaining steam in America. Robeson worried that going abroad at this juncture would render him "irrelevant" in his peoples' struggle. Paul Jr. tried to reassure him at the time but, several years later, considered his father's sentiment to be "prophetic."

By all accounts, Robeson received a hero's welcome at the airport in London. A crowd of about two hundred came out to welcome Paul and Eslanda back to England. A dispatch to the *Sunday Worker* described the moment when the beloved artist landed: "As the plane door opened a great silence fell . . . One by one the passengers appeared, and a great sigh of relief was followed by the traditional British '3 cheers' as Paul waved to the crowd." It was as if his supporters could not really believe he had made it until seeing him in person. Settling into London, the British embrace of Robeson was expressed daily. Taxi drivers refused payment and asked for autographs instead. Cedric Belfrage remembered that on Robeson's morning walks, there were "hands to shake on every block." Reflecting later on the welcome he received, Robeson commented, "I have never been met with more warmth. . . . The reception that I have had here has passed all bounds." Right away, Robeson's calendar filled with appearances. He officially accepted the offer to portray Othello for the hundredth anniversary season in Stratford-upon-Avon. Several television appearances were booked, a signing was organized for his book *Here I Stand*, and there was a dinner hosted by a Nigerian minister. Robeson visited the Welsh Eisteddfod music festival and sang to a packed house at London's Albert Hall with Lawrence Brown on piano. A few critics chided Robeson for using a microphone, but the audience was "thrilled" by his "warm humanity." Interestingly, a young Harry Belafonte was making his London debut the same night. A longer British concert tour was scheduled for Robeson in the autumn season.

In mid-August, the Robesons headed to the Soviet Union for a tour sponsored by the Ministry of Culture. In Moscow, Robeson received an eager welcome. Crowds gathered at both the airport and their hotel, and they offered the couple flowers and heartfelt greetings. People on the street and going by in buses waved and called out to Robeson. He made a television appearance, and eighteen thousand people crammed into an enormous sports complex to hear him sing. The Robesons also visited Eslanda's brother, Frank, who had been living in the Soviet Union since the 1930s and was raising a family there. After a quick visit to the capital of Uzbekistan for a film festival, the Robesons traveled to the Crimean coast for some rest. Stopping first at Sochi on the Black Sea, they then made their way to Yalta to relax at a government rest house for two weeks. Toward the end of August, Paul and Eslanda received an invitation to visit Khrushchev's summer retreat where he was entertaining several heads of state. At dinner, Robeson and Khrushchev chatted in Russian about various issues, including their shared acquaintance with India's leader Jawaharlal Nehru and the freedom struggle in the United States. Back home, some newspapers charged that Robeson's visit with Khrushchev was proof that he was a stooge of the Soviets, while other media outlets cited the dinner as evidence of Robeson's esteemed artistic stature overseas.

Returning to the United Kingdom in September, Robeson embarked on a three-month tour with Lawrence Brown. Adoring fans filled auditoriums across England, Scotland, Wales, and Ireland to demonstrate their enduring love for Robeson. Critics were also pleased. They wrote about Robeson's "zest and friendliness of manner" and the "lovable creative touches" in the program. Most found his voice to be "little impaired by the years" and marveled at the way in which Robeson's "mixture of dignity and charm" held audiences "spell bound." In October, Robeson became the first layperson to read scripture at St. Paul's Cathedral in London during a recital at an evening service. Reporting on the special event for the Associated Negro Press, Eslanda noted that Paul must have been thinking of his father, Reverend William Drew Robeson, and his brother, Reverend Benjamin Robeson, when he stood behind the lectern. Paul sang several selections, including "We Are Climbing Jacob's Ladder," "Every Time I Feel the Spirit" and "Balm in Gilead," with Lawrence Brown playing by his side. In her account, Eslanda observed that the capacity crowd was remarkably diverse, with many Africans and West Indians in attendance. During one hymn, a collection was taken in support of the defendants in a trial currently going on in South Africa. Known collectively as "the treason trial," over one hundred antiapartheid activists had been charged by the government with committing treason. Following the service, Robeson was besieged by fans and supporters. He signed autographs for the choir and tried to slip out a side door but found a crowd of about five hundred people waiting for him outside. Fairly overwhelmed, Robeson remarked to a reporter, "I am terribly moved by this tremendous demonstration for me. I am close to tears about it."

In late December 1958, the Robesons flew to Moscow, where they celebrated the New Year holiday at a formal event. W. E. B. Du Bois and his wife, Shirley Graham, were also there as they were spending some time abroad following the restoration of Du Bois's passport. The plan was for the Robesons to continue to India before returning to England for *Othello* rehearsals. However, both Robesons fell ill and were hospitalized in Moscow. Paul suffered from dizzy spells and flu-type symptoms that possibly stemmed from exhaustion. Eslanda was diagnosed with a precancerous condition in her uterus. She would have to stay to undergo a series of treatments. Eslanda urged Paul to cancel the theater engagement at Stratford and to rest instead. Glen Byam Shaw was devastated by the news that Robeson was not going to appear in *Othello*. He pushed back rehearsals until March and entreated Robeson to reconsider. After undertaking a month of diet, exercise, and rest at the Barvikha Sanatorium, Robeson felt well enough to reacquaint himself with Shakespeare's Moor. In March, he headed to England while Eslanda stayed in Moscow to finish the round of treatments.

Back in England, Robeson traveled to the bucolic village of Stratford-upon-Avon in the Cotswolds to begin rehearsals at the Shakespeare Memorial Theatre. He was headlining the production of *Othello*, which opened a historic anniversary season that also included Laurence Olivier's portrayal of Coriolanus. The *Othello* revival premiered in April, the month when the beloved playwright's birth was celebrated in his hometown. During the run of the play, Robeson settled into a suite of rooms that he rented in a farmhouse in nearby Shottery. His landlady owned the house and lived on the property with her family, who promptly took Robeson into their fold. The *Othello* production was rather unorthodox under the direction of the young, up-and-coming Tony Richardson. He used what critics ended up viewing as a lot of extraneous gimmicks that detracted from the overall pathos of the play. In this high-energy production, there were fireworks exploding, swords clashing vigorously, and Great Danes loping across the stage. Unfortunately, this nontraditional approach contrasted with Robeson's dignified interpretation of Othello. Joining Robeson onstage were Sam Wanamaker as Iago and Mary Ure, who played Desdemona. Some critics were irritated that the two principle roles were portrayed by Americans, and some complained about Wanamaker's accent. Ure was rather inexperienced, and numerous reviewers hastened to critique her interpretation of Othello's wife.

Despite these drawbacks, reviewers were satisfied with Robeson's performance, which was widely praised although the revival as a whole received mixed notices. The public seemed to love the show, which remained sold out for much of its run from April to November. Opening night was nothing short of a triumph for Robeson. Coming out of an illness and into an unconventional production, he had nonetheless enchanted the audience. One longtime reporter who had been to most of the openings at Stratford observed that the ovation for Robeson was like none he had ever seen. The writer for London's *Daily Worker* felt that the thunderous applause could have shaken the very brickwork of the building. Robeson disclosed to a reporter that he was "overwhelmed" by the reception of the crowd. After the cast offered Robeson a backstage birthday toast, he declared that it had been one of the greatest nights of his life.

Following an intense opening schedule, Robeson was committed to *Othello* only two or three nights a week. Eslanda took a flat in London, and Paul could go back and forth between there and Stratford. Numerous friends stopped through Stratford, including Du Bois and his wife, Alphaeus Hunton, Sam and Helen Rosen, and Bob and Clara Rockmore. Paul Jr. came over for an extended visit with his wife and children. His son remembered Robeson seeming "fulfilled and at peace" in Stratford. The townspeople enjoyed having him around, and he got along well with his acting colleagues. Robeson also found time to put in other appearances in London at the West Indian Festival, an African Freedom Day event, and a disarmament rally in Trafalgar Square. He also visited the May Day celebrations in Glasgow and the World Youth Festival in Vienna. Robeson was practically mobbed by African and Asian young people when he arrived at the airport in Austria. The World Youth Festival had left-wing sponsors but included a variety of young delegates from all over the world who came together under the theme of friendship and peace. Robeson's remarks focused on the growing civil rights movement in the United States and the antiapartheid campaigns in South Africa.

The *Othello* production wrapped up in late 1959, and Robeson was pondering a tour of Australia and New Zealand for the next year. He felt pulled toward returning home at times, but the prospects for work in the United States were not reliable. He also felt a certain obligation to his fans around the world now that he could travel. In addition, there was the issue of FBI surveillance, which was occurring in Britain and would probably be intense back in the United States. Above all, Robeson needed rest. It had been a long and tumultuous decade for him both personally and professionally. After a long period of repression, there had been some extremely rewarding moments once Robeson had regained the right to travel. Completing the engagement in Stratford had been particularly satisfying. However, the passport fight and other stresses of the 1950s had taken a toll. When he was visiting Stratford, Robeson revealed to his son that he was "getting tired inside."

6

FINAL CURTAIN

In January 1960, Paul and Eslanda Robeson headed to Moscow, where they both had medical check-ups. Paul was found to be in good health, although he could stand to lose a few pounds. Essie had been suffering from an ulcer, and treatment kept her in the Soviet Union for a few extra weeks. While in town, Paul made a number of public appearances and especially enjoyed visiting the workers at a ball-bearing plant. In an article in the *Moscow News*, Robeson was quoted as saying that he was "very happy and proud" to see the "advances of the Soviet people." "Come and see this exciting Socialist land," he urged readers. In February, Robeson flew back to England for a spring concert tour with Lawrence Brown. The tour visited over thirty cities and lasted until May. British audiences were thrilled to once again have Robeson in their midst. The audience's enthusiasm prompted a reporter in Liverpool to describe the show as a "succession of encores" that was interrupted by a musical program. Reviewers were equally ebullient. Most found his voice to be "as powerful" and "as majestic as ever." A critic from Yorkshire admired the "infinite variety" that characterized Robeson's programs. While some preferred that Robeson sing more and talk about politics less, one critic from Newcastle reached a thoughtful conclusion. "He never lets us forget that his father was a slave," the reviewer summarized, "but he does make us feel that the road to complete emancipation and race equality can be travelled with less weariness and bitterness because of the gift of song."

When Eslanda returned to London, she settled into the flat at 45 Connaught Square. That summer, after slimming down a bit, Robeson set off for appearances in Paris and Budapest. Essie accompanied him on a trip to East Berlin, where Paul was awarded an honorary doctorate from Humboldt University. Although Robeson was tempted to visit the newly independent nation of Ghana in West Africa, he took an offer for a concert tour of Australia and New Zealand instead. The tour would be lucrative, and Eslanda hoped that the money would enable him to retire. In October, the Robesons journeyed with Lawrence Brown for the eight-week engagement. Overall, his visit was very warmly received. Several reviews remarked that Robeson's presence had long been anticipated. "A legend had come true," one review commented. Another noted that "probably no overseas artist" had "been more eagerly awaited than Robeson." The varied program included spirituals, world folk songs, classical selections, and a recitation of Othello's final monologue, which illustrated "how compelling and commanding he must be on the dramatic stage."

Many of the reviewers especially appreciated his onstage presence, which they found to be "charged with sincerity," "shaped with an intuitive feeling," and projecting an "aura of benevolence and goodwill." Two outdoor appearances must have been highlights. More than two thousand people crowded a railroad junction to hear Robeson, while children climbed trees and young people peeked out of nearby balconies to get a glimpse the performer. He also gave an "unscheduled" and "unrehearsed" show for the workmen and seagulls at the Sydney Opera House, which was still under construction. The tour was a professional and financial success. (He made around $150,000 for concerts and other appearances.) However, the traveling and hectic pace of the tour had exhausted Robeson by the time he returned to London in December. After a period of rest, he began to consider his itinerary for 1961. He was ready to go back home, but Eslanda was concerned about his safety and tried to dissuade him. Robeson pondered a trip to Moscow followed by several stops in West Africa and a possible appearance in Cuba before going on to the United States. He headed to Moscow in March 1961 but did not end up continuing on to Africa or Cuba.

While Robeson had been touring, major events were unfolding globally. The United States now had a young Catholic president from Massachusetts. It was not quite clear to what extent John F. Kennedy was committed to supporting civil rights for African Americans. Early in 1960, four African American college students started the sit-in movement that spread quickly across the South and garnered northern support from politicians such as Adam Clayton Powell Jr., who urged a national boycott of stores that segregated their lunch counters. This campaign culminated in the formation of the Student Nonviolent Coordinating Committee (SNCC) in the spring of 1960. While civil rights activists were on the move, Africa was transitioning as well. By 1960 over a dozen countries on the continent had achieved independence from Europe. A wind of change, as British prime minister Harold Macmillan famously observed, was blowing across Africa. Robeson perceived from Australia that "a new day has dawned in Africa." He also looked forward to peace, complete disarmament, and "friendship and understanding with our neighbors."

Indeed, Cold War dynamics were evolving at this time. In 1959 friendlier relations between the United States and the Soviet Union seemed to be on the horizon. The two countries exchanged exhibitions that illustrated their national values. Khrushchev and then vice president Richard Nixon even engaged in an informal dialogue about material culture while standing next to a mock-up of a modern U.S. home. This became known as the "kitchen debate." Meanwhile, the United States had been secretly sending spy planes into Soviet airspace. When one of these planes was shot down in the spring of 1960, the relationship between the two competitors quickly turned acrimonious once again. In the Western hemisphere, Fidel Castro had taken over leadership of Cuba after the successful revolution in 1959. Late in 1960 he announced that Cuba, which was less than one hundred miles from the Florida coast, was aligning with the Soviet Union. The CIA, among other groups, began plotting to oust Castro.

It was in this climate, then, that Castro and Khrushchev attended the UN session in New York in the autumn of 1960. Castro held court at the Hotel Theresa in Harlem, where large crowds came out to greet Khrushchev when the two leaders met. Paul Robeson Jr. was invited to meet with two of Castro's aides, who extended an invitation for his father to visit Cuba. Paul Jr. suggested that travel arrangements be made with his father in London. Security for such a trip would be important as Robeson was being monitored by intelligence agencies. Paul Robeson Jr.'s meeting with the Cubans in New York and the invitation they offered to his father were carefully noted in Robeson's FBI file. The report on a possible trip to the island referred to an invitation from "the guy" (presumably Castro) to visit Cuba. In fact, Castro himself telephoned Robeson's flat in London in March 1961. When a friend of Robeson's answered the phone and disclosed who it was, Robeson decided not to take the call. Given the current Cold War tension, discussing such a trip over the phone probably was not safe.

As Robeson sensed, the political climate had become hazardous. In January 1961 the CIA had been involved in the murder of Patrice Lumumba, who was the first prime minister of an independent Congo and had a left-leaning, Pan-African perspective. In April, the CIA supported an invasion at the Bay of Pigs to overthrow Castro. The incursion was repelled, but relations between the United States and Cuba as well as the Soviet Union deteriorated even further. In 1962 a crisis ensued when Khrushchev decided to install missiles in Cuba that could reach the United States. Thus, Robeson had been inadvertently contemplating a trip to Cuba during a period of intense U.S. covert activity. A report in Robeson's FBI file from April 1961, the same month as the Bay of Pigs invasion, commented on the possible international ripple effects of Robeson's death. "In view of the past exploitation of Robeson's popularity by the communists," the document noted, "it is expected that the death of Robeson would be much publicized . . . and highlighted even more in propagandizing on behalf of the international communist movement." The report closed by mentioning that Robeson's activities would continue to be monitored. Was this mere speculation, or were plans against Robeson being devised? Paul Robeson Jr. wrote that he was alerted in 1964 by a former CIA agent that an idea to solve "the Robeson problem" had been proposed in the late 1950s. He also suggested that the CIA could have been involved in his father's collapse in Moscow in March 1961.

When Robeson arrived in the Soviet Union in the spring of 1961, issues of security were paramount in his mind. He knew about Lumumba's assassination and that he was under surveillance. Feeling energetic, Robeson made numerous appearances once he arrived in Moscow. He also stated publicly that he planned to visit Ghana, Guinea, and Cuba as well as Hungary and the German Democratic Republic that year. On the evening of March 26 he retreated to his hotel room for bed, but the next morning he was found on the bathroom floor of his suite with lacerations on his wrists. Eslanda flew from London right away, and Paul Jr. came from New York a few days later. Paul refused to see his wife in the hospital. Doctors diagnosed him as suffering from paranoiac psychosis accompanied by depressive symptoms and arteriosclerosis. Martin Duberman wrote that a bipolar depressive disorder could have been aggravated in Robeson by the prolonged government harassment that he had endured. Duberman noted that probably anyone subjected to the kind of repression Robeson had encountered could be susceptible to a breakdown whether or not one had a "predisposition" to depression. In his biography, Paul Jr. explored the possibility that his father's suicide attempt could have been induced by a drug such as LSD.

When he was in Moscow, Paul Jr. did some investigating around the mysterious circumstances of his father's breakdown. Paul had, for example, told the translator traveling with him that he planned to retire early on the night of the twenty-sixth because he had an early appointment in the morning. However, other guests complained about the noises of a loud party coming from his room late into the night. Paul Jr. was suspicious about the party and wondered whether his father had been deceived into hosting some guests, one of whom could have slipped something into his drink. The CIA had been running experiments on various mind-altering drugs, including LSD, since the 1950s under the auspices of the MKULTRA project. According to John Marks in *The Search for the "Manchurian Candidate,"* this secret program carried out the "ultra-sensitive" work of investigating "whether and how it was possible to modify an individual's behavior by covert means." Since LSD tends to exaggerate a person's existing traits, any nascent depression or anxiety could have been intensified by the drug and helped instigate Robeson's breakdown. The CIA was actively plotting against Castro at this time, and perhaps the agency wanted to prevent Robeson from traveling there. According to Robeson's FBI file, information on his health status that year had been forwarded to the CIA and other departments. Whether or not the CIA was in any way involved in his breakdown, Robeson certainly never made it to Cuba.

His wrist wounds were healing, and Robeson was well enough to enjoy a small birthday celebration in the hospital in early April. Paul Jr. recorded that engaging his father in conversation could sometimes be difficult, as he was "suspicious of everyone." Paul Jr. continued to ask around about his father's breakdown while he was in Moscow. For instance, he wondered whether drug tests been done on Paul when he entered the hospital. Who were the people who had been at the party in his room? Had anyone tried to talk to them? Yet he was advised by Soviet officials to leave the matter alone. Moreover, Eslanda did not buy the drugging scenario at all. In the midst of these events, Paul Jr. suffered a breakdown himself while in Moscow that he believed was drug induced. He chronicled feeling strangely after a banquet at the hotel where he was staying. That night, he experienced hallucinations, suffered from acute paranoia, and threw a chair through a pair of French doors. He wandered the streets, afraid that he was being followed, was straightjacketed, and woke up in a psychiatric hospital. Paul Jr. traveled to join his parents at Barvikha Sanatorium when he was sufficiently recovered. The Soviet doctors had recommended that a full retirement from public life would be the most effective road to long-term recovery for Paul. They also suggested that the familiar environment of America would aid his recuperation, and Paul had expressed a desire to go home. His immediate recovery at the sanatorium was going well. In early June, he and Eslanda went back to their flat in London where life carried on pretty routinely. Paul undertook musical rehearsals with Lawrence Brown and was considering a trip to Ghana. Kwame Nkrumah had personally invited Robeson to contribute to the music and drama program at the University of Accra.

However, Robeson relapsed into a debilitating depressed state that summer, and Eslanda took him back to the Soviet Union for treatment. After another period of hospitalization followed by convalescence at Barvikha, Robeson returned to England in September 1961. Upon returning to London, Robeson's anxiety became incapacitating. Eslanda telephoned Helen Rosen in New York, who came over to help right away. Because he was in no condition to fly back to the Soviet Union, Paul was checked into the Priory, a psychiatric hospital in London. In retrospect, Paul Jr. questioned the choice of the consulting psychiatrist who cared for his father as well as the failure of the doctors in England to contact the doctors in the Soviet Union, or even Robeson's primary care physician from New York, for case histories. Nevertheless, Robeson was provisionally diagnosed as suffering from chronic depression and being suicidal.

The London doctors believed that electroconvulsive therapy (ECT) could be immediately beneficial for Robeson. ECT uses an electric current directed into the brain to generate a brief seizure. It can lead to memory loss, but it can also offer short-term benefits quickly to patients who are not responsive to other treatments. The therapy was first introduced in Europe in the late 1930s and was used fairly widely through the 1940s and 1950s. It was viewed as more controversial in the 1960s and 1970s, and public perception became more negative especially after the publication of Ken Kesey's novel *One Flew over the Cuckoo's Nest* in 1962, which, interestingly, was when Robeson was receiving ECT in England. While scientists today are still not exactly sure how it works, ECT can be effective for some patients with severe depression and it is still used, often in conjunction with drug therapy and psychoanalysis. In mid-September of 1961 Robeson was started on a course of ECT, and another followed in October. Eslanda signed the consent forms for the ECT but did not tell her son about these treatments. Over the course of the next twenty months, Robeson received fifty-four ECT treatments. Paul Jr. was alarmed at the length of this treatment when he learned of it years later. He also noted that the doctors who initially treated Robeson in the Soviet Union were strongly against using ECT on Robeson. Additionally, Martin Duberman pointed out that Robeson was started on ECT only days after arriving at the Priory. Perhaps other treatments could have first been explored before undertaking rounds of therapy that could have had very serious side effects.

Nevertheless, Robeson seemed to respond positively to the ECT. He was taking day trips to the Connaught Square flat by November and left the hospital for Christmas. In January 1962, however, he again entered the Priory for depression and insomnia. Thereafter, Robeson experienced "up cycles" when he functioned fairly well and dealt with "down cycles" when depression and anxiety could be virtually incapacitating. This would be a long-term struggle. More ECT treatments were prescribed in early 1962, and these were, at times, supplemented by a variety of powerful medications. By March, Robeson had improved and wanted to go along with Eslanda to an Ella Fitzgerald concert. The outing was a success, with Fitzgerald even dedicating a song to Robeson, who visited her backstage after the show. Robeson was also up to attending a production of *The Cherry Orchard*, which starred Peggy Ashcroft, who had portrayed Desdemona to his Othello in 1930. Robeson chatted amiably with Ashcroft backstage following the play. In April 1962, Robeson received birthday greetings from all over the world. Kwame Nkrumah once again extended an invitation to Ghana. Two of Robeson's colleagues from the Council on African Affairs,

W. E. B. Du Bois and Alphaeus Hunton, had settled in Ghana in the early 1960s. Unfortunately, he would not be able to visit them there.

Robeson's passport needed to be renewed in May, which necessitated a visit to the U.S. embassy in London. Accompanied by Bob and Clara Rockmore, who were in town, Robeson's passport application was successfully filed. Yet the State Department informed Eslanda in July that she and her husband would have to sign non-Communist affidavits in order to have their passports renewed. Without passports, the Robesons could not renew their resident permits in England. Given Robeson's delicate state of health, Martin Duberman suggested that what should have been a routine matter was extended to the point of harassment. While Duberman did not find any evidence pointing to government complicity in Robeson's breakdown, he pointed out that U.S. agencies "proved perfectly willing to assist" the further decline of his health. Eslanda fired off a statement immediately as to her political affiliation. Robeson, on the other hand, was conflicted since this had been a sticking point in his passport case in the 1950s. Eslanda was concerned that this issue could impact Paul's mental health, and she enlisted help. Ben Davis and others friends were able to convince Paul that he had done his share of struggling with the State Department, and others would now continue the fight. He reluctantly agreed to sign an affidavit.

Robeson spent time between the Connaught Street flat and the Priory throughout the autumn and winter of 1962. He showed signs of recovery, though somewhat unevenly. The doctors experimented with drug treatments, and in early 1963 Robeson underwent another course of ECT. Eslanda worried that news of Bob Rockmore's untimely death in the spring of that year would send Robeson into a down cycle, so she waited a month to tell Paul. Rockmore had been a close friend and manager of Robeson's career for many years. Robeson wrote a heartfelt letter to Clara upon hearing the news. Eslanda encouraged friends and associates from around the world to send messages for Paul's birthday that April. Ironically, this had the opposite effect than what she had intended. Paul became very anxious by the flood of mail and was concerned that he could not meet the expectations of his well-wishers.

Around this time, Paul Jr. called a meeting in New York with several doctors to discuss his father's health. He felt that his father might respond more positively to an environment like the Barvikha Sanatorium, which provided some social stimulation for patients. The idea of relocating Paul to the Buch Clinic in the German Democratic Republic was proposed, and the next step was to convince Eslanda. Claire Hurwitt, a former psychiatric nurse who had also been involved in progressive politics, agreed to talk with Essie and visit Paul at the Priory. Hurwitt was dismayed by the considerable doses of strong drugs that were being administered to Paul and was surprised by the high number of ECT treatments that had been prescribed. She urged Essie to move Paul to the Buch Clinic in East Berlin as soon as possible. Eslanda visited the German clinic and liked what she saw there. She was also impressed by Dr. Alfred Katzenstein, who had been trained in the United States and had worked with concentration camp survivors after the war.

Arrangements were made in late August 1963 to move Paul as efficiently as possible without alerting the press. Avoiding the media was vital, as stories had been recently circulating that Robeson was disillusioned with Moscow. Newspapers would want verification even though Eslanda had stressed that "Paul is no longer a public figure." Eslanda, along with a cluster of allies, cleverly orchestrated the logistics of getting the Robesons to the airport along with their eleven pieces of luggage without tipping off the reporters outside the Connaught Square flat. When Paul and Eslanda arrived at the airport, they were helped onto the plane while the cooperative director of the airline had guided the press to a VIP lounge. One enterprising reporter managed to get onto the flight, which angered Eslanda, who restricted him to two questions. Paul proved willing to engage with the reporter and assured him that he had not changed his political views. He also remarked that the March on Washington that month represented a "turning point" for African Americans.

Robeson stayed at the Buch Clinic for about four months. The doctors there dramatically slimmed down the number of medications Paul was prescribed, put him on a diet, and encouraged him to interact with the other patients. Soon he became more attentive and was sleeping better. Katzenstein was pleased that there did not seem to be any brain damage but was unsettled by the prolonged use of ECT and strong sedatives on Paul. He additionally surmised that Robeson's confidence had been undercut by the treatments in London and that might have increased his anxiety. Paul began socializing more as he improved, even visiting with Ollie Harrington, a cartoonist he knew from Harlem who now lived in Berlin. The outlook for Eslanda's health, however, was not good when she had a medical exam. She was told that cancer was spreading even though doctors in London had assured her that she was healthy. She chose not to share the gloomy diagnosis with her husband. For several weeks Eslanda also hesitated to tell Paul that his brother Ben had died of cancer in late 1963. It seemed to be time to return home. The doctors suggested a complete retirement, and it would be beneficial to be closer to friends and family. The couple flew to New York by way of London a few days before Christmas.

When the Robesons landed in the United States for the first time since 1958, Paul Jr. and other members of the family were there to greet the couple. According to the *Detroit News* account, "deep lines" were apparent on Robeson's "emaciated face," but he still "strode briskly" to the terminal. A group of reporters showered him with questions. Some questions were ignored or answered by Eslanda. However, when he was asked if he would take part in the civil rights fight, Robeson pointedly replied, "Yes, I was part of the civil rights movement all my life." Paul settled back into the brownstone at Jumel Terrace with Eslanda. Paul Jr. visited daily and found that his mother was insistent about her husband's care. However, Paul Jr. considered the hospitalization in London to have been detrimental and became very involved in supporting his father's health. Without the full burden of care on her shoulders, Eslanda could get back to covering the United Nations and making public appearances as her health allowed. At a tribute to W. E. B. Du Bois, who died in the summer of 1963 at the age of ninety-five, she received extended applause from the audience. Paul Jr. encouraged friends such as Clara Rockmore to visit his father. Lloyd Brown would stop by and sometimes take Paul to call on other friends. Paul Jr. drove him to Pennsylvania to see his older sister. Paul's sister, Marian, a retired schoolteacher, was widowed and lived in Philadelphia with her daughter. He felt comfortable in Marian's twelve-room house at 4951 Walnut Street on the west side of the city. Her house, in fact, became a refuge where Paul felt secure and nurtured. Philadelphia, then, became a second home to Paul. By June 1964, he was sleeping better and gaining weight. His doctor proclaimed that he was again "the Paul Robeson" who had a "lively interest in life."

Bad news came in August when Ben Davis died of pancreatic cancer. Robeson had visited his friend in the hospital and spoke at his funeral in

Harlem. In his remarks, Paul reflected on the period when he and Ben had first met thirty-five years earlier. As young men, they had been focused on their future law careers as well as the game of football. Passersby were bemused when the two athletes practiced football tactics on the sidewalk. Robeson also used this opportunity to remember W. E. B. Du Bois and Ben Robeson, who had passed away at a time when his health prevented him from offering a proper good-bye. This was for him "a time of deep sorrow." Soon after Davis's funeral, Robeson made his first public statement to the African American press. Characteristically, he framed the brief essay as a response to a man on the street who asked how Paul had been feeling and what he had been doing. He thanked everyone who had wished him well during his "period of exhaustion." While he was improving, he wrote that he would stay in retirement but that he felt "deeply involved with the great upsurge of our people." Robeson admired and was proud of the thousands of "Negro Freedom Fighters" who were now mobilizing. He also mourned for Medgar Evers and the four girls killed by the church bomb in Birmingham. "The 'long hot summer' of struggle for equal rights," Robeson hoped, had "replaced the 'Cold War' abroad as the concern of our people."

Even though he had been advised to retire completely, Robeson felt compelled to appear publicly on occasion. In the autumn of 1964 Robeson put in visits to a Soviet reception at the United Nations and a mass meeting at Carnegie Hall for the National Council of American-Soviet Friendship. By now, Khrushchev had been replaced by Leonid Brezhnev, who ended many of his predecessor's reformist efforts. Robeson was greeted warmly at Carnegie Hall, where he highlighted the importance of friendship in his brief comments. He also wrote a reminiscence of Du Bois for *Freedomways* journal. *Freedomways*, a quarterly publication, had recently been started to document the contemporary civil rights struggles. As the name implied, it was a progressive descendent of *Freedom* newspaper. Robeson's essay on his friend and colleague appeared in the first issue of the new periodical in the winter of 1965. Robeson recalled his first memory of Du Bois as a student when he felt proud of Du Bois's scholarship on Africa and race relations. Young people spoke of Du Bois as "the Doctor" or "the Dean," and always did so with great respect. Robeson contextualized Du Bois's statesmanship through his pioneering organizing of the Pan-African Congresses in the early twentieth century. Not only was his book *The World and Africa* an important analysis of postwar Africa, but the Council on African Affairs was "very fortunate and proud" when the Doctor became a member. During the years that *Freedom* was operating, Du Bois had been a frequent and "brilliant" contributor. Finally, Robeson reflected on his last memory of his friend, which occurred during "less happy circumstances." Marveling at the elder scholar's remarkable longevity, Robeson explained that Du Bois stopped through London in 1962 between trips to China and Ghana, and, at age ninety-three, "visited *me* in a nursing home!"

Another sad occasion occurred in January 1965 when the acclaimed writer Lorraine Hansberry died of cancer at the age of only thirty-four. Hansberry had gotten her feet wet as a writer while reporting for *Freedom* newspaper. Robeson, Louis Burnham, and the newspaper staff had also bequeathed a political education to Hansberry. She was the first black woman playwright to have a play produced on Broadway when *A Raisin in the Sun* shook audiences in 1959. Scores of people from all over the city paid tribute to Hansberry at her funeral in Harlem. Robeson offered a few brief but heartfelt remarks on her writing and "her deep roots in her people." Invoking poet Langston Hughes, Paul observed, "Her soul had grown deep like rivers." Interestingly, black Muslim leader Malcolm X was also at the event and expressed a desire to Paul Jr. to meet his father. Malcolm preferred a private meeting rather than talking at the funeral, and plans were to be made soon for two of the most provocative figures of the century to converse in person. Unfortunately, the meeting never took place since Malcolm was assassinated the next month before a speech at the Audubon Ballroom.

More uplifting events also unfolded that year. In the spring of 1965 Robeson was feted by *Freedomways* journal at the Americana Hotel in New York. Over two thousand people attended the event, which included a four-hour cultural presentation. The reporter for the *Amsterdam News* noticed that the crowd was about four-fifths white, and Paul Robeson Jr. observed that some black leaders, such as Roy Wilkins, still chose to distance themselves from Paul. However, there did not seem to be any trouble filling the ballroom to capacity. Some people even opted to sit on the steps. Actors Ossie Davis and Ruby Dee hosted the affair, which included music from Billy Taylor's jazz quintet, anti-Vietnam songs from Earl Robinson, and freedom songs by Pete Seeger. Lawrence Brown was on hand to play spirituals, and Robert Nemiroff read a tribute to Robeson by the late Lorraine Hansberry. The

FBI, which was still keeping tabs on Robeson, duly noted the event and looked into the *Freedomways* organization.

Writers James Baldwin and John O. Killens also paid homage to Robeson, as did John Lewis of SNCC. The eloquent Baldwin praised Robeson for speaking "in a great voice" at a time when there seemed to be no possibility of "raising the individual voice" or applying the "rigors of conscience." Lewis thoughtfully referred to the student activists of SNCC as Robeson's "spiritual children." Martin Duberman pointed out, however, that Lewis had to get help preparing his remarks because he was not familiar with Robeson's legacy. The torch passing from one generation of freedom fighters to the next, it seemed, had not been entirely seamless. A generational divide was also in evidence in the coverage of the event. The story in *Liberator*, a more militant journal of the black freedom movement, complained that rather than welcoming home a "leader," the event paid tribute to a "legend." Legends, the writer mused, "were part of any struggle" but could not "substitute for the kind of fearless and uncompromising leadership which Robeson exerted before his departure." The event might have felt, as this reporter suggested, more like a memorial than a salute. Robeson's delicate health meant that his years in the active struggle were now behind him.

Nevertheless, Robeson was deeply touched by the outpouring of warmth and support for him at the *Freedomways* event. His long career of art and activism was being formally acknowledged in a way that he had not previously experienced. "I've never had a reception anything like this at any time that I can remember," he remarked upon taking the platform. This was his last major public speech, but it resonated with the themes that he had advocated throughout his public career. He offered an assessment of contemporary events in the diaspora. Robeson was glad to see that the freedom movement was uniting people in America as illustrated by the Selma to Montgomery march that year. Additionally, self-determination for Africa was important now that independence was becoming a reality. He stressed that "peaceful coexistence" was paramount, so that the newly emancipated nations of Africa could "decide for themselves" which "economic system best fits their needs." Closing on a positive note, Robeson assured the audience that he would "certainly go home . . . feeling more deeply" that "we shall overcome some day."

Perhaps capitalizing on momentum from the *Freedomways* salute, in May 1965 Paul and Eslanda disembarked for California to take part in tributes in

Los Angeles and San Francisco. The trip started out promisingly. Robeson enjoyed the social interaction, and people packed black churches to honor the veteran activist. However, the pace of traveling and making public appearances quickly took a toll on the couple; Eslanda began to experience acute back pain, and Paul became exhausted and withdrawn. The couple flew back to New York early. Paul became more depressed back at Jumel Terrace and showed signs of possibly trying to injure himself again. He was checked into Gracie Square psychiatric hospital in June where he began to improve. By early July he was discharged, but he suffered a recurrence later in the summer when Eslanda was admitted to the hospital. Paul went back to Gracie Square but was not getting better after a few days. Paul Jr. was concerned about his father's worsening condition and pushed for answers. Two new doctors found that Paul was being dangerously overmedicated and was suffering from other conditions due to the drugs that had been administered. He was close to death but improved upon being transferred to another hospital. When he returned home, Eslanda was also home recovering, though her doctors estimated that the cancer would probably take her life in only a matter of months.

Friends were enlisted to help care for the couple along with Paul Jr., who remained vigilant. Even so, one October evening Paul slipped out of the house undetected and was lost for the whole night. Paul Jr. and Lloyd Brown searched for hours without luck. The next morning the police were called about a figure lying in a clump of bushes. Paul was taken to the hospital to treat some bruises and a cut, but he had no memory of being out of the house. He remained under hospital care until stabilizing in early November. At that time, Paul Jr. took him to Marian's, where he seemed to relax right away. Back in New York, Eslanda reentered the hospital in December, where she ultimately succumbed to her battle with cancer. Always energetic and resolute, she had asked her son to bring her typewriter from home when she checked into her hospital room. No doubt there were many letters and another article or two she had in mind to write that had never made it down on paper. The stacks of boxes stored at Jumel Terrace filled with correspondence, clippings, and memorabilia documenting Paul's career and their lives offered a vital testimony to her industriousness and attention to detail.

After Eslanda's death, Paul Jr. and his wife and children experimented sharing a living space with Paul. They tried going between their apartment

Paul Robeson after his retirement from public life. Special Collections Research Center, Temple University Libraries, Philadelphia, Pennsylvania.

and Jumel Terrace, and then attempted living all together in a larger apartment. Neither option turned out to be quite satisfactory, so Paul ended up moving permanently to Philadelphia in the autumn of 1966. He was fortunate to have in Marian a devoted caretaker. His health stabilized, though some days were better than others. Paul lived a quiet life on Walnut Street reading the newspapers, watching television, and visiting occasionally with friends. He applauded Martin Luther King's stand against the Vietnam War in 1967 and was saddened when the reverend was murdered in April 1968, the same month that Paul turned seventy.

Marian and Paul Jr. were cautious about having too many callers stop by the house. Preventing demands from being made on Paul seemed a wise course considering his frail health. Some acquaintances were annoyed that access to Robeson was so carefully guarded. Yet, Paul Jr. maintained that his father wanted to be remembered as he was when he performed and spoke publicly. Lloyd Brown, along with his wife and sometimes his daughters, were regular visitors, as were close friends such as Sam and Helen Rosen, Clara Rockmore, and Freda Diamond. Reflecting on this period in his friend's life, Brown wrote that Paul was pleased when a new edition of *Here I Stand* was released in the early 1970s. Brown also conducted research on the Robeson family tree for the biography that he later published. He shared what he uncovered about their ancestors with both Paul and Marian.

During the 1970s, there was a "gradual lifting" of the "blackout" against Robeson, as Lloyd Brown explained. For example, *Ebony* magazine named Robeson to be one of the ten greatest African American men, and *Sports Illustrated* ran a piece on his athletic career. Lincoln University, his father's alma mater, bestowed Robeson with an honorary degree. C. L. R. James penned a Robeson tribute for *Black World*, and *Freedomways* published a collected volume reflecting on Robeson's career called *The Great Forerunner*. The New York Urban League gave him an award, as did the Congressional Black Caucus, and the Theater Hall of Fame inducted Robeson. Even the FBI curtailed its investigation of Robeson. In 1973, *Freedomways* hosted a benefit honoring Robeson at Carnegie Hall. Paul Jr. and Harry Belafonte collaborated on the program, which included appearances by Sidney Poitier, James Earl Jones, Dizzy Gillespie, Pete Seeger, Ossie Davis, Ruby Dee, Angela Davis, and Coretta Scott King. In addition, written tributes were mailed from around the world. Many leaders from throughout the African diaspora, such as Michael Manley of Jamaica, Cheddi Jagan in Guyana, and Julius Nyerere from Tanzania, recognized Robeson's legacy in the anticolonial struggle. Robeson himself sent a recorded message to the gathering as well. He reassured the crowd that he was "the same Paul" who was "dedicated as ever to the worldwide cause of humanity for freedom, peace and brotherhood." Robeson also saluted "the colonial liberation movements of Africa, Latin America and Asia" and the "heroic example of the Vietnamese people." Though his health had compelled his retirement, Robeson affirmed that "in his heart" he was still singing: "But I keeps laughing / Instead of crying / I must keep fighting / Until I'm dying, / And Ol' Man River / He just keeps rolling along!"

Robeson's long-time musical collaborator Lawrence Brown died in New York around this time. Lloyd Brown had delivered a message from Paul to his old accompanist, who urged him to "take it easy" and "come on over and see us" when he could. Robeson also imagined a day when they could "sing a song for dear old Africa" together. In the autumn of 1975, Lloyd Brown interviewed Robeson with the intention of publishing an article to dispel the rumors that Paul was "hiding out in disgrace." They chatted about sports and the honors recently conferred on Robeson. Paul stressed that he simply did not "feel up to going out much any more" and that he had "decided to let the record speak for itself." Anyone further interested in his point of view should consult his memoir. Brown, however, held off on releasing the interview when Robeson suffered a stroke in late 1975. He was hospitalized and, on January 23, his spirit joined his brothers, his parents, and all of his ancestors going back to his African forebears.

A chilly rain was falling the day of Paul Robeson's funeral at Mother AME Zion Church in Harlem. This church, where Benjamin Robeson had been pastor, was one of the oldest African American places of worship in America. After its founding, in 1796, it became part of the Underground Railroad for escaping slaves, and even Frederick Douglass, a hero of Robeson's, had passed through these doors. Thus, the community bid farewell to a freedom fighter in a sanctuary that had long been a symbol of freedom. Hundreds of mourners huddled under umbrellas waiting to offer their respects to the man in the mahogany coffin. Scores of others had filed past the casket at the two-day viewing in a neighborhood funeral parlor. The people in the crowded vestibule listened to eulogies from spiritual leaders and friends of Robeson's. Bishop J. C. Hoggard reminded the audience that Paul often sang of Joe Hill, a fallen union organizer, who had entreated those who came after him not to mourn but to organize. Hoggard captured this sentiment in the wake of the artist's passing. "Don't mourn for me, but live for freedom's cause" would have been Robeson's entreaty. Paul Robeson Jr. closed the service by pondering his father's legacy. That legacy, he asserted, belongs "to all those who decide to follow the principles by which he lived," "to oppressed peoples everywhere," "to those of us who knew him best," and "to the younger generation that will experience the joy of discovering him." It was still drizzling as the pallbearers bore the flower-covered casket out of the church. The somber notes of "Deep River" in Robeson's unparalleled voice reverberated throughout the church and reminded the audience that his home was over Jordan.

The spiritual "Deep River" evoked Robeson's concert career and his commitment to interpreting the music of African Americans with pride. The depth of emotion conveyed through the spiritual recalled Robeson's early writing on black culture and his contention that it was the African ancestry of black Americans that imbued them with unique gifts that could enrich American culture. The song also called to mind a painful history further removed by time but no less salient because of that distance. This was a music born out of the anguish of enslavement, but this was a connection of which Robeson was never ashamed. He hastened to remind audiences that his father had been enslaved and that meant that his family had helped build America. The first generations who sang "Deep River" around fires by streams or while paddling canoes through marshes longed to cross a figurative Jordan River to a place of comfort. These people had been forced to endure a terrible journey across an ocean when they were kidnapped from their homeland in Africa. This was another relationship that Robeson firmly embraced. He wanted to "carry always" the "central idea" to be African. He expressed that idea in his tireless advocacy for African liberation and African American freedom as well as his efforts to portray the culture of the diaspora with dignity. Robeson was a nationally recognized athlete, a pioneering interpreter of spirituals and folk music, and a trail-blazing actor in film and on stage. Perhaps most importantly, he had dedicated his prodigious talents to the struggle for freedom. That history was whispered between the notes that resonated through the sanctuary when Paul Robeson sang "Deep River."

A NOTE ON SOURCES

Several archival collections were useful in preparing this manuscript, especially the Robeson collections at the Moorland-Spingarn Research Center (MSRC) at Howard University. The Schomburg Center for Research in Black Culture in Harlem has a microfilm collection on Robeson as well as collections on several of his associates, including Lawrence Brown, W. Alphaeus Hunton, and Doxey Wilkerson. The Max Yergan Papers at MSRC and the Margaret Webster Papers at the Library of Congress were also consulted, as was the mammoth W. E. B. Du Bois repository at the University of Massachusetts, Amherst. The Shakespeare Birthplace Trust in Stratford-upon-Avon provided material related to the 1959 *Othello* production under the auspices of the Royal Shakespeare Company. The file on Paul and Eslanda Robeson available through the FBI electronic reading room also imparted interesting perspectives on Cold War surveillance. The Special Collections at Rutgers University has material on Robeson's undergraduate years at the institution. A number of newspapers and periodicals provided commentary on and helped to contextualize Robeson's endeavors, including: *Afro-American, Crisis, Daily Worker, Chicago Defender, Freedom, Freedomways, International African Opinion, The Keys, London Times, New Africa* and *Spotlight on Africa, New York Times, People's Voice,* and the Associated Negro Press (in the microfilm edition of the Claude A. Barnett Papers).

The body of scholarship related to Paul Robeson is vast and growing all the time. What follows is a list of many of the general works that have been particularly illuminating in the preparation of this biography. Topical sources are then included for each chapter. I will mention two of my own monographs that deal with Robeson only because the years I spent researching those projects informed my approach to this book: *The Politics of Paul Robeson's Othello* (Jackson: University Press of Mississippi, 2011) and *Southern Roots of Radicalism: African American Activism from the Depression to the Early Cold War* (Gainesville: University Press of Florida, forthcoming). I also attended a conference on Robeson hosted by Lafayette College in 2005 that helped me to better understand several facets of Robeson's life and work.

Robeson's unique memoir *Here I Stand* (Boston: Beacon Press, 1988), which was written in collaboration with friend and writer Lloyd Brown, is a piece that a reader can return to again and again and always take away something new. Anyone interested in Robeson is indebted to historian Philip Foner for the marvelous collection of writings and speeches titled *Paul Robeson Speaks* (New York: Kensington, 2002) that he edited. Roberta Yancy Dent edited another collection of Robeson's works: *Paul Robeson Tributes and Selected Writings* (New York: Paul Robeson Archives, Inc., 1976). There are several key biographies to which I have frequently referred: Martin B. Duberman's *Paul Robeson: A Biography* (New York: Ballantine, 1989), which was for years the chief academic study of Robeson, and Sheila Tully Boyle and Andrew Bunie's detailed work *Paul Robeson: The Years of Promise and Achievement* (Amherst: University of Massachusetts Press, 2001). Paul Robeson Jr.'s two-volume set titled *The Undiscovered Paul Robeson: An Artist's Journey, 1898–1939* (New York: John Wiley and Sons, 2001) presents Robeson's life from the thoughtful perspective of one who lived through many of the events chronicled and knows his subject well. Volume one, *An Artist's Journey, 1898–1939*, came out in 2001 and volume 2, *The Quest for Freedom, 1939–1976*, was released in 2010. Also informative is Duberman's article on the response to his biography titled "Writing Robeson" in the collection *Left Out: The Politics of Exclusion/ Essays, 1964–1999* (New York: Basic Books, 1999). Reading Duberman and Paul Robeson Jr.'s books side by side is interesting in that they offer different perspectives on some events and issues. Other instructive biographies written by people close to Robeson include Eslanda Robeson's volume, *Paul Robeson Negro* (New York: Harper and Brothers, 1930) and Lloyd

Brown's *The Young Paul Robeson: On My Journey Now* (Boulder, CO: Westview Press, 1997). These two books focus on Robeson's early years. Robeson's granddaughter, Susan, collected a pictorial biography titled *The Whole World in His Hands: A Pictorial Biography of Paul Robeson* (Secaucus, NJ: Citadel Press, 1981) that is a joy to thumb through. The Columbia College (Chicago) Paul Robeson 100th Birthday Committee put together a detailed compilation titled "Paul Robeson Rediscovered: An Annotated Listing of His Chicago History, 1921–1958" that is very informative.

Since he was admired by many people around the world, it is not surprising that there are numerous collections about Robeson and tributes to him in print. A few of these are *Paul Robeson: The Great Forerunner* by the editors of *Freedomways* journal (New York: International Publishers, 1998) and *Paul Robeson: Essays on His Life and Legacy* edited by Joseph Dorinson, Henry Foner, and William Pencak (Jefferson, NC: McFarland and Company, 2002). Jeffrey C. Stewart edited *Paul Robeson: Artist and Citizen* (New Brunswick, NJ: Rutgers University Press, 1998), which was part of the Paul Robeson Centennial Project. Robeson has also been the subject of multiple documentary films. Gil Noble's early effort *The Tallest Tree in Our Forest* was produced in 1977 just a year after Robeson's death. Director St. Clair Bourne's *Paul Robeson: Here I Stand* (Menair Media, 1999) is an excellent starting point for anyone who is not familiar with Robeson's life.

Fortunately, Robeson's artistic legacy has been preserved for those of us who never got to see him stride across the theater stage or hear him entrance a crowd with his voice. A few album highlights include: *Paul Robeson Live at Carnegie Hall: The Historic May 9, 1959, Concert* (Vanguard Records, 1987); *Paul Robeson: The Peace Arch Concerts* (Folk Era Records, 1998); *Songs of Free Men: A Paul Robeson Recital* (Sony, 1997); *William Shakespeare, Othello: Cast Recording* (Columbia Records, 1951); and *Paul Robeson: The Original Recording of "Ballad for Americans"* (Vanguard Records, 1991). In 2008, Freedom Archives produced a collection of Robeson interviews and speeches on compact disc called *Paul Robeson: Words Like Freedom*. Not to be missed is the DVD box set *Paul Robeson: Portraits of the Artist* (Criterion, 2007) that brings together a documentary and several of Robeson's films. There are interesting commentary features to accompany some of the films.

INTRODUCTION

Paul Robeson's memoir and Philip Foner's collection of Robeson's articles and speeches were referenced in this section. The descriptions of the viewing and funeral came from *Ebony* magazine and the *New York Times*, and the collection *The Great Forerunner* includes several of the eulogies. C. L. R. James's thoughts can be found in *Spheres of Existence: Selected Writings* (Westport, CT: Lawrence Hill and Co., 1980, 256–64).

CHAPTER 1

For this chapter, Robeson's memoir and Lloyd Brown's book were consulted, as was Eslanda Robeson's biography of her husband. I also referred to volume 1 of Paul Robeson Jr.'s biography, Duberman's monograph, and Boyle and Bunie's book. Robeson's senior thesis and commencement address are in Philip Foner's collection, along with an interview in the *New York Times*, "Robeson Remembers," in which Robeson discussed playing football at Rutgers. An article by Lamont Yeakey, "A Student without Peer: The Undergraduate College Years of Paul Robeson," from the *Journal of Negro Education* also discusses Robeson's college years. (His thesis on Robeson's early life is available in the Rutgers's archives.) Jack Washington's book *The Long Journey Home: A Bicentennial History of the Black Community of Princeton, New Jersey 1776–1976* (Trenton, NJ: Africa World Press, 2005) does a fine job of characterizing the community in which Robeson spent his early years. Other books that provided context on the black urban experience in the north around the turn of the twentieth century are W. E. B. Du Bois's classic study *The Philadelphia Negro* (Philadelphia: University of Pennsylvania Press, 1899), St. Clair Drake and Horace Cayton's study of Chicago in *Black Metropolis: A Study of Negro Life in a Northern City* (New York: Harper Torchbooks, 1962), and *Following the Color Line: American Negro Citizenship in the Progressive Era* by Ray Stannard Baker (New York: Harper Torchbooks, 1964). Leon Litwack's books on the postemancipation years, *Been in the Storm So Long: The Aftermath of Slavery*, and the rise of segregation, *Trouble in Mind: Black Southerners in the Age of Jim Crow*, focus mainly on the South but do an excellent job of contextualizing the African American experience during these pivotal eras. Background on the significance of the church in the African American community came from C. Eric Lincoln and Lawrence H. Mamiya's *The Black Church in the African American Experience* (Durham, NC: Duke University Press, 1990) and *Black Religion and Black Radicalism: An Interpretation of the Religious History of African Americans* by Gayraud S. Wilmore (Maryknoll, NY: Orbis Books, 1998).

CHAPTER 2

In addition to the biographies and the Foner collection, this chapter drew upon coverage of Robeson's endeavors and reviews of his films and recitals in the *New York Times*. Two books helped frame the historical context of the New Negro Renaissance (or Harlem Renaissance): David L. Lewis's book *When Harlem Was in Vogue* (New York: Penguin Books, 1997) and Lewis's edited collection *The Portable Harlem Renaissance Reader* (New York: Penguin Books, 1994). This volume includes an article by Robeson reflecting on the plays of Eugene O'Neill. Alain Locke's collection, *The New Negro*, from the time period is fundamental to any discussion of black art in the 1920s (New York: Simon and Schuster, 1997). Pearl Bowser has done a lot of scholarship on Oscar Micheaux, including the book *Writing Himself into History: Oscar Micheaux, His Silent Films and His Audiences* (New Brunswick: Rutgers University Press, 2000). Her commentary on *Body and Soul* in the Criterion edition of the DVD was quite informative.

Several books provided background information on the musical form of the spirituals. Eileen Southern's overview is useful in *The Music of Black Americans: A History* (New York: W. W. Norton and Co., 1997). W. E. B. Du Bois writes eloquently of the significance of the spirituals in several of his books: *Dusk of Dawn* (New York: Schocken Books, 1968), *The Gift of Black Folk: The Negroes in the Making of America* (New York: Oxford University Press, 2007), and *The Souls of Black Folk* (New York: Oxford University Press, 2007). Thomas Wentworth Higginson was one of the first collectors of spirituals, and he captured some of the early written history of spirituals in *The Magnificent Activist: The Writings of Thomas Wentworth Higginson*

(New York: Da Capo Press, 2000). *Dark Midnight When I Rise: The Story of the Jubilee Singers, Who Introduced the World to the Music of Black America* by Andrew Ward (New York: Farrar, Straus and Giroux, 2000) recounts the history of the Fisk Jubilee Singers, who helped popularize the spirituals. James Weldon Johnson and J. Rosamond Johnson collected arrangements of the spirituals and commented on the form in *The Books of American Negro Spirituals* (New York: Da Capo Press, 1969).

CHAPTER 3

In addition to the biographies and the Foner collection, Robeson's memoir, *Here I Stand*, discusses themes from the 1930s. Eslanda Robeson's book, *African Journey*, recounts her trip across the continent in the summer of 1936. Theater, concert, and film reviews from newspapers in the United States and abroad helped to evoke Robeson's performances. A number of the films discussed in this chapter (*Borderline, The Emperor Jones, Sanders of the River, Song of Freedom, Jericho, Proud Valley*) are available in the Criterion collection. For West Indian perspectives on London in the thirties, see C. L. R. James, *Letters from London* (Port of Spain: Prospect Press, 2003). James reminisces on his collaboration with Robeson for the play about Toussaint L'Ouverture in the essay "Paul Robeson: Black Star" in *Spheres of Existence: The Selected Writings of C. L .R. James* (Westport, CT: Lawrence Hill and Co., 1980). A revised version of James's play can be found in the *C. L. R. James Reader* (London: Blackwell, 1992). Howard Zinn's chapter, "Self Help in Hard Times," in *A People's History of the United States* (New York: Harper Perennial, 1995) provides a good overview of labor militancy in the United States in the 1930s.

Additional context on the U.S. Communist Party during the Depression is available in: Philip Foner and Herbert Shapiro, eds. *American Communism and Black Americans: A Documentary History, 1930–1934* (Philadelphia: Temple University Press, 1991); Mark Naison, *Communists in Harlem during the Depression* (New York: Grove Press, 1984); Michael Denning, *The Cultural Front: The Laboring of American Culture in the Twentieth Century* (New York: Verso, 1996); Fraser Ottanelli, *The Communist Party of the United States from the Depression to World War II* (New Brunswick, NJ:

Rutgers University Press, 1991); and Mark Solomon, *The Cry Was Unity: Communists and African Americans 1917–1936* (Oxford: University Press of Mississippi, 1998). Examinations of African Americans in the Soviet Union include: Kate Baldwin, *Behind the Color Line and the Iron Curtain: Reading Encounters Between Black and Red 1922–1963* (Durham, NC: Duke University Press, 2002) and Joy Gleason Carew, *Blacks, Reds and Russians: Sojourners in Search of the Soviet Promise* (New Brunswick, NJ: Rutgers University Press, 2010). James Meriwether analyzes the African American response to the invasion of Ethiopia in *Proudly We Can Be Africans: Black Americans and Africa 1935–1961* (Chapel Hill: University of North Carolina Press, 2002).

Quite a bit of scholarship explores Robeson's theater and film work from this period, including: Scott Allen Nollen, *Paul Robeson: Film Pioneer* (Jefferson, NC: McFarland Books, 2010); Richard Dyer, *Heavenly Bodies: Film Stars and Society* (New York: Routledge, 2002); Lois Potter, *Othello* (Manchester, UK: Manchester University Press, 2002); and Virginia Mason Vaughan, *Othello: A Contextual History* (Cambridge: Cambridge University Press, 1994). Donald Bogle's scholarship on film helps to contextualize Robeson's film career: *Toms, Coons, Mulattoes, Mammies and Bucks: An Interpretive History of Blacks in American Films* (New York: Continuum, 2001). Errol Hill's work on black theater is excellent: *Shakespeare in Sable: A History of Black Shakespearean Actors* (Amherst: University of Massachusetts Press, 1984), as is *A History of African American Theatre* with James Hatch (Cambridge: Cambridge University Press, 2003).

CHAPTER 4

In addition to the Robeson biographies and the Foner collection, several books helped contextualize World War II and the immediate postwar era: Martha Biondi, *To Stand and Fight: The Struggle for Civil Rights in Postwar New York* (Cambridge, MA: Harvard University Press, 2003); Robert Dallek, *The Lost Peace: Leadership in a Time of Horror and Hope 1945–1953* (New York: HarperCollins, 2010); Maurice Isserman, *Which Side Were You On? The American Communist Party during the Second World War* (Middletown, CT: Wesleyan University Press, 1982); and Ronald Takaki, *Double Victory:*

A Multicultural History of America in World War II (Boston: Little, Brown, 2000). Mainstream, African American, and left-wing newspaper coverage of Robeson's activities were also important in framing this chapter.

Biographies of some of the activists with whom Robeson interacted and collaborated provide insight: David Henry Anthony, *Max Yergan: Race Man, Internationalist, Cold Warrior* (New York: New York University Press, 2006); Carole Boyce Davies, *Left of Karl Marx: The Political Life of Black Communist Claudia Jones* (Durham, NC: Duke University Press, 2008); Gerald Horne, *Red Seas: Ferdinand Smith and Radical Black Sailors in the United States and Jamaica* (New York: New York University Press, 2009); Gerald Horne, *Black Liberation/Red Scare: Ben Davis and the Communist Party* (London: Associated University Presses, 1994); David L. Lewis, *W. E. B. Du Bois: The Fight for Equality and the American Century 1919–1963* (New York: Henry Holt and Co., 2000); David L. Lewis, Michael H. Nash, and Daniel J. Leab, eds., *Red Activists and Black Freedom: James and Esther Jackson and the Long Civil Rights Revolution* (New York: Routledge, 2010); Gerald Meyer, *Vito Marcantonio: Radical Politician 1902–1954* (Albany: State University of New York Press, 1989); Hugh Mulzac, *A Star to Steer By* (New York: International Publishers, 1972); William Patterson, *The Man Who Cried Genocide: An Autobiography* (New York: International Publishers, 1991); Earl Robinson and Eric A. Gordon, *Ballad of an American: The Autobiography of Earl Robinson* (New York: Scarecrow Press, 1998); and Graham White, *Henry A. Wallace: His Search for a New World Order* (Chapel Hill: University of North Carolina Press, 2009). Jackie Robinson's memoir also reflects on this time period: Jackie Robinson with Alfred Duckett, *I Never Had It Made: An Autobiography of Jackie Robinson* (New York: G. P. Putnam and Sons, 1972).

Charles H. Wright's book *Robeson, Labor's Forgotten Champion* (Detroit: Balamp Publishing, 1975) offers an overview of Robeson's interaction with labor. Books on other labor and left-wing groups with which Robeson worked include: Gerald Horne, *Communist Front? The Civil Rights Congress 1946–1956* (Cranbury, NJ: Associated University Presses, 1988) and June Levine and Gene Gordon, *Tales of Camp Wo-Chi-Ca: Blacks, Whites and Reds at Camp* (Walnut Creek, CA: Avon Springs Press, 2002). In addition to their newsletters, *New Africa* and *Spotlight on Africa*, these works discuss the work of the Council on African Affairs in the 1940s: Hollis

Lynch, *Black American Radicals and the Liberation of Africa: The Council on African Affairs 1937–1955* (Cornell University: Africana Studies Research Center, 1978) and Imanuel Geiss, *The Pan African Movement: A History of Pan-Africanism in America, Europe, and Africa* (New York: Africana Publishing Co., 1968). Two books by W. E. B. Du Bois, who worked with the Council in the late 1940s, also provide context: *Color and Democracy: Colonies and Peace* (New York: Harcourt, Brace and Co., 1945) and *The World and Africa* (New York: International Publishers, 1946). Concerning Peekskill, firsthand accounts were published in the *Daily Worker*'s extensive coverage. There is an unpublished account in the papers of Louise Thompson Patterson at Emory University, and the Westchester Committee for a Fair Inquiry published a detailed pamphlet called "Eyewitness to Peekskill." Howard Fast's account was published as *Peekskill USA: Inside the Infamous 1949 Riots* (Mineola, NY: Dover Publications, 2006).

In addition to Paul and Eslanda Robeson's FBI file, Kenneth O'Reilly's work analyzes the FBI's surveillance of the black community: *Black Americans: The FBI Files* (New York: Carroll and Graf Publishers, Inc., 1994) and *Racial Matters: The FBI's Secret File on Black America, 1960–1972* (New York: The Free Press, 1989). With regard to Robeson's artistic career, there is an interesting discussion of "Ballad for Americans" in Michael Denning's book *The Cultural Front: The Laboring of American Culture in the Twentieth Century*. Two books by director Margaret Webster provided insight into the Broadway *Othello* production: *Don't Put Your Daughter on the Stage* (New York: Alfred A. Knopf, 1972) and *Shakespeare without Tears* (New York: McGraw-Hill, 1942). Milly S. Barranger's biography of Webster was also useful: *Margaret Webster: A Life in the Theater* (Ann Arbor: University of Michigan Press, 2004).

CHAPTER 5

In addition to the biographies, Robeson's memoir, and the Foner collection, there is a lot of coverage of Robeson during these years in left-wing and black newspapers such as the *Daily Worker*, the *Afro-American*, the Associated Negro Press, and, of course, the newspaper Robeson started, *Freedom*. Robeson's articles in *Spotlight on Africa* are also useful. There is extensive coverage of Robeson's tours in the United Kingdom and the 1959 *Othello* in British papers such as the *Times*. The genocide petition Robeson presented to the United Nations has been published as *We Charge Genocide: The Historic Petition to the United Nations for Relief from a Crime of the United States Government against the Negro People*, 2nd ed. (New York: International Publishers, 1971). Marie Seton's biography of Robeson is from this era: *Paul Robeson* (London: Denis Dobson, 1958).

Context for the Cold War era, anticolonialism, and the peace movement can be found in books such as Murali Balaji, *The Professor and the Pupil: The Politics and Friendship of W. E. B. Du Bois and Paul Robeson* (New York: Nation Books, 2007); Cedric Belfrage and James Aronson, *Something to Guard: The Stormy Life of the* National Guardian *1948–1967* (New York: Columbia University Press, 1978); Thomas Borstelmann, *The Cold War and the Color Line: American Race Relations in the Global Arena* (Cambridge, MA: Harvard University Press, 2001); W. E. B. Du Bois, *In Battle for Peace: The Story of My 83rd Birthday* (New York: Masses and Mainstream, 1952); W. E. B. Du Bois, *The Autobiography of W. E. B. Du Bois: A Soliloquy on Viewing My Life from the Last Decade of Its First Century* (New York: International Publishers, 1968); Gerald Horne, *Black and Red: Du Bois and the African American Response to the Cold War* (Albany: State University of New York Press, 1986); W. Alphaeus Hunton, *Decision in Africa* (New York: International Publishers, 1957); Victor Navasky, *Naming Names* (New York: Viking Press, 1980); Brenda Plummer, *Rising Wind: Black Americans and U.S. Foreign Affairs 1935–1960* (Chapel Hill: University of North Carolina Press, 1996); Penny von Eschen, *Race against Empire: Black Americans and Anticolonialism 1937–1957* (Ithaca, NY: Cornell University Press, 1997); Odd Arne Westad, *The Global Cold War: Third World Interventions and the Making of Our Times* (Cambridge: Cambridge University Press, 2005); and Richard Wright, *The Color Curtain: A Report of the Bandung Conference* (Jackson, MS: Banner Books, 1994).

There are discussions of people involved with *Freedom* newspaper in Judith Smith, *Visions of Belonging: Family Stories, Popular Culture and Postwar Democracy 1940–1960* (New York: Columbia University Press, 2004); Dayo F. Gore, *Radicalism at the Crossroads: African American Women Activists in the Cold War* (New York: New York University Press, 2011); Lorraine Hansberry, *To Be Young, Gifted and Black: An Informal*

Autobiography of Lorraine Hansberry (New York: Signet Books, 1970); and Bill V. Mullen and James Smethurst, eds. *Left of the Color Line: Race, Radicalism and Twentieth Century Literature of the United States* (Chapel Hill: University of North Carolina Press, 2003). Alice Childress's column from *Freedom*, "Conversations from Life," was collected in *Like One of the Family: Conversations from a Domestic's Life* (Boston: Beacon Press, 1986). The Carnegie Hall concert from May 1958 and the Peace Arch concert recordings also informed this chapter.

CHAPTER 6

Martin Duberman and Paul Robeson Jr.'s biographies as well as Foner's collection were important to this chapter. Lloyd Brown's biography also discusses Robeson's retirement years in Philadelphia and includes the final interview. Reviews of Robeson's last concert tours and obituaries in major newspapers helped contextualize this chapter. The tribute compilation, *The Great Forerunner*, by the editors of *Freedomways*, was consulted for this chapter. A lot of interesting work has been done on the CIA during the Cold War in books such as John Marks, *The Search for the "Manchurian Candidate": The CIA and Mind Control* (New York: New York Times Book Co., 1979); Thomas Powers, *The Man Who Kept the Secrets: Richard Helms and the CIA* (New York: Alfred A. Knopf, 1979); and Tim Weiner, *Legacy of Ashes: The History of the CIA* (New York: Doubleday, 2007). Hugh Wilford's book *The Mighty Wurlitzer: How the CIA Played America* (Cambridge, MA: Harvard University Press, 2008) discusses Robeson in the chapter on African Americans.

INDEX

ABOUT THE AUTHOR

Lindsey R. Swindall completed her doctorate in Afro-American Studies at the University of Massachusetts, Amherst, and is currently visiting assistant professor of history at Sam Houston State University in Huntsville, Texas. She has also written *The Politics of Paul Robeson's Othello*.